ETHICAL DIMENSIONS
OF THE PROPHETS

ETHICAL DIMENSIONS
OF THE PROPHETS

Joseph Jensen, O.S.B.

A Michael Glazier Book

LITURGICAL PRESS
Collegeville, Minnesota

www.litpress.org

A Michael Glazier Book published by Liturgical Press.

Cover design by Joachim Rhoades, O.S.B.

Abbreviations, sigla, and other conventions follow those given in Patrick H. Alexander, et al., eds., *The SBL Handbook of Style: For Ancient Near Eastern, Biblical, and Early Christian Studies* (Peabody, MA: Hendrickson, 1999).

1   2   3   4   5   6   7   8   9

Library of Congress Cataloging-in-Publication Data

Jensen, Joseph, 1924–
   Ethical dimensions of the prophets / Joseph Jensen.
      p.   cm.
   Includes bibliographical references and indexes.
   ISBN-13: 978-0-8146-5983-0 (alk. paper)
   ISBN-10: 0-8146-5983-7 (alk. paper)
    1. Bible. O.T. Prophets—Criticism, interpretation, etc.   2. Ethics in the Bible.   I. Title.

BS1505.6.E8J46 2006
224'.06—dc22

2006004678

To my dear sister Loretta

CONTENTS

PREFACE

The remote origin of this book is a course taught several years ago at Princeton Theological Seminary. I was asked to teach a course on the prophets, which had been my specialty for several years, and since I had also been working on biblical ethics I designed the course more or less in the shape the present book manifests.

Cyrus H. Gordon has spoken of the Hebrew Bible as being unique in its moral superiority to other ancient Near Eastern cultures.[1] It may be that not all would hasten to endorse that position. (See, for example, the passage quoted from James H. Breasted below in Chapter Three, contrasting Israelite and Egyptian moral teaching.) But assuredly the prophetic contribution in this area is tremendous. Although the number of introductions to the prophetic literature is legion and no small number of writings address this or that aspect of prophetic morality, not many attempt to approach in a systematic fashion the overall achievement of at least those prophets who have contributed most significantly. Furthermore, I believe there are a number of methodological issues that are often not adequately addressed, and so the first two chapters of this book are largely given to them.

The title speaks of "Ethical Dimensions" because there is no attempt to cover all the prophets or to address exhaustively all that all the prophets have said in the area of ethics, but I believe the most significant areas have been covered. Most of the prophets have something to say in the area of what we call social justice, but repetitious presentation has largely been avoided. This is possible because each of the prophets has his own unique approach: Amos, Hosea, Micah, Isaiah, etc., each address the matter we call "social justice," but each from a somewhat different point

---

[1] Cyrus H. Gordon, "The Background to Jewish Studies in the Bible and the Ancient Near East," *Shofar* 12 (1944) 1–46.

of view. The prophets who seem not to have made a major contribution are covered only briefly.

The present work is intended to be "scholarly" in the sense of being useful to scholars but not technical to the point of being beyond the general reader. The positions expressed and conclusions drawn are based on critical scholarship, sometimes on what can be considered a scholarly consensus, sometimes on the work of specific individuals, sometimes on my own. The research on which these positions are based is often documented, but not always. Hebrew terms are used (in transliteration) but always with explanation for the general reader.

The book is written by a Christian but not intentionally from a Christian perspective; the Old Testament, and indeed the whole Bible, is understood to be the word of God and therefore inspired and authoritative, but, as is well known, both terms allow a great deal of latitude of interpretation. My own understanding, at least of what is meant by "authoritative," will emerge in Chapter One. The Old Testament is taken on its own terms for the contribution it can make to the moral life of people of good will. It is hoped there will be little here to which a Jew who accepts a critical methodology in approaching the Bible would need to take exception, though undoubtedly a Jew would have done it differently, perceiving a different relation between the Law and the Prophets and probably giving important consideration to materials from the Talmud.

"Ethical dimensions of the prophets" could undoubtedly be presented in a series of themes rather than in a prophet-by-prophet exposition, but the latter approach is followed as better able to preserve the unique contribution of each prophet. Raymond F. Collins notes the multiplicity of theologies in the Bible and comments:

> That there exists a similar diversity of viewpoint within the Scriptures with respect to morality must also be acknowledged. . . . Should one attempt a systematic presentation of a specific theme related to moral theology from the biblical perspective, one must take into account not only the diversity of biblical teaching but also the development of that teaching. In his classic criticism of the methodology employed by the authors of the articles in the *Theological Dictionary of the New Testament*, James Barr correctly noted that even the meaning of terms varies considerably from generation to generation.[2]

---

[2] Raymond F. Collins, *Christian Morality: Biblical Foundations* (Notre Dame: University of Notre Dame Press, 1986) 7–8.

He also speaks of the need to take into account the development of moral standards. The same can be said of the Old Testament.

There is no intention of providing here the information that can be found in a general introduction to the prophets; however, in most cases some information is given on the background of the prophet and the structure of the book for the sake of the general reader.

The present work is presented in the conviction that the prophets, who had so great an impact on Israel's ethics, should also have an impact on ours. The approach will not be to attempt to make application at each step to our contemporary situation. The prophets deserve to be heard on their own terms, as they address their contemporaries. It is my conviction that much of what they say will have its obvious implications for our own situation. Thus, although in the final chapter of this book some conclusions will be drawn and some applications made, this is a secondary rather than primary approach.

I would like to thank Michael Glazier, an honored friend for many years, for accepting this book for publication under his imprint. And I would like to thank Linda M. Maloney, Academic Editor for the Liturgical Press, and also a good friend, for generous help in preparing the manuscript for publication.

Chapter One

PRELIMINARY NOTIONS

A necessary starting point in approaching the topic of the ethical teaching of the prophets is a definition of terms. A dictionary may be of only limited help. An earlier edition of Webster's Unabridged gave several definitions for the word "ethics," the third of which is "moral principles, quality, or practice; a system of moral principles." There is quite a latitude in this definition that, we should note, can lead to ambiguities.[1] The "principles" and "practices" that will be discussed in this book will be those of the Old Testament, specifically those of the prophets, but in this introductory section we will deal with the topic of Old Testament ethics in a more general sense, as a way of putting the prophets in context. Whether it is possible to speak of a "system" of ethics in the Old Testament is something that will be touched on later.

It would be well to mention at the outset that in terms of the *biblical* material it does not seem appropriate to distinguish between ethics and ascetics.[2] Those addressed in Scripture are addressed as God's people and, as such, are called to holiness ("a kingdom of priests, a holy nation," Exod 19:6). In the New Testament the Beatitudes are addressed not to some spiritual elite, but to those called to be disciples. If in times past (happily *long* past) courses in moral theology dealt in large part with

---

[1] *Webster's New International Dictionary of the English Language, Second Edition Unabridged* (Springfield, MA: Merriam, 1944). The same dictionary gives, among others, the following definitions of "morality": (1) "knowledge of moral principles, moral wisdom"; . . . (4) "the science, or a system, of morals"; (5) "moral practice or action; rectitude of life." If the terms "ethics" and "morality" are sometimes used interchangeably, it is because their definitions are not always that clearly distinguished.

[2] To turn to the dictionary again: "ascetics" is equated with "ascetical theology" and defined as "the science which treats of the practice of virtue and the means of obtaining holiness and perfection."

principles for hearing confession, with distinguishing between what is and what is not sin, and between mortal and venial sin,[3] that approach did not respond to the biblical reality.

"Old Testament morality" is sometimes used in a derogatory fashion, but the Old Testament knows the call to holiness,[4] which is one of the reasons it is relevant to the Christian as well as to the Jew. It is relevant also because much of what it enjoins in the interests of moral living (e.g., in terms of social justice, sanctity in marriage, sanctity of life) remains the same for the Christian as for the Jew.

OLD TESTAMENT ETHICS AND NATURAL LAW

How one relates biblical ethics to natural law will depend to a large extent on how one defines or understands natural law. John Barton sees "natural law" as the basis of what Isaiah teaches:

> Isaiah, then, begins with a picture of the world in which God is the creator and preserver of all things, and occupies by right the supreme position over all that he has made. The essence of morality is cooperation in maintaining the ordered structure which prevails, under God's guidance, in the natural constitution of things, and the keynote of the whole system is order, a proper submission to one's assigned place in the scheme of things and the avoidance of any action that would challenge the supremacy of God or seek to subvert the orders he has established. Such is the basic premise from which all of Isaiah's thinking about ethical obligation begins.
>
> If this analysis of Isaiah's ethical teaching is correct, we have in him an early example of that way of approaching ethics which begins with a hierarchically ordered universe whose moral pattern ought to be apparent to all . . . whose reason is not hopelessly clouded, and derives all particular moral offenses from the one great sin, a disregard for natural law. Of course, what we have in Isaiah is a theological form of natural law, as were most natural law theories before the Enlightenment: one might perhaps speak equally well of a theory of "general revelation."[5]

---

[3] Or as one professor is reputed to have put it grossly when asked about a more perfect way: "This course is not about perfection but about how to get into heaven with your tail singed."

[4] As attested in Exod 19:6, cited above. See also "Be holy, for I the LORD, your God, am holy," found like a refrain in the Holiness Code (Lev 19:2; and cf. 20:26; 21:8, 15, 23; 22:16, 32), to give just one additional example of the many that could be given.

[5] "Ethics in Isaiah of Jerusalem," *Understanding Old Testament Ethics: Approaches and Explorations* (Louisville and London: Westminster John Knox, 2003) 139–40 (originally published in *JTS* 32 [1981]).

To maintain his view Barton resorts to referring to "a theological form of natural law" and alludes to a "theory of 'general revelation.'" Even with those qualifications I do not think his explanation of the basis of Isaiah's teaching can be defended, and in any case it is not in that sense that I understand "natural law."

An encyclopedia might define natural law as "a system of right or justice held to be common to all mankind and derived from nature rather than from rules of society, or positive law."[6] The article on "Natural Law" in *The New Catholic Encyclopedia* explains it as follows: "a law or rule of action that is implicit in the very nature of things." It explains that while the term is sometimes used of laws that regulate nature, properly speaking it "designates a prescriptive rule of conduct naturally received by and measuring human reason which enables human reason rightly to measure human action." The article traces the historical development of the concept and the various ways it has been understood from the "pagan period" through "the debates of the late 20th century." Some of the earlier Greek philosophers had a concept of natural law that is divine, universal, and known to all. Aristotle saw "the naturally just and virtuous as a function of conforming to the natural order that is derived from its divine origin," though his concept tends to subordinate the individual to the Greek city-state. Zeno and others emphasized the nature of the human being as such and not merely as related to political society; here the individual "comes to be recognized as a moral unit who is governed by universal law, which prescribes a pattern of conduct that is discoverable by reason."[7] It is in this sense that I would understand "natural law." If we are to use that term, it seems that it should apply to what is discoverable by reason and be able to be justified by reason. Thus natural law, in the sense I am using it here, must operate from universally valid principles, be applicable to all, must necessarily be "reasonable" (in the sense, that is, that it can be deduced by reason and be defensible by reason). The position I am taking here is that once the religious factor has been admitted into the definition, the concept has escaped from that which is controllable on a purely rational level and therefore is no longer strictly natural law.

The broadest statement of natural law would be "good is to be done and evil is to be avoided." Who would quarrel with that? And yet value

---

[6] *Encyclopedia Britannica*, 15th ed. (1993), *Macropaedia*, 8:559.

[7] B. F. Brown and A. Long, "Natural Law," *New Catholic Encyclopedia*. 15 vols. (2d ed. Detroit: Thomson/Gale; Washington, DC: Catholic University of America, 2003) 10:179–86.

judgments are involved. The question is whether all would agree on what things are "good" and what "evil." Certainly some cultural conditioning is involved in the judgments most of us would give. Cannibalism would be abhorrent to most of the readers of this book, but in some cultures, until very recently at least, it was part of the accepted ritual practice, more of a virtue than a vice.

The natural law approach is legitimate and even necessary; for example, it is certainly needed in seeking solutions to moral problems the Bible says nothing about. But the point I wish to make is that it is not identical with or to be confused with biblical ethics.[8] The biblical conviction is that God has revealed something of the divine moral will, has specified something about behavior, has said something about what "good" and "evil" are; that divine authority, not simply human reason, comes into it. The point needs to be made, for there is the danger that a morality based purely on human reason will, to some extent at least, be affected by the "follow the crowd" mentality that is apparent in almost any culture. From this approach biblical morality would deliver us, for it understands that those who are called to be God's people will also often be called to stand quite apart from the judgments and mores of the surrounding milieu.[9] In both the Old and New Testaments we find the conviction that those who are members of the covenant community ought to bear witness by holy lives to those outside the community. This they will never do simply by cultivating the virtues the Stoics cultivated.

In biblical terms, as we will see, there is a strong connection between religion and morality. More than half a century ago this was expressed by

---

[8] The term "ethics" itself, in the view of some, does not go with "biblical." Ze'ev Falk, *Religious Law and Ethics: Studies in Biblical and Rabbinical Theonomy* (Jerusalem: Mesharim, 1991), seems to equate "ethics" with natural law: "Ethics, being based on human reason and the questioning of all assumptions, is therefore in conflict with this kind of authoritarian system. Indeed, ethics is part of human thought, it is *anthropocentric,* and according to Kant stands for human *autonomy.* Biblical thought, on the other hand, is *theocentric* and *theonomic,* so that a priori there can be no encounter between the two. . . . We may say that the system of the Torah defines right and wrong as that which has been declared as such by God, while ethics would demand that God declared right and wrong that which is so according to human reason" (p. 8). "Biblical reflection on the Torah seems to affirm the incompatibility of the latter with ethics" (p. 9). "In other words, the only basis of justice is *theonomy,* not ethics or any other human-centered thought" (p. 10).

[9] The biblical tradition is explicitly conscious about this with reference to Israel and Canaan (e.g., Deut 12:29-31; 14:1-2; 18:9-14) and "Gentiles" in general (Phil 2:15; 1 Pet 4:1-6), not to mention the exhortations against idolatry and worship of pagan gods.

William B. Greene, a distinguished professor of biblical ethics at Princeton: "The Old Testament knows nothing of religion without morality, nothing of faith which does not issue in right life and character. Neither does it . . . know anything of morality without religion, anything of conduct or character whose rightness or wrongness is independent of its relation to God. Hence, in the Old Testament the irreligious men are the immoral men, and the immoral men are the irreligious men."[10] And he cites Ps 14:1: "The fool says in his heart, 'There is no God.'" His words may strike us today as stilted, yet they are basically true to the biblical idea. More recently Johannes Lindblom has said much the same in different words: "Prophetic ethics are theonomic[11] ethics. Ethics divorced from religion would be an absurdity to the Old Testament prophets. Behind all that they apprehended as right and good they set Yahweh as Authority and Guardian. The ideal of humanity in the classical or modern sense was quite alien to them. Every offense against moral demands was at the same time an offense against Yahweh's holy will. In the prophetic teaching we do not find any rational motivation of moral demands. They accepted the best elements in the moral tradition of their people and regarded them as Yahweh's commands."[12]

Louis Dupré has expressed very well what I am here trying to say:

> The call to transcendence has taught man ever new ways of being human. His attentiveness to this call which is now so often decried as retarding the humanization process, may well have been the most creative factor in the building of culture. The reason why moral principles have become so commonly ineffective in the daily conduct of our affairs is not so much the inappropriateness of past formulations for a new society, but the almost unprecedented tendency to reduce morality to a purely immanent code of behavior. By some strange law man has to concentrate on what goes beyond what he is, or can ever hope to be, in order to gain and retain

---

[10] William B. Greene, Jr., "The Ethics of the Old Testament," *Princeton Theological Review* 27 (1929) 156.

[11] I.e., ethics subject to God's government.

[12] Johannes Lindblom, *Prophecy in Ancient Israel* (Philadelphia: Fortress, 1965) 346. One might object that both Greene and Lindblom neglect the wisdom tradition, which often seems to operate in a sphere that gives much more emphasis to human experience and reason than to religious convictions. Yet Proverbs and all the other compositions in this category make frequent reference to the deity and to divine sanctions. The final sentence in the above quotation from Lindblom says it well.

his humanity. If he restricts his existence to the mere preservation of the immanent, he finds the extent of his value system shrinking ever further, for there is no other way of satisfactorily defining the good life but by introducing what surpasses the good life.[13]

This transcendent dimension, which is seen to be so important for an effective ethic, the Bible claims to know firsthand.

Finally, to quote from a more recent author who clearly sees a distinction between biblical teaching and a philosophical approach to ethics:

> When theologians turn to Scripture for moral guidance they are not acting like moral philosophers. They do not begin with a theory of ethics but with a canonical text which is authoritative because it is inspired by God. . . . Systems of ethics begin with a fundamental principle or value. The Gospel begins with a person who claims that he himself is the "norm" we are to follow when he calls: "come, follow me."
>
> In both the Old Testament and the New a new way of life is presented to God's people to follow which is inseparable from the history that has revealed God.[14]

SOME METHODOLOGICAL CONSIDERATIONS

Here we need to make some distinctions, offer some cautions, and present some methodological considerations. The following chapter on "Source of Prophetic Ethical Teachings" will also involve important methodological considerations.

There was a time when, especially among some more liberal scholars, the prophets were thought to be the great discoverers (or at least the first proponents) of the distinctive Israelite morality.[15] Now almost all recognize that their contribution has to be seen within a much broader perspective. That is why, before we can speak specifically about the prophets, we need to say something about Old Testament ethics as such.

---

[13] From an unpublished position paper entitled "The Impact of Religious Transcendence Upon Moral Values," given at a symposium, June 24, 1975, as background for the American Bishops' pastoral on moral values. See also his *Transcendent Selfhood* (New York: Seabury, 1976).

[14] William C. Spohn, *What Are They Saying about Scripture and Ethics?* (fully rev. and expanded ed. Mahwah, NJ: Paulist, 1995) 1–2.

[15] The name of Julius Wellhausen frequently comes up in this connection. See the enlightening discussion on this by Joseph Blenkinsopp, *Prophecy and Canon: A Contribution to the Study of Jewish Origins* (Notre Dame: University of Notre Dame Press, 1977) 7.

Earlier we noted that the latitude involved in the definition of ethics allows some ambiguity. Therefore various authors attempt distinctions in order to introduce greater precision. For example, Barton points out that by "Old Testament ethics" (1) we can be referring to the historical development of *ideas about morality* or *actual moral conduct* or (2) we may be thinking of the Old Testament essentially as a book that forms part of the Christian Scriptures and be asking what, in its finished form, it has to say to us about ethical issues; and he thinks it is important that we be clear in our minds which of these two types of inquiry we are engaged in.[16] H. L. Bosman, on a somewhat different tack, begins by distinguishing between *ethos* and *ethics*. *Ethos* denotes the concretization of moral life as it occurs in a particular society; it concerns the way of life of individuals and groups insofar as they are governed by moral rules, norms, and values; it is not a matter of conscious reflection. *Ethics* is concerned with the study of *ethos* and does entail conscious reflection; it may be aimed at the description, explanation, or validity of moral behavior. "Old Testament ethics" would mean not only the study of its *ethos* but also the ethical reflection one actually encounters in the Old Testament. He then provides a threefold division: ethics can be the study of (1) what is good and bad human conduct ("normative ethics"); (2) what conduct is considered good or bad by a particular group of people ("descriptive ethics"); or (3) the validity and meaning of moral pronouncements ("meta-ethics").[17]

In my judgment the distinction between "descriptive ethics" and "normative ethics" is less significant in the prophetic material than it would be, for example, in the narrative tradition. When the biblical author tells the story of Jephthah's sacrifice of his daughter or of Abraham letting Sarah be taken into Pharaoh's harem or of Jacob cheating Esau or of Judah taking up with Tamar in the belief that she was a prostitute, all without comment, we *may* have material for "descriptive ethics," but when Jeremiah, in his Temple sermon, accuses the people of stealing, murdering, committing adultery, swearing falsely, etc., the address is to people who are understood to *know* that those things are wrong.

---

[16] John Barton, "Approaches to Ethics in the Old Testament," in John Rogerson, ed., *Beginning Old Testament Study* (Philadelphia: Westminster, 1983) 114.

[17] Hendrick L. Bosman, "Taking Stock of Old Testament Ethics," *OTE* 1 (1983) 97–104. The discussions of Barton and Bosman are not that far apart, for Bosman's "normative ethics" can be compared to Barton's "ideas about morality," his "descriptive ethics" to Barton's "actual moral conduct," and his "meta-ethics" to Barton's "what the Old Testament has to say about ethical issues."

Another important distinction made by both Barton and Bosman is that between "ethics in ancient Israel" and "Old Testament ethics." In this they follow the distinction proposed by Henry McKeating in an article that is of interest to us for its methodological content.[18] McKeating begins by citing Old Testament laws against adultery and the sanctions they propose. The apodictic[19] laws in the Decalogue (Exod 20:14; Deut 5:18) appeal to no explicit sanctions, but the casuistic laws of D and H[20] (Deut 22:22; Lev 20:10) prescribe death for both man and woman and do not envisage any alternative (i.e., mitigated) penalty, such as a fine. These laws are generally taken as giving the overall Old Testament manner of dealing with adultery. However, McKeating looks at indications from the narrative, wisdom, and prophetic texts and concludes that there is little evidence to show that death was *regularly* inflicted as a legal penalty. He thinks the D and H laws on adultery cannot be shown to be earlier than the seventh or sixth century. D and H did not invent the death penalty for adultery (it is found in earlier non-Israelite codes, though always as a *possible* penalty); what they do is make it mandatory. In effect, the D and H legislators are attempting to make adultery into a sacral crime by attaching penal sanctions to a divine prohibition that had been there for a very long time. There is plenty of evidence that the intention of taking adultery out of the area of family law and turning it into a sacral crime was no more than a partial success. From this McKeating draws the methodological conclusion that one needs to be very careful in interpreting the evidence provided by laws. We cannot simply read off our assessment of a society's ethical values from the laws it produced. He says we must consider what was the effectiveness of Israel's religion in determining the people's moral attitudes.

The Old Testament appears to establish as fact that Israel's religion was the decisive influence in moral matters. But the Old Testament is a body of largely religious documents, edited and put together by people for whom religion was a dominant interest, and McKeating concludes that Old Testament ethics is a theological construct, that "Old Testament ethics" and "the ethics of ancient Israelite society" do not necessarily coincide. The distinction is legitimate and one to be kept in mind, though

---

[18] Henry McKeating, "Sanctions against Adultery in Ancient Israelite Society, with Reflections on Methodology in the Study of Old Testament Ethics," *JSOT* 11 (March 1979) 57–72.

[19] The terms apodictic and casuistic, for those not familiar with them, are explained below, in Chapter Two.

[20] D and H designate the deuteronomic law code (Deuteronomy 12–26) and the Holiness Code (Leviticus 17–26) respectively.

it is much more relevant to law than to the prophets. To the extent that we have the witness of the prophets as living people addressing other living people, they are not dealing in "theological constructs" but, again, are speaking of obligations the people do recognize or the prophets feel they should recognize; or, if the ethical norms have indeed been rejected (and the prophets often accuse the leaders of doing this), that itself becomes the substance of their accusations. It can be noted, however, that editors have sometimes imposed on prophetic words behavioral ideals from later times.

Another methodological concern relates to the chronology of the sources *and* the particular groups involved—those two familiar and inevitable companions, the *diachronic* and *synchronic* approaches. That is to say, one must keep in mind both that things were different in the tenth century than in the sixth and that, in any period, different ethical concerns are to be found in different cultural circles (e.g., shepherds, city dwellers, court officials, priests, merchants, etc.); each group may have its own particular *ethos,* though obviously not with deviations so great that it would be impossible to speak of a general *ethos* for the people as a whole. Barton criticizes J. Hempel for attempting to trace a line of development through tenth-century historiography (J), ninth-century saga (Elijah and Elisha stories), eighth-century prophecy (Amos and Hosea), and seventh-century law (Deuteronomy).[21] Since quite different sorts of groups are involved, the criticism appears valid.

IS THE BIBLE NORMATIVE FOR ETHICS?

In approaching this thorny question it is important to establish what one means by "normative," for it can be taken in different senses; the disagreements among various authors sometimes stem from different understandings of the term "norm." For example, *Webster's Third New International Dictionary of the English Language Unabridged* (1993) gives "an authoritative rule or standard" as a first definition, "a standard of conduct or ethical value; a principle of right action" as a second, and "an ideal standard binding upon members of a group and serving to guide, control, or regulate proper and acceptable conduct" as a third. The distance between "authoritative rule" and "ideal standard" is considerable.

---

[21] "Understanding Old Testament Ethics," *JSOT* 9 (1978) 48. The reference is to J. Hempel, s.v. "Ethics in the OT," *Interpreter's Dictionary of the Bible,* ed. G. A. Buttrick (New York: Abingdon, 1962–1976).

Another aspect of this question of normativity has to do with whether we judge ethics to be teleological or deontological, that is, whether an action is to be judged by the result it produces or whether there is an antecedent obligation commanding or forbidding.[22] Although the biblical tradition undoubtedly judges that good actions have good results and bad actions bad results, especially in the wisdom tradition, it looks to the authority of God as the ultimate criterion of good and evil; must it therefore be judged to be deontological?[23] Robert J. Daly *et al.* hold that "the Bible is at least inceptively normative for Christian ethics." Presumably this is explained from what they go on to quote from Bernard Häring, who points out that a norm refers back to a *value* "which is much richer than what the verbal form of a norm can ever express," with the further assertion that "a norm which is not based on a value and does not direct one to a worthwhile action has no moral binding force." Some are willing to recognize the Bible as the (or a) proper source for the *values* on which the practical norms of Christian morality are based, but not as the proper source for the practical norms in themselves.[24] This is a step away from Lindblom's "theonomic ethics" (see above), but is an eminently defensible position. The behavior promoted and insisted on in the biblical tradition (such as social justice, concern for the oppressed and disadvantaged, respect for marriage, respect for truth, for life, etc.) provides norms for behavior at least in the sense that it imparts values on which the morality of concrete actions can be judged.

Somewhat similar but different is the distinction between "heteronomous" and "autonomous" ethics. Autonomous ethics relates to the position that "the moral dimension of human life has a form and structure of its own that is independent of religion, of custom and convention and

---

[22] In Robert J. Daly and others, eds., *Christian Biblical Ethics: From Biblical Revelation to Contemporary Christian Praxis: Method and Content* (New York and Ramsey: Paulist, 1984), the terms are explained as follows: "According to the *teleological* theory, the rightness or wrongness of an action is 'always determined by its tendency to produce certain consequences which are intrinsically good or bad,' while the *deontological* theory argues: 'Such and such a kind of action would always be right (or wrong) in such and such circumstances, *no matter what its consequences might be'"* (p. 81).

[23] The term comes from the Greek *to deon,* the neuter participle of the impersonal *deî* (from *deō,* to tie or bind), and means "that which is binding, needful, right."

[24] Daly, *Christian Biblical Ethics,* 74–77. The work of Häring cited is *Das Gesetz Christi,* 1:260 (English: *The Law of Christ: Moral Theology for Priests and Laity,* tr. Edwin G. Kaiser [Westminster, MD: Newman, 1961–1967]). Note that while the title and quotation refer to "Christian ethics," what is said is equally applicable to biblical ethics in general.

indeed of any other sphere of life or form of authority."[25] Heteronomous ethics would approximate deontological ethics in that it holds that the ultimate norm of morality comes from outside the human person. Daly *et al.* see these positions as mutually exclusive:

> The ultimate norm of morality is either outside of the human person *(heteronomy)* or within the human person *(autonomy)*. Rational ethics, esp. when dependent on Kant, has, of course, insisted on autonomy. Christian ethics, holding that God (the will of God / divine revelation) is the ultimate norm of morality, has insisted on heteronomy. This is sometimes called *theonomic moral positivism.* In its biblical form, it insists that the *Bible alone* is the norm of morality. In its "authority-form," it insists that official Church or community teaching is the ultimate practical norm of morality.[26]

But they argue that in some modern ethicists much of the "mutual exclusivity of the old positions" has broken down.[27]

The objections against taking the Bible as normative in any absolute sense are formidable, no matter how we approach it.[28] Exception may perhaps be made for the Orthodox Jew for whom the Torah is absolute, but even here there is no small amount of rabbinical exegesis and casuistry to save from the imposition of a literal carrying out of many prescriptions, and no little reinterpretation to apply the law to modern situations.[29] For the rest of us certain Old Testament legislative provisions create problems. Were we to encounter any Amalekites we might be loath to "blot out their memory from under the heavens" (Deut 26:19; cf. 1 Sam 15:1-3), to exclude Egyptians from the Lord's community until the third generation (Deut 23:8-9), to chop off someone's hand as a penalty (Deut 25:11-12), or

---

[25] Daly *et al., Christian Biblical Ethics,* 78–79, quoting J. E. Smith, "Autonomy of Ethics," *Dictionary of Christian Ethics,* ed. John Macquarrie (London: SCM, 1967) 25.

[26] Daly *et al., Christian Biblical Ethics,* 79.

[27] See also the discussion by John Rogerson, "The Old Testament and Social and Moral Questions," in M. Daniel Carroll, ed., *Theory and Practice in Old Testament Ethics.* JSOTSup 405 (London and New York: T & T Clark, 2004) 13–20.

[28] See the more detailed discussion, referring only to the Old Testament, in John Barton, *Ethics and the Old Testament* (Harrisburg, PA: Trinity Press International, 1998) 1–7.

[29] For example, Immanuel Jakobovits, "Jewish Law Faces Modern Problems," in Leon D. Stitskin, ed., *Studies in Torah Judaism* (New York: Yeshiva University Press, 1969), speaks of establishing all of Manhattan as an *Eruv,* i.e., "a legal device enacted by the rabbis whereby a large urban area, within boundaries properly designated and constituted, may be regarded as one corporate domain for the purpose of removing the prohibition against carrying outside private property on the Sabbath" (p. 344).

to impose the death penalty for violation of the Sabbath (Exod 35:2; cf. Num 15:32). Many Christians who like to think they observe the Sabbath strictly do not advert to the fact that they have substituted Sunday for Saturday and observe it in ways that bear little resemblance to biblical legislation.

If we turn to the narrative tradition, we might conclude from the Israelite invasion of Canaan that the Lord sanctions wars of conquest and the wholesale destruction of cities with their entire populations (Jos 6:21; 10:28-39; cf. Deut 7:1-4; 20:16-18). In fact, some parts of the Old Testament praise conduct that other parts condemn, as when the deuteronomistic historian praises Jehu's bloody zeal in dealing with Ahab's line and Baal worshipers (2 Kgs 10:15-30), an approach that Hosea condemns (Hos 1:4-5). So also some passages (such as some of those just cited) display the utmost hostility to pagans and an exclusivistic spirit (e.g., Isa 25:10-12; Ps 137:7-9), while others manifest a very open universalism (e.g., Isa 19:18-25).

These last examples make us aware that there was substantial ethical development during the time span within which biblical revelation took place. Things that were applauded by earlier generations were judged differently by later ones.[30]

SYSTEM OF ETHICS?

In view of the diversity of the Old Testament materials it is difficult even to think of attempting to erect anything like an overarching system from it. And Barton early insists that "there is no one 'ethics of the Old Testament.'" Nevertheless, he does end by presenting a synthesis that is at least worth reporting. In spite of the diversity within the Old Testament, he thinks there is "a strong family likeness about the Old Testament in all its parts." By and large the Old Testament registers only religious attitudes toward morality and shows that, at least for those who produced it, God was very much the center of ethical obligation. The simplest form of religious morality is one in which people think that ethics is a matter of doing what God tells them—and they devise ways of discovering God's will (oracles, etc.) or else they interpret laws as being the expression of the will of God. Wisdom literature likes to present morality as a matter of fitting one's life to the order and pattern observable in the world,

---

[30] The chronologically later text is not always the ethically more advanced. The deuteronomistic historian who praised Jehu's "zeal" for the Lord comes after the prophet Hosea who condemned it.

which is God's creation. And Barton brings in a third pattern, the imitation of God. The Old Testament can only make coherent sense within a particular religious system that can be specified and described, even if only in very general terms. There are certain common assumptions: for example, that YHWH is a God who demands total allegiance and whose purpose must not be resisted by humans. In the Old Testament God is the fountainhead of ethical obligation. This does not mean that ethics is straightforwardly "obedience to God's commands," for it involves a subtle synthesis of a number of ways of understanding this obedience. The basic category for ethics in the Old Testament is "Law," but law understood as *tôrâ*, i.e., not primarily as providing information about morality but as providing materials that, when pondered and absorbed into the mind, will suggest the pattern or shape of a way of life in the presence of God. But the Old Testament contains much more than laws or rules. Readers are meant to be directed in obeying God's will and living in fellowship with God, not simply by carrying out laws but also by reading the narratives, by worshiping God with the help of the psalms, and by meditating on the sayings of the sages and prophets. Thus practical moral conduct is inextricably linked with what we would call "spirituality": it is a matter of a style of life, not just of particular rulings. "Torah" is a system by which to live the whole life in the presence of God rather than a set of detailed regulations to cover every individual situation in which a moral ruling might be called for. The motive behind this is the desire to bring the whole of life under control of God's rule. Those parts of the Old Testament that deal with "theodicy," the attempt to vindicate the justice and goodness of God,[31] urge that God is just even on human terms, that God adheres to the same moral principles that humankind is expected to observe. To do good, on such a view, is to imitate God, to do the things God would do if God were a human being. What these things are can be read in some measure from the things God *has* done, especially the acts of love and faithfulness toward Israel. It is just for this reason that it is essential for Israel to keep record of these events. The rules God requires Israel to observe can be seen to be congruent with the character of the deity only if the events that show what that character is are also recounted. God's purposes for the future, in which that character will continue to be consistently manifested, also need to be included. And

---

[31] Found especially in the wisdom literature, some of the psalms, and even in some prophetic passages.

so the historical books run off without a break into prophetic books that confirm for the reader that God will continue to be in the future as in the past, true to the sorts of moral principles laid upon humans.[32]

There are undoubtedly a number of questions one might raise concerning this non-system, but one can only applaud the manner in which Barton attempts to make all the Old Testament traditions, including the narrative tradition and the Psalter, contribute to its ethics.

---

[32] Barton, "Approaches to Ethics," 113–30.

Chapter Two

SOURCE OF PROPHETIC ETHICAL TEACHINGS

At this point it will be useful to discuss a number of Old Testament traditions that have been proposed by various authors as the source of the contents of the prophets' ethics, such as covenant, law, wisdom, and prophetic experience. We could easily play at "sic" and "non" here in the sense that each of those traditions has a role to play in *some* prophetic ethical teaching but none of them is the exclusive source for any prophet. The relative importance of any of them can be assessed only with regard to an individual prophet. We should note at the outset that although "covenant" is given in the above list, and we will discuss it in some detail, it cannot be a *source* in the sense of providing content (even though some authors treat it that way), but can only define the relationship between God and Israel and thus would provide a *basis* for Old Testament morality.[1]

COVENANT

We will begin by saying something about the nature of covenant. First of all, it should be remembered (though it is often not adverted to at all) that the application of the covenant concept to the Yhwh-Israel relationship involves analogy. If we conceive of God as transcendent we can speak of him/her only by analogy because, by definition, a transcendent God exceeds our power to conceptualize, formulate, express: by analogy some concept known from our human experience is applied to God. To speak of God as "Father" (or "Mother") is possible only because we are familiar

---

[1] This distinction between the *source* of (the content of) Old Testament morality and the *basis* for it will be clarified in what follows.

with human parenthood. When this concept is purified of its imperfec-
tions and raised to the highest degree it can be used to say something
about the sort of love and mercy God manifests toward us, the sort of
relationship we enjoy with God. So also with covenant: its application to
divine-human relations supposes the human institution of covenant.

Although many begin the discussion of covenant with George E.
Mendenhall's comparison of Israel's covenant to international suzerainty
treaties,[2] I think a far better starting place is with Johannes Pedersen. Pedersen begins his discussion of covenant with the concept of community,
which he sees to be characterized by a common participation in blessing.
He speaks of the various kinds of community: that of the family, that of
the people, that based on friendship. He points out that the distinction
between the relationship of kin and friendship is a vague one, that it
is called both *šālôm* and *bĕrît* (or sometimes both together: Ezek 34:25;
37:26), words of different origins that do not designate different kinds of
relationships. The covenant must always contain a certain community of
will and those united by it have a common aim, though it is the stronger
who imparts his character to the fellowship, the weaker who enjoys his
strength. Pedersen also speaks in this connection of the importance of
righteousness *(sĕdāqâ),* the mental quality on the strength of which peace
is maintained and which is therefore the kernel of peace and blessing.[3]
On this point Gerhard von Rad gives Pedersen credit for new insights
on *sĕdāqâ* but questions his concept of it as "health of the soul."[4]

When approached from this direction, the analogy of the YHWH-
Israel covenant can be seen to involve a relationship that, on many levels,
calls for a response of obedience: Israel as recipient of "blessing" needs
to respond in gratitude; obedience is also implied in that there must
be just one will in the covenant community, that of the greater; to act
rightly, Pedersen says, means that the soul acts in accord with its nature
by maintaining the covenant.[5]

---

[2] George E. Mendenhall, "Covenant Forms in Israelite Tradition," an article originally
published in *BA* 17 (1954) and reprinted many times; available in Edward F. Campbell and
David N. Freedman, eds., *The Biblical Archaeologist Reader* 3 (Garden City, NY: Doubleday,
1970) 25–33.

[3] Johannes Pedersen, *Israel, Its Life and Culture, I–II* (London: Oxford University Press,
1926); these matters are discussed in the chapter on "Peace and Covenant," pp. 263–310.

[4] Gerhard von Rad, *Old Testament Theology* (Edinburgh and London: Oliver and Boyd,
1962) 1:376, n. 14.

[5] Erhard Gerstenberger, "Covenant and Commandment," *JBL* 84 (1965) 38–51, also
takes a rather different tack from Mendenhall. He speaks of covenant (= treaty) declara-

While the "community" referred to here is (in the covenant analogy) between Yʜᴡʜ and Israel (the vertical dimension), there are important implications for relations within the community of Israel itself: whatever is true of the Yʜᴡʜ-Israel relationship in terms of quasi-familial intimacy, sharing of blessing, *šālôm,* interaction characterized by *ṣĕdāqâ,* etc., ought also to be extended to the relationship between members of the Israel community (thus, the horizontal dimension). Covenant *per se* does not specify what duties Israel undertakes by entering into relationship with Yʜᴡʜ, though obviously concluding a covenant involves specifying it in some way.[6]

Mendenhall's approach[7] to the matter, as is well known, is very different. It has been treated so frequently that here it will be sufficient to summarize it very briefly. His starting point is the Hittite suzerainty (vassal) treaty and the form in which it is cast, which exhibits certain characteristic parts, including preamble, historical prologue, stipulations, periodic reading, list of witnesses, and curses and blessings. He then attempts to identify these characteristic parts (or most of them) in the Decalogue and concludes that Israel's Sinai covenant was formulated in terms of a suzerainty treaty. This is done not without some apologetic intent, for he asserts that this form was not in vogue in the ancient Near East after the thirteenth century and that, therefore, Israel's covenant (and the Decalogue) go back to the time of Moses.[8] Mendenhall obtained a very wide following, including

tions that begin "You are my brother (friend) and I am your brother (friend)." He sees this two-way binding as an essential characteristic of ancient Near Eastern covenants. The terminology just described "would define the covenant relationship as a cordial agreement between partners—no matter how superior one of them might be—to promote peace and to combat common enemies" (pp. 41–42). See also Frank Moore Cross, "Kinship and Covenant in Ancient Israel," in idem, *From Epic to Canon; History and Literature in Ancient Israel* (Baltimore and London: Johns Hopkins University Press, 1998) 3–21.

[6] As per the quotation from Gerstenberger, given below.

[7] See above, n. 2; as noted below, Mendenhall has modified his position somewhat in his article on "Covenant" in *ABD.*

[8] "It must be emphasized again, that this particular structure of covenant is not attested for any other subsequent period. Though it is to be expected that survival of the form outlasted the Hittite Empire, it is perfectly clear that the home of this form is in the 2nd millennium ʙ.ᴄ. and cannot be proven (outside Israel) to have survived elsewhere" ("Covenant Forms," 36). Mendenhall modified his position on some points in his article on "Covenant" in *ABD* (co-authored with Gary A. Herion). He acknowledges the debate, but claims that the answer centers on one point: "whether the Sinai covenant was indeed a historical reality known to the Israelite population in the premonarchic period (ca. 1200–1000 ʙ.ᴄ.), or whether it was instead nothing more than a pious literary fabrication of the later monarchic period. . . ." (*ABD* 1:1183). This appears to be a case of *petitio*

Delbert Hillers[9] and others. Dennis McCarthy,[10] however, pointed out that the suzerainty treaty was much more widely distributed in space and time than Mendenhall realized and that therefore its use would not necessarily relate the covenant to Moses or his time. More importantly, the Decalogue bears too slight a resemblance to the treaty forms: the preamble and historical prologue are practically nonexistent and other parts (aside from stipulations), including the indispensable curses and blessings formula, are not found in the Exodus setting.[11] This is not to deny that covenant is ancient in Israel or that it goes back to the Sinai context; it simply means that the Sinai covenant was not thought of in terms of or formulated on the pattern of a vassal treaty. McCarthy would see Israel's covenant assimilated to the treaty form at a later period, reflected very clearly in Deuteronomy, both in its overall structure and in individual sections of it.

Covenant *per se* does not bespeak ethical/moral teaching, but it does imply a relationship. And as Gerstenberger points out, "no entente, cordial though it may be, can operate in the long run on general prescriptions which define attitudes rather than actions. . . . Guidelines for appropriate behavior as well as denunciations of unlawful acts have to be formulated."[12] In the later development virtually all of Israel's legislation, in virtue of being placed in the Mount Sinai context, came to be understood as specifying the covenant,[13] but even in the earliest period there must have been some specification. While there are weighty arguments that suggest that the complete Decalogue as we know it does not

---

principii. It is possible to hold that the covenant at Sinai is historical without conceiving it as patterned on a suzerainty treaty, as in fact McCarthy and many others, including the present writer, do; only later, e.g., in Deuteronomy, is Israel's covenant with Yhwh presented as structured along treaty lines.

[9] As seen, e.g., in Delbert Hillers, *Covenant: The History of a Biblical Idea* (Baltimore: Johns Hopkins University Press, 1969).

[10] Dennis McCarthy, *Treaty and Covenant* (2d ed. Rome: Pontifical Biblical Institute, 1978). Or see the more popular work, *Old Testament Covenant* (Richmond: John Knox, 1972).

[11] See further the criticism by Dale Patrick, *Old Testament Law* (Atlanta: John Knox, 1985) 224–25, with the summary statement, "Such flaws vitiate the treaty thesis and prompt me to leave it out of the exposition of the covenant texts" (p. 224). See also my own treatment in "Apodictic Law and the Eighth-Century Prophets," in Maurya Horgan and Paul Kobelski, eds., *To Touch the Text: Biblical and Related Studies in Honor of Joseph A. Fitzmyer, s.j.* (New York: Crossroad, 1989) 103–17.

[12] "Covenant and Commandment," 43.

[13] Not to mention much that was not legislation in any normal sense of the word; reference can be made, in particular, to the liturgical and priestly lore and customs that make up the bulk of Leviticus.

go back to the beginning, as will be pointed out below, I would suggest that the earliest specifications (i.e., at Sinai) included commitment to the worship of Yhwh alone[14] and Sabbath observance.

Covenant, as already explained, is not the source of the *content* of Old Testament moral teaching, but it does operate as an influence in the ethical sphere in at least two ways: first in that the relationship it implies is a motive for fidelity and obedience; second in that it may be specified by laws that now come to be closely connected with it and derive authority from it, though the different codes come to be connected with it at different times (e.g., H comes to be associated with it at a much later date than the Covenant Code, in all probability). Furthermore, the question of the relationship of the prophet to the covenant has to be answered separately in the case of each individual prophet.[15] For example, Hosea seems to have the covenant analogy as background in his presentation of Israel as Yhwh's bride, while in Isaiah there is no discernible covenant thought. Thus it is necessary to view with reserve the approach of those who assume a pervasive influence of covenant on all the prophets. The covenant concept seems to have had a greater impact on the northern tribes than it did on Judah, and this was especially the case after the division of the united monarchy. We can easily accept covenant influence on Jeremiah, both because of his northern roots and because of the Deuteronomic reform, which took place during his ministry, and on those prophets who followed him, but the case is rather different with Isaiah.

ISRAEL'S LEGAL TRADITION

Law is so prominent a feature of Old Testament ethics and of the Old Testament itself that sometimes it is the only thing that is looked at. In sheer bulk it looms very large, constituting probably half the Pentateuch. A useful starting point would be the listing of the various codes:

---

[14] See the terms of the Sinai agreement as suggested by Jo Ann Hackett, "There Was No King in Israel," in M. D. Coogan, ed., *The Oxford History of the Biblical World* (Oxford and New York: Oxford University Press, 1998) 158.

[15] Ronald E. Clements, *Prophecy and Tradition* (Atlanta: John Knox, 1975), especially in his Chapter 2, explicitly modified the stance of his earlier *Prophecy and Covenant*. SBT 1/43 (London: SCM, 1965), that of bringing together "a considerable variety of Israel's religious traditions into a relatively uniform covenant theology." In this same section he also rejects the arguments of those who see the prophets as exercising an office of covenant mediator, who see prophetic denunciations based on treaty curses, and who find a distinctive "covenant lawsuit" behind some prophetic passages (pp. 8–23).

(*Ethical*) *Decalogue:* Exod 20:2-17; Deut 5:6-21
Ritual Decalogue: Exod 34:17-26
Covenant Code: Exod 20:22–23:19(33)
Deuteronomic Code: Deuteronomy 12–26
Holiness Code (H): Leviticus 17–26
Priestly Code: the laws in P are scattered throughout the Pentateuch; see
   especially Exod 12:1-20, 40-50; 35:1-3; Leviticus 1–16; 27; Numbers 5–6;
   15; 18–19; 27–30.

In the present Pentateuchal context all of these are closely joined to
the covenant, all but Deuteronomy placing them at Sinai, even though
historically their origins were quite diverse. This says something very
important theologically about Israel's perception of morality: covenant
is that which makes Israel Yhwh's people; law is that which specifies its
response—or at least part of its response. Nevertheless, as was indicated
earlier, it is also necessary to keep things in synchronic and diachronic
perspective, i.e., to keep in mind when a particular code came into existence and what group(s) it would have related to.

THE INDIVIDUAL COLLECTIONS

The brief comments that follow are not intended as expositions of
the various collections but only to indicate what code or codes might or
might not have been in force in a given place or time, as background for
the prophets we will discuss.

The Decalogue

There is a large body of opinion that would date the Decalogue (sometimes called the Ethical Decalogue to distinguish it from the Ritual Decalogue) to the time of Moses and of Sinai; we have seen that Mendenhall's
thesis attempted to demonstrate that it dated to Mosaic times. Harold
H. Rowley also developed a fairly elaborate argument for its antiquity.[16]
Some of those who have argued for an early date have based their arguments in part on prophetic texts. In Hos 4:2 and Jer 7:9 condemnations

---

[16] In *From Joseph to Joshua* (London: Oxford University Press, 1950) he attempted to
take into account the fact that the Ritual Decalogue appears to be more primitive than
the Ethical Decalogue (which would therefore argue that the latter could not be Israel's
earliest legislation). He built upon the "Kenite hypothesis," according to which the name
Yhwh and certain elements of Yahwism were mediated to Moses through the Kenites. He
went on to argue that the Ritual Decalogue was a Kenite code, and this therefore left the
way open for holding that Moses produced the Ethical Decalogue through adaptation of
the Kenite code.

of three sorts of actions that correspond to prohibitions found in the Decalogue come immediately together, and it has been urged that these prophets know or are citing the Decalogue. But three are far short of ten, all three are common crimes, and neither prophet cites them in the same order as they occur in the Decalogue:

> Hosea: murder, theft, adultery
> Jeremiah: theft, murder, adultery
> Decalogue: murder, adultery, theft

Further, they do not appear in "commandment" form in the prophetic texts; in Hosea they are part of a catalogue of crimes, in Jeremiah part of a rhetorical question. Georg Föhrer, working from those prophetic texts and others like them, has argued that we have here a brief series of three precepts of similar content (i.e., not injuring the neighbor) and probably, in their original formulation, similar in form (in the Decalogue each is simply *lōʾ* plus the verb in the imperfect). Such apodictic series tend to be short (two or three), and in any case to be restricted to one particular sphere of behavior. Thus, although in Lev 18:7-17 we have a series of eleven (originally ten), they all relate to prohibitions of sexual relations within the larger family (including grandmother, aunt, mother-in-law) such as would have occupied one tent in a semi-nomadic group. The tendency to cover a broader area of morality in a single series of commandments (if that is the correct term) would appear to be a secondary development. Fohrer argues for the Decalogue being composed of a number of smaller series (he speaks explicitly of 1–2, 6–8, and 9–10—in which we can note diverse grammatical forms). But it clearly intends to be a brief summary of general obligations and as such would be a later development. He would date it to the time of the Elohist.[17]

It is very difficult to attain to any certitude on the question of date. As indicated above, my own position is that worship of Yʜwʜ alone was probably part of the Sinai specification; the prohibition of images[18] and Sabbath command perhaps also belong there. The Pentateuchal narrative

---

[17] Georg Föhrer, "Das sogenannte apodiktisch formulierte Recht und der Dekalog," *KD* 11 (1965) 49–74. Reprinted in idem, *Studien zur alttestamentlichen Theologie und Geschichte (1949–1966).* BZAW 115 (Berlin: de Gruyter, 1969). See also Helen Schüngel-Straumann, *Der Dekalog—Gottes Gebote?* SBS 67 (Stuttgart: Katholisches Bibelwerk, 1973).

[18] If the prohibition of images is primitive, it was not always strictly observed. See William G. Dever, *What Did the Biblical Writers Know, and When Did they Know It? What Archaeology Can Tell Us About the Reality of Ancient Israel* (Grand Rapids and Cambridge: Eerdmans, 2001) 234–37 and the sources cited there.

tradition that has the tablets of the Decalogue placed in the ark suggests that the time of the Elohist is the latest possible date,[19] thus a time considerably earlier than Hosea and Jeremiah, on the usual dating of the Pentateuchal documents.

The Ritual Decalogue

This collection is introduced into the text in a rather surprising way. Sometime after Moses had broken the tablets containing the Decalogue given him on Mount Sinai he is told to provide two new tablets upon which God is to write the commandments that were on the former tablets (Exod 34:1); the commandments God now utters are identified as "the words of the covenant, the ten commandments" and Moses is commanded to write them down (v. 28), but they are not the same as those previously given as the text on the tablets in Exod 20:2-17. Evidently the editors used the story about the breaking of the tablets to introduce another collection they did not wish to be lost (34:17-26).

This collection is sometimes called the Yahwist Decalogue (just as the Ethical Decalogue is sometimes called the Elohist Decalogue),[20] but more often the Ritual (or Cultic) Decalogue. This is because, aside from the first command ("You shall not make for yourselves molten gods"; v. 17), the provisions relate to the celebration of feasts, the offering of the firstborn, Sabbath observance, and similar matters. Reference has already been made to Rowley's suggestion as to its origin (see above, n. 16).

The Covenant Code

This collection has often been dated to the early period of the Tribal League and said to be intended for a society composed largely of shepherds and farmers without extensive commercial activities; it is asserted to be the code that goes with the covenant enacted under Joshua at Shechem (Joshua 24). It may have been mainly a northern code, and whether it was ever in force in Judah is questioned.[21] Many recent authors hold it to be of somewhat mixed provenance, coming in part from older sources but redacted in its present form during the monarchy;

---

[19] As already noted, Fohrer sees the time of the Elohist as the *terminus ad quem* for development of the Decalogue.

[20] For a brief discussion of the possible attribution of these two codes to those Pentateuchal traditions see Patrick, *Old Testament Law,* 17–18, 35–38.

[21] For a brief summary of opinion see Patrick, *Old Testament Law,* who supposes that "the Covenant Code with its framework was . . . a northern document which was combined with the Elohist prior to the fall of the Northern Kingdom" (pp. 63–65).

J. Albert Soggin speaks of the legislator's concern as "a typical rural society, relatively well-to-do."[22] It appears to be earlier than Deuteronomy (see below).

The Deuteronomic Code

The date of the Deuteronomic Code is widely accepted by Scripture scholars as late seventh century, the "book of the law" discovered in the eighteenth year of King Josiah (622), as reported in 2 Kings 22–23. This "book of the law" is generally identified with the core Deuteronomy. This does not, however, exclude the probability that many of its provisions were current before that date. In fact, there are reasons for arguing that many of its provisions were taken over from the Covenant Code.[23] In any case the general opinion is that the traditionary circle in which it was formulated and passed on (variously identified as levitical or prophetic) originated in the north and migrated to Judah around the time of the fall of Israel; in Judah the traditions were crystallized and written down, perhaps in the days of Hezekiah.

The Priestly Code and the Holiness Code

Although the Holiness Code (H) is currently imbedded in the complex of the Priestly Code (P) in Leviticus, many hold that it was originally a separate collection. It is so named because its provisions aim at maintaining the ritual cleanness that ought to be preserved by a holy people; it is characterized by the formula, "Be holy, for I, the LORD, your God, am holy" (Lev 19:2; 20:7). Although to a great extent this holiness is seen in terms of separation from what is considered profane, some of its provisions express high ethical ideals (see below, p. 31). H was probably made up of several smaller collections before its insertion into P.

Relatively late dates are usually assigned for both H and P (late monarchy and postexilic times, respectively), but much of the material in each is far older. Priestly circles are generally quite conservative and while P in its present form reflects the hierarchy and practice of postexilic times, that is a *terminus ad quem* for the development, with origins that reach back into the early days of the Jerusalem priesthood and perhaps

---

[22] J. Albert Soggin, *Introduction to the Old Testament,* tr. John Bowden (3d ed. Louisville: Westminster John Knox, 1989) 84.

[23] For an early detailed exposition and comparison see Samuel R. Driver, *An Introduction to the Literature of the Old Testament* (10th ed. revised and enlarged. New York: Scribner's, 1902) 73–76; for a recent summary see Patrick, *Old Testament Law,* 65, 97–101.

beyond. It should be remembered that it is priestly lore and tradition and much of it would not have been common coin in other circles at any period. It probably did not come into the Pentateuch (and so into the Sinai context) until the latest stages of redaction. The amazing thing is that it ever did: that rubrics for offering sacrifices and ordaining priests should ever have been put under the formula, "The Lord told Moses: thus shall you speak to the Israelites . . . " (Exod 20:22) as though they were intended as law for the people as a whole.

NATURE OF ANCIENT NEAR EASTERN LAW

Reference has already been made to apodictic law in the foregoing discussion and will be in what follows, so it is necessary to explain the term and to distinguish it from casuistic law, the form most commonly encountered in ancient Near Eastern law codes. "Apodictic" is applied to the peremptory sort of formulations we have in the "Thou shalt [not] . . ." type of commandment and the imperative.[24] "Casuistic" is applied to laws in the conditional formulation "if a person does [specification of the crime], then [specification of the punishment]." The origin of casuistic (from the Latin *casus*, "case") is easy to discern. A particular case is brought to the attention of the authorities for a judgment; for example, someone's grain field is set afire by a neighbor who was burning out weeds in his own field and the first person demands restitution for the destroyed grain. When the authorities (royal officials, village elders, etc., depending on the social context) render judgment, their decision may establish a certain precedent, so that when something similar happens, the same judgment is likely to be rendered, possibly with appeal to the earlier case. When this has happened often enough to establish a custom, it can be formulated "if . . . then . . ." (cf. Exod 22:4-5). It is obvious that such laws arise only in response to a particular need; laws governing agriculture are not needed in a purely pastoral nomadic culture. For this reason it is equally obvious that many of Israel's laws would not have come from the time of Sinai but would have arisen only after the Israelites had entered the land and settled down.

---

[24] The term "apodictic" has been applied more or less broadly by different scholars and is sometimes applied to other types of formulation, for example, "the one who does X will be put to death," though that can perhaps more accurately be reduced to a casuistic law that carries the death penalty ("if a man does X, then he will be put to death"). A better case can be made for "cursed be the one who does X," for in that case no penalty is prescribed, but the wrath of the deity is invoked.

Although we have been calling these formulations "laws," they are not really that in our sense of the word. These case laws simply gave indication of what was the customary disposition of this or that sort of case. They were for the guidance of the judge without necessarily being binding on him;[25] much less, then, did they simply dictate to the ordinary citizen how he or she must (or must not) live—though they did indicate what would be likely to happen to those who engaged in certain types of behavior. All this relates to casuistic law, the form in which virtually every provision of the ancient Near Eastern law codes (Code of Hammurabi, Middle Assyrian Laws, Code of Eshnunna, Hittite Laws, etc.) is cast. It is not surprising that we have a great many of them in the biblical legal collections, both because of the way such laws came into being and because Israel was subject to cultural influence from the peoples who created these other ancient Near Eastern codes.

However, in Israel we also find the apodictic form, a command in the second person imperative (singular or plural) or future (singular or plural). This *second person* apodictic as a *law form* is unique to Israel.[26] How it came to be incorporated into Israel's legislative tradition is disputed. Again the influence of Mendenhall has been tremendous. One of the characteristic elements of the Hittite suzerainty treaties was the stipulations, and these were often second person apodictic formulations; thus, in arguing that Israel's covenant was formulated on the pattern of such treaties Mendenhall claimed that apodictic law appears in Israel as specification of the covenant and is patterned on the treaty stipulations. However,

---

[25] George E. Mendenhall, "Ancient Oriental and Biblical Law," *Biblical Archaeologist Reader* 3:3–24 (originally published *BA* 17 [1954] 26–46), speaking mainly of the Code of Hammurabi, says: "In the past they [law codes] had been regarded naturally as 'legislation' established as law by the king who was responsible for the codification [of it]. . . . Recently it has been necessary to give up this position. Landsberger has . . . demonstrated that not only are the codes not law in the modern sense of the term, but also that the concept of a written binding law code was completely lacking in old Mesopotamian law. It seems clear that the judges of ancient times had neither the custom nor the techniques for arriving at a decision by means of interpreting and applying an authoritative written law code. . . . Whatever the purpose of the code, it cannot have been positive law binding on all judges in their decisions, but was simply a description of a legal tradition resting, it is believed, largely upon earlier collections of laws" (pp. 9–12).

[26] The two phrases are stressed because third person apodictic laws do occur (though only rarely) in other Near Eastern law codes and because second person apodictic formulations do occur in other contexts (treaty stipulations, wisdom instructions, royal instructions, sepulchral inscriptions, etc.). See Rifat Sonsino, *Motive Clauses in Hebrew Law: Biblical Forms and Near Eastern Parallels.* SBLDS 45 (Chico, CA: Scholars, 1980) 37–38.

if one rejects the treaty analogy, as many scholars do (see above), that explanation of the origin of apodictic law also falls through.

A number of important studies have pointed in a different direction. Erhard Gerstenberger, investigating prohibitions, argues that the stylization of the second person address as Yнwн-speeches at Sinai is secondary and that the original context for the prohibitions is not a covenant renewal ceremony (against Albrecht Alt and others) but must be sought elsewhere.[27] He sees that most of the prohibitions, which he finds concentrated in parts of the Covenant Code, Holiness Code, and Deuteronomic Code, do not regulate duties toward God but relate to right behavior toward other people[28]—for the most part those things that have parallels in the wisdom literature. He sees them as originally addressed to the individual, present and listening. As to the origin of the form, he rejects Mendenhall's treaty form argument,[29] suggesting that most of the prohibitions suppose a semi-nomadic or small town society. He sees them rooted in clan ethic *(Sippenethos),* with the Semitic clan as the place of origin. Thus the prohibitions were the authoritative orders of the clan or family head, but they take their worth not primarily from the power of the clan chieftain but rather from the sanctified rule of life they represent. Gerstenberger appeals to the example of the Rechabites (Jer 35:6-7); they refuse to drink the wine Jeremiah offers them, citing the words of Jonadab, their forefather, who forbade them to drink wine, build houses, or engage in agriculture, and his words are couched in a series of *lō$^{\circ}$* + imperfect (future) formulations,[30] just as are most of the commandments of the Decalogue. Here, then, it is a matter of a precept given

---

[27] Erhard Gerstenberger, *Wesen und Herkunft des "apodiktischen Rechts"* (Neukirchen-Vluyn: Neukirchener Verlag, 1965).

[28] Gerstenberger also recognizes that there are a number of cultic prohibitions but finds that these are of the sort that relate to a cultic functionary who is the head of a family or clan, that the kind of authority speaking here is patriarchal rather than civil or priestly.

[29] He follows McCarthy in this and points out that treaty stipulations are all ordered to the end for which the treaty was made; they redound to the advantage of the suzerain. (Of the Old Testament prohibitions he sees only those against "other gods," images, and cursing, and the law of the altars as possibly being rooted in a covenant ceremony.)

[30] There are five in this series, all of which, as in the early apodictic series, relate to the same sphere of activity. Jonadab seems to have been more famous than the eponymous ancestor Rechab; see 2 Kgs 10:15-27, where he accompanies Jehu for the extermination of Baal worshipers. Jeremiah's encounter with the Rechabites was intended to contrast their obedience to the precepts of their ancestor with the Israelites' disobedience toward the Lord (Jer 35:12-14).

by the clan father in the same apodictic form we find in some Israelite laws; the substantive (v. 18) is *miṣwâ,* "precept, commandment," a term at home both in the wisdom and legal traditions. Gerstenberger looks at the wisdom literature and speaks of the similarities to be found, and concludes that negative wisdom admonitions and the legal prohibitions had the same origin, namely, the *Lebensordnung* (rule of life), from which they developed independently. Once released from its natural origin, this sort of formulation was taken into a new context and developed further; this further development explains why the prohibition ultimately manifests a different form in the legal tradition than that generally found in the wisdom tradition.

The apodictic formulation prescribes no punishment, and in the clan context this was in order, for the clan was responsible for the three closely joined functions of education, regulation, and the judicial; punishment, when needed, could be imposed by the clan father. But when the Israelites settled in Palestine, Gerstenberger theorizes, the influence of Canaanite practice (based on casuistic law, as in Mesopotamia) appeared more useful for legal proceedings "at the gate." Apodictic formulations also were taken up into the legal tradition, but now are placed into the context of Sinai where the speaker is understood to be the Lord.

Another influential work that broke ground in the same general area was by Wolfgang Richter.[31] He pays a great deal more attention to the difference in form between the wisdom and legal traditions. Following von Soden, he uses "prohibitive" for *lōʾ* + imperfect (future), found mainly in law, and "vetitive" for *ʾal* + jussive, found mainly in wisdom, though also in the prophets.[32] Without going into his investigation in detail, we can say that he looks carefully into the law collections and finds the prohibitive there closely related to the wisdom admonition *(Mahnspruch),* both in terms of content and in having motivation attached to it. Richter concludes that there is a connection between the two forms in that they have a life setting in the wisdom school of the upper middle class. The significance of all this for understanding the prophets should become apparent later.

---

[31] Wolfgang Richter, *Recht und Ethos. Versuch einer Ortung des weisheitlichen Mahnspruches.* STANT 15 (Munich: Kösel, 1966).

[32] The vetitive, when supplied with a motivation, is called "admonition," *Mahnspruch* in German, which explains the title of his book.

UNIQUE AND COMMON ASPECTS OF ISRAELITE LAW

The two primary grammatical law forms (casuistic and apodictic) already illustrate that Israel has something in common with the legal traditions of the surrounding cultures and something unique. This is true also of the content. The rejection of, e.g., murder and adultery, found in apodictic law in Israel (as in the Decalogue) is common in the ancient Near Eastern law codes. What is certainly unique is the prohibition of worshiping other gods and of images. Unique also are some of those things that relate to cult and worship, such as the observance of the Sabbath. Obviously these are not things that are apt for being the content of casuistic law.

It can also be asserted that the *strong* concern for social justice, for the defense of the weaker members of society (stranger, widow, orphan, etc.) is fairly unique *in law*. Such concern is found in non-biblical traditions, especially in wisdom literature, but it does not receive the emphatic attention in law that we find in Israel. That is to say, individual laws exist in favor of those in need of protection, but that is somewhat different from making them beneficiaries of very generic laws, laws that amount almost to exhortations. Again the casuistic form, in which virtually all non-biblical laws are cast, does not lend itself to such concerns.

I would also say (though this may be disputed by others) that Israel's understanding of law as revealing God's will, and thus being enforced by divine authority, is unique. Hammurabi claims responsibility for the laws he promulgated,[33] but the provisions of the Pentateuch are regularly preceded by "The LORD said to Moses, thus shall you say to the children of Israel . . ." or some such expression. Thus in Israel the law was understood (at least by the time the Sinai narrative reached something like its present form) to be the revelation of God's will. That would mean

---

[33] It is sometimes asserted that the Code of Hammurabi was mandated to the famous king by a god. It is indeed true that the diorite stele from Susa on which the text of the Code of Hammurabi is inscribed shows Shamash handing something to Hammurabi, and this is often taken as settling the case; but what is being handed to him is certainly not the stele containing the laws! Theophile Meek, referring to the relief, simply describes the king as "in the act of receiving the commission to write the lawbook from the god of justice, the sun god Shamash." What Hammurabi asserts in the Prologue is that, called by Marduk, "I established law and justice in the language of the land." Although late in the Epilogue he identifies himself as the one "to whom Shamash committed law," a whole series of expressions ("the laws of justice, which [I] set up," "I wrote my precious words . . . ," "the law of the land which I enacted ") indicate that he is responsible for the content (*ANET,* 164–65, 177–80).

that the vertical and horizontal dimensions go together, equally expressions of God's will;[34] and this in turn means that where the horizontal dimension (social justice, etc.) is lacking, the vertical dimension (worship, sacrifice) is impossible. This concept is very important and lies behind those prophetic denunciations of the cult that we know so well.

Thus was achieved in Israel the union of morality and religion that to us seems so natural but was hardly known elsewhere. Walther Eichrodt has this to say:

> This divine authority is concentrated in a single personal will, which takes complete hold of the man addressed by it, and tolerates no other claim. Here the obligation imposed by the Law is unconditional, and cannot be avoided by recourse to any other divine court of appeal more kindly disposed to human interests, like the personal tutelary gods of paganism. Nor can it be avoided by magical practices or exorcisms which compel the desired result. In the strict "thou shalt" of the Decalogue . . . it is not some human lawgiver but the divine Lawgiver himself who speaks and makes his will the absolute norm. . . . Thus not only the Law of the cult but also the civil Law acquires the character of a direct demand from God.[35]

It remains to say a few words about one other unique feature of Israelite law, namely the motivations found in it. Although others have written more extensively on the subject,[36] an early study by Berend Gemser provides a useful summary.[37] He found that Israelite law codes manifested an increasing tendency to provide their provisions with motivations. That is, seventeen percent of the laws in the Covenant Code, sixty percent in the Deuteronomic Code, and sixty-five percent in the Holiness Code are provided with motivations; the various Decalogues have between twenty-five percent and thirty-three percent, which leads him to suggest they come between the Covenant Code and Deuteronomy. He finds this a striking feature when compared to the non-Israelite law

---

[34] This is aptly epitomized in the inclusion in the Decalogue, the summary of Israel's basic obligations, of matters that relate to both God and neighbor. Traditionally this is expressed by depicting the "two tablets of the Law" as referring, respectively, to these two areas, but, as Raymond F. Collins, *Christian Morality: Biblical Foundations* (Notre Dame: University of Notre Dame Press, 1986) 51, correctly notes, the Bible gives us no information on this score.

[35] Walther Eichrodt, *Man in the Old Testament.* SBT 1/4 (Chicago: Regnery, 1951) 15–16.

[36] See the reference to Sonsino in n. 26 above.

[37] Berend Gemser, "The Importance of the Motive Clause in Old Testament Law," International Organization for the Study of the Old Testament, *Congress Volume.* VTSup 1 (1953) 50–66.

codes in which, he says, not a single instance of motive clauses can be discovered. This assertion is challenged by Sonsino, but his discussion indicates that motive clauses in non-Israelite codes are rare and of a rather different nature and origin from those in Israel.[38] The reason Gemser gives for the frequency of the motive clause in Israel is that the laws are directed to the people rather than to the judges or jurists and, like Sonsino (see previous note), he relates the practice of providing motivations to the wisdom tradition.

POSITIVE AND NEGATIVE ASPECTS OF LAW

Derogatory references to "Old Testament morality" usually come with reference to law and usually from people who know little about it. Many aspects of Old Testament law are extremely enlightened.[39] Some of them are so lofty, in fact, that they cannot even be called "law" in any normal sense of the term because they relate to things that cannot be imposed from without; in those cases they inculcate an attitude (and perhaps a moral obligation) rather than imposing any strictly legal obligation. In some of these more positive aspects Israelite legislation reveals a close connection with the wisdom tradition. Among the examples of these positive aspects we find, in the Covenant Code, the command against oppressing the alien, the widow, or the orphan (Exod 22:20-23—and see 23:9), a provision found frequently also in the Deuteronomic Code; the prohibition against taking interest on a loan to a poor neighbor or keeping overnight the cloak taken in pledge (22:24-26;

---

[38] He finds relatively few motive clauses in ancient Near Eastern codes; only in the Code of Hammurabi (eighteen instances, about six percent) and in the Middle Assyrian Laws (seven instances, about five percent. The cuneiform law motivations regularly refer to inner-legal matters and commonly achieve their aim by underscoring the key element in the case; in biblical law, on the other hand, in a large majority of the cases, motive clauses "add new information and actually spell out the presuppositions of the laws to which they are attached." Unlike biblical law, "no cuneiform law is ever motivated by reference to an historic event, a promise of well-being or, for that matter, a divine will. In fact, in these laws the deity is completely silent, yielding its place to a human lawgiver whose main concern is economic rather than religious." He finds that the motive clauses in biblical law come probably under the influence of the wisdom literature, which does not seem to be the case with the cuneiform laws (pp. 153–75).

[39] This discussion relates only to the content of the provisions of the individual laws. Within Jewish tradition and Jewish piety there is also the conviction that obedience to the law is itself a good thing and worshipful service to God, quite apart from anything that we, in our human wisdom, recognize in the laws as "good."

cf. Deut 24:6, 10-13);[40] a series of admonitions about truth and justice in testifying at or judging lawsuits (23:1-3, 6-8); and an injunction to render assistance when an enemy's beast has gone astray or has fallen beneath its burden (23:4-5). It is in these last two examples especially that we can see how these injunctions go beyond anything that can be called law in the proper sense of the word. It is surprising enough that assistance is *enjoined* (somewhat as if our laws contained provisions for helping any motorist we saw with a flat tire or engine trouble), but here it is precisely to be given to "your enemy" (v. 4), "one who hates you" (v. 5)! It is the most difficult case that is singled out; clearly what is intended here is the promotion of an attitude that goes far beyond simply helping a friend in need.[41] So also the prohibition against *following the crowd* to do wrong (23:2) is intended to deter us from an all-too-frequent fault rather than presenting an enforceable law.

The Deuteronomic Code is well known for its humanistic concern in several areas, some of which have been alluded to above. In the seventh year debts are to be forgiven and slaves are to be given their freedom (Deut 15:1-11, 12-18; cf. Exod 21:1-6); the mother bird is not to be taken with her eggs (22:6-7) and the ox treading the grain is not to be muzzled (25:4).

The Holiness Code, so often judged to be too exclusively concerned with ritual purity, contains quite a number of admirable provisions, primarily in chapters 19 and 25. The Israelites are forbidden to reap fields or pick vines too thoroughly, but are to leave something for the poor to glean (Lev 19:9-10; and cf. Deut 24:19-22). More of the same is found in the following verses (Lev 19:11-18), where the objects of concern are the day laborer, the deaf, and the blind (and, in 19:32, the aged). Slander is forbidden (19:16), and we find injunctions against taking revenge and cherishing a grudge, as well as the command "you shall love your neighbor as yourself" (v. 18). Although it is frequently asserted that the "neighbor" *(rēʿăkā)* would be a fellow Israelite, a little later the same expression *(ʾāhabtā . . . kāmôkā)* is used with reference to the resident alien, who, it is explicitly stated, is to be treated "no differently than the natives born among you" (19:34).

---

[40] Deuteronomy 23:20-21 likewise prohibits the taking of interest, though the prohibition relates to taking it from an Israelite (with no reference to financial status), but not from a foreigner.

[41] The Deuteronomic Code, on this point, does not maintain the same high standard; the injunction to help in the case of strayed or fallen animals is given, but they belong to the "kinsman," not the "enemy" (Deut 22:1-4).

There are also some aspects to the law that modern Gentiles will be tempted to judge to be less praiseworthy. Deuteronomy, in particular, could be harsh and vindictive toward pagans (Deut 7:1-4, 16-26; 12:29-31; 25:17-19),[42] and there is something very disconcerting about men under the Holy War discipline striving to keep their camp and themselves ritually pure (Deut 23:10-15) and then putting enemy cities under the ban, which would involve slaughtering all their men and, in some cases, the women and children as well (20:10-20). The death penalty could be meted out for quite an array of offenses, including breaking the Sabbath (Exod 35:2). A variety of circumstances for which the individual was not culpable could exclude one from membership in the community (Deut 23:2-9). Quite a bit of attention is given to matters we might judge as taboos, such as mixing clothes, seeds, animals, or threads (Deut 22:5, 9-11; Lev 19:19), including the designation of a number of things as unclean, such as certain animals (Lev 11:1-47; Deut 14:3-21), or as rendering one ritually unclean, such as childbirth (Leviticus 12), a variety of blemishes classified as leprosy (Leviticus 13–14), genital discharges (Leviticus 15), or touching a corpse (Num 19:11-22).

THE PROPHETS AND THE LAW

It has already been suggested that no blanket judgment of how the prophets related to the law is possible; one must examine each prophet individually. This is not always done. One author has suggested that "everything the prophets have to say on social responsibility seems to presuppose the tradition of the law. This makes it possible to discuss the subject of social responsibility in the OT without looking into the prophets."[43] A clear example of failure to ask questions about what law might be in force in the time and place of a given prophet can be seen in Richard Bergren's book, *The Prophets and the Law*.[44] He also seems to suppose that if a prophet speaks about the same thing as the law, he must be alluding to the law. Bergren explores the connection between apodictic law and prophetic accusation and asserts that the prophetic accusation presupposes a standard, namely the apodictic law of the

---

[42] According to 1 Sam 15:2-3, 17-18, Samuel sends Saul on an expedition to exterminate the Amalekites, just as this passage commands.

[43] H. Eberhard von Waldow, "Social Responsibility and Social Structure in Early Israel," *CBQ* 32 (1970) 182. In spite of this unpromising beginning, the article is a good discussion of Israel's concern for *personae miserabiles* (the poor, widows, orphans, etc.) and why laws concerning them are in apodictic formulation.

[44] Richard V. Bergren, *The Prophets and the Law.* HUCAMS 4 (Cincinnati and New York: Hebrew Union College-Jewish Institute of Religion, 1974) 76.

covenant, to which those the prophets accuse are bound. Bergren claims that wherever a prophetic judgment speech is based on law (the prophets he deals with are Amos, Micah, Isaiah, and Jeremiah), the reference is to apodictic law. He accepts Mendenhall's distinction between "policy" and "technique"[45] with reference to law and asserts that the prophetic judgment speech presupposes a situation in which legal sanctions and legal techniques have failed: the community failed to protect itself from divine punishment by punishing the offender, and the prophetic judgment speech says that God himself will punish the offender. He says that it is the Sinai covenant that validates the laws or even that "the law was part of the covenant."[46] However, objections must be raised against his methodology and therefore against his conclusions. For example, Bergren alleges parallels between various prophetic passages and apodictic laws found in the Code of the Covenant, the Deuteronomic Code, and the Holiness Code, without asking about the age of these codes or when and where they might have been recognized as authoritative. More seriously, it seems that only a general similarity in content (e.g., concern for the poor, bribery) between a prophetic condemnation and a law is sufficient for him to claim that the prophetic passage reflects the law; in fact, only close terminological similarity would provide the basis for such a claim, which even then would have to be tentative, since other explanations are possible. Finally, Bergren does not ask whether parallels can be found outside the legal tradition, for example in wisdom, which manifests many of the same concerns as those found in the prophetic and legal traditions, such as concern for the poor and weak, honest weights, bribery.[47]

---

[45] "Ancient Oriental and Biblical Law," 3.

[46] *The Prophets and the Law,* 91, 101, 125. Bergren bases his statement on an earlier work by R. Bach, "Gottesrecht und weltliches Recht in der Verkündigung des Propheten Amos," in Wilhelm Schneemelcher, ed., *Festschrift für Günther Dehn* (Neukirchen: Verlag der Buchhandlung des Erziehungsvereins Neukirchen Kreis Moers, 1957) 23–34, which dealt only with the prophet Amos. Bergen argues for the connection between apodictic law and covenant on the basis of the use of *peṣaʿ* and *yādaʿ,* treaty curse parallels in prophetic announcements of disaster, and examples of the so-called "covenant lawsuit" in the prophets. Some of these points have been dealt with above. For an assessment of Bach see Gene M. Tucker, "Prophecy and Prophetic Literature," in D. A. Knight and G. M. Tucker, eds., *The Hebrew Bible and Its Modern Interpreters* (Philadelphia: Fortress, 1985) 325–68.

[47] This criticism applies also to Bach and others who follow much the same approach; see my "Eighth Century Prophets and Apodictic Law," in *To Touch the Text,* 103–17.

Much more helpful is what Henry McKeating has to say, especially in his methodological observations.[48] He holds that it is unwise to use the law as a starting point for any discussion of Israelite ethics (*a fortiori* of ethics in the prophets), pointing out that some Old Testament "laws" are really statements of principles or ideals. He recognizes that the wisdom writings also play their part in indicating how Israelites actually behaved. He points out that it is normal, in any society, for the same offense to be discouraged by a whole battery of sanctions, operating in a variety of social spheres. In our modern context, e.g., we might point to civil law, religious persuasion, parental authority, peer pressure, etc. The fact that in relation to a given offense the lawmakers, the prophets, and the wisdom writers may all appeal to different sets of sanctions does not mean, of course, that these various groups of people subscribe to different ethical standards. It is simply that they were concerned with operating different bits of the machinery of social control.

---

[48] Henry McKeating, "Sanctions against Adultery in Ancient Israelite Society, with some reflections on Methodology in the Study of Old Testament Ethics," *JSOT* 11 (March 1979) 57–72, discussed in greater detail in Chapter 1.

Chapter Three

THE BASIS OF
OLD TESTAMENT ETHICS

Now that I have said something about the *content* of Old Testament ethics, it is necessary to speak of the *basis* of Old Testament ethics because this is, in large measure, what sets Old Testament ethics and biblical ethics in general (and ultimately Christian ethics) apart from other systems. People throughout the world have consciences. They have convictions concerning the need to do good and avoid evil, and sometimes their ideas of "good" and "evil" are very enlightened. What is it that distinguishes Old Testament ethics, biblical ethics, that makes them different? Perhaps a good starting point would be a quotation from James H. Breasted:

> Like most lads among my boyhood associates I learned the Ten Commandments. I was taught to reverence them because I was assured that they came down from the skies into the hands of Moses, and that obedience to them was therefore sacredly incumbent upon me. I remember that whenever I fibbed I found consolation in the fact that there was no commandment, "Thou shalt not lie," that the Decalogue forbade lying only as a "false witness" giving testimony before the courts where it might damage one's neighbor. In later years when I was much older, I began to be troubled by the fact that a code of morals which did not forbid lying seemed imperfect; but it was a long time before I raised the interesting question: How has my own realization of this imperfection arisen? Where did I get the moral yardstick by which I discovered this shortcoming in the Decalogue?[1]

Breasted goes on to speak of being even more troubled when he learned that Egypt possessed standards of morals far superior to the Decalogue, and then comments:

---

[1] James H. Breasted, *The Dawn of Conscience* (New York: Scribners, 1961 [c1933]) xi.

It is now quite evident that the ripe social and moral development of mankind in the Nile Valley, which is three thousand years older than that of the Hebrews, contributed essentially to the formation of the Hebrew literature which we call the Old Testament. Our moral heritage therefore derives from a wider *human* past enormously older than the Hebrews, and it has come to us rather *through* the Hebrews than *from* them. The rise of man to social idealism took place long before the traditional theologians' "age of revelation" began. It was a result of the social experience of *man himself* and was not projected into the world from outside.[2]

If we accept that estimate without qualification we have come around full circle and are back to a "natural law" kind of ethic that I deny we find in the prophets of the Old Testament or in the Scriptures in general.

We certainly do find a very lofty ethic in some Egyptian wisdom texts (also in some from Mesopotamia), as we shall have occasion to observe later. But the noteworthy thing is that they are in wisdom texts rather than in specifically religious ones.[3] It is universally agreed that people should do good and (among those who believe in God) that this is what God commands them. It can also be asserted that in many cultures there is a large measure of agreement on what is "good." But that is why there is need to distinguish between the *content* of Old Testament ethics and the *basis* for it. People want to do what is right just because they recognize it as right or because they conceive of it as something God commands (not mutually exclusive perceptions, of course). But because various cultures and different individuals within those cultures have different ideas of God, one can say that what is unique about Old Testament ethics is not so much the content as it is Israel's understanding of God and of their relation to God.

To put this in more concrete terms, we could say that the basis for Old Testament ethics lies in the answers to the two questions:

1. What kind of God does Israel perceive the Lord to be?
2. How did Israel conceive its relation to God?

In the answer to those questions lies the explanation of why Israel came to unite religion and morality in a way we do not find in the cultures around them. Our own personal lives can be improved by asking ourselves similar questions; in the light of the proper answers to them, many moral "dilemmas" will find a resolution.

---

[2] Ibid. xv.

[3] In a later section of the work cited Breasted goes on to say that in its primitive stages religion has nothing to do with morals as we understand the term today (p. 18).

Even modern, contemporary cultures attest to quite diverse concepts of what God requires (and therefore to quite diverse visions of what God is like). The Ayatollah Khomeini, it was reported, sent unarmed boys, aged 12 to 17, across Iraqi mine fields to trigger the mines and thus leave the way open for attack by Iranian tanks. These young volunteers, it was said, had been indoctrinated in the Shiite tradition of martyrdom; they carried small keys that, if they are killed by the mines or machine-gun fire they advanced against (and many thousands of them were), they would use to go directly to heaven. They wore on the backs of their shirts, "I have the special permission of the Imam to enter heaven."[4] In the United States, on September 11, 2001, terrorists hijacked commercial airliners filled with innocent, unarmed civilians and flew them into the twin towers of the World Trade Center in New York City and the Pentagon in Washington, D.C., destroying them and taking the lives of almost three thousand other innocent, unarmed civilians, along with those on the airliners. The evidence indicates that the terrorists were indoctrinated in the same tradition of martyrdom. That sort of indoctrination suggests one view of what God is like and of God's relationship to a believer in a particular sect. It is a view that most would find ugly and repulsive. Even within Israel cruel and highly nationalistic conceptions of God were entertained, especially in the early period—some three thousand years ago, let us say; but that represents a starting point for development to loftier ideals. This is another reason for keeping things in chronological perspective.

No attempt will be made here to give specific answers to the two questions raised above; they will be repeated at various places in the following pages. However, it will be useful at this point to sketch what the Exodus tradition says about the Lord's nature and his relationship to Israel.

Israel's God is presented as one, holy, mighty, jealous, and compassionate (Exod 19:3-6; 34:6-7). That God is *one* certainly sets him apart from the gods of the surrounding peoples, with their pantheons of gods numbering in the hundreds. For those peoples, if it were a matter of asking what God wanted, they would have to ask "which one?" And indeed these gods were very different in character and not always very edifying. That the God of Israel acts in history (delivering Israel from Egypt in accord with promises already made to Abraham, Isaac, and Jacob) sets him apart from the nature gods. That the Lord is a "jealous" God already

---

[4] Terence Smith, "Iran: Five Years of Fanaticism," *New York Times Magazine* (February 12, 1984) 21.

says something about Israel's relationship to him. God lays claim to Israel and will not abide divided loyalties. At a later date Elijah calls for a clear choice between Yhwh and Baal (1 Kgs 18:21). The people, who refused to answer him, probably would have preferred a little of each, but that is not an option. It is within this context of relationship that the concept of election can mean so much. Later a more developed understanding of God would lead to the realization that all nations pertain to God, but at this moment (and throughout its history), election indicates to Israel the manner and the strength of the claim the Lord imposes on loyalty and obedience. Within this context the many expressions that carry personal import become intelligible. "Seek the Lord," while it originally had a cultic meaning, is used by the preexilic prophets for the right worship of the Lord in a deeper sense, one that implies right behavior (Amos 5:6); related expressions are "look to," "think of," "remember," contrasted with "forsake," "spurn," "forget."[5]

It is within this context, too, that covenant receives its deepest meaning, for covenant intends to solidify and make permanent a relationship that begins with deliverance from Egypt. And it deserves to be emphasized again that the understanding we have of what covenant is and means will have a great impact, especially if, with Pedersen, we hold that it implies relationship, *šālôm*, the sharing of blessing, and the prevalence of one will, and if, with Cross, we recognize a close relationship between covenant and kinship.[6]

The cult is important in this regard because it helps us to understand how the individual Israelite conceived of the Lord and of his/her relationship to God. The fact that in the psalms Israel, and individual Israelites, worship the Lord already expresses dispositions of submission and obedience. Nor should we forget that the language of the psalms is not infrequently (to our ears) impertinent: "How long, Lord?" (13:2). "Why do you stand at a distance?" (10:1). "Listen, God, to my prayer!" (55:2). "Awake, why do you sleep, O Lord?" (44:24).[7] All this suggests a feeling of great familiarity with God, but along with it, a desire to be instructed: "Make known to me your ways, Lord; / teach me your paths" (25:4). There is the desire to do God's good will by watching one's

---

[5] Johannes Lindblom, *Prophecy in Ancient Israel* (Philadelphia: Fortress, 1965) 341.

[6] See reference above, Chapter Two, nn. 3 and 5.

[7] Alongside this comfortable familiarity, however, stands great reverence and numinous fear. Uzzah was struck dead for having touched the ark of the covenant (2 Sam 6:6-7); no one can see the Lord's face and live (Exod 33:20; and cf. Isa 6:5).

conduct: "Yes, like the eyes of a servant / on the hands of his master / . . . / So our eyes are on the LORD, our God, / till we are shown favor" (123:2). There is the conviction that being heard depends on proper living: "Had I cherished evil in my heart, / the LORD would not have heard" (66:18). There is the awareness of the need for prayer to foster a moral life; it is the wicked who say, in effect, that God does not exist (10:4), whose "eyes are closed to the fear of God" (36:2), while it is the just and obedient who have "God's teaching . . . in their hearts" (37:31; cf. 40:9). There is the conviction that mercy is to be had for sins repented, that God does not "spurn a broken, humbled heart" (51:19). There is even fervent expression of desire for fellowship with God: "Whom else have I in the heavens? / None beside you delights me on earth" (73:25). Such dispositions may represent the spiritual elite of Israel, but those whom the prophets addressed would not have been strangers to them.

Chapter Four

THE EARLY PROPHETS

It has long been common practice to distinguish between the "early prophets" on the one hand and the "classical prophets" on the other.[1] The most objective basis for that distinction is the Old Testament canon itself. The term "classical" suggests the high point of a movement between a beginning and a decline, and there are grounds for defending that view. Generally speaking, the term is considered synonymous with "canonical prophets," that is, those who have collections of oracles ("books") attributed to them that have been accepted into the Old Testament canon; they have also been called "writing prophets" or "literary prophets," terms now seldom used. The use of the term "canonical prophet" is also somewhat misleading. It seems to identify the book with the prophet whose name it bears, whereas some of the books represent collections of oracles from two or more people. Thus the anonymous prophet of the Babylonian exile, referred to as Second Isaiah or Deutero-Isaiah, to whom Isaiah 40–55 is attributed, deserves to be considered as much a "classical prophet" as Isaiah or Jeremiah, though in fact he has no collection in the canon named after him. Something analogous can be said of the ones who stand behind the book of Zechariah, which is generally divided into at least two different collections.

Of the words of the early prophets, very little was preserved; they were more particularly people of action.[2] While the distinction between "classical prophets" and "early prophets" is useful, it should not obscure

---

[1] Not all are happy with this sort of distinction; cf. Joseph Blenkinsopp, *A History of Prophecy in Israel* (rev. and enlarged ed. Louisville: Westminster John Knox, 1996) 86–87 and elsewhere. Blenkinsopp's objection stems in part, and rightly so, from the tendency to demean ecstaticism and attribute it almost exclusively to the early prophets; hopefully that error is avoided in the present treatment.

[2] As Blenkinsopp, *History of Prophecy*, has it, "The most obvious difference [between 'primitive' and 'classical' prophecy] is, of course, at the literary level: we have a book of

the continuity in the development of the prophetic movement in Israel or foster the idea that, beginning at some particular time, prophetism as such exhibited "classical" traits. The canonical prophets stand in the same line as those who preceded them, adopting many of the same conventions as they had used in formulating their message along with much continuity in content. And although the canonical prophets are singled out as having collections of oracles that have been taken into the canon of Scripture, there existed during their ministries many others recognized as prophets. These other prophets are sometimes named (as in the case of Hananiah, Jeremiah's contemporary), but more often are not; frequently they appear to have proclaimed a message at odds with the prophets we know and were opposed by them. To speak of "early" and "classical/canonical" prophets does not suggest any simplistic division such as "charismatic" and "vocational" or anything of the sort. A distinction can be made (see below), but only in broad, general terms.

Frequently these early prophets are totally skipped in treatments of prophetism or given short shrift,[3] but it is well worth treating them in this study because they were prophets, after all, because there certainly were "ethical dimensions" to what they contributed, and because in many points they anticipated the teachings of the later prophets or, more accurately, the later prophets continue in lines begun by them.[4] Not all that we will find here can be commended, and on some points they contrast unfavorably with the classical prophets.

SAMUEL

Just as in the case of several other early prophets, the figure of Samuel has been so overlaid with later traditions that we are tempted to ask, "Will the real Samuel please stand up?" The narratives that relate to him are contained mainly in 1 Samuel 1–3; 7–14; 15–16; 19:18-24; 28. Within these passages Samuel appears under a number of different guises: dedicated

Amos but no book of Elijah and, correspondingly, we have more emphasis on sayings and less on prophetic biography or hagiography" (p. 66).

[3] This is a criticism that can be leveled against Abraham Joshua Heschel's *The Prophets* (New York: Harper & Row, 1962), excellent as it is in so many ways. While intending to deal with the characteristics of Israelite prophetism (from which ecstaticism was ruled out by the author), Heschel neglected the early prophets almost completely.

[4] Johannes Lindblom, *Prophecy in Ancient Israel* (Philadelphia: Fortress, 1965), speaking of the "classical" prophets, says: "It would be a serious mistake to dissolve the connection between these prophets and those whom we have called the primitive or early prophets" (p. 105).

to service at the altar by his mother from the womb, he is a nazirite (1:10-11, 22); he is a "judge" in the sense of administering justice (7:15-17); he is one who brings military victory like the judges of old (7:5-14); he is a spiritual leader acknowledged by all Israel (ch. 8); a small-town seer *(rōʾeh)* to whom Saul and his servant can turn for help in finding some lost donkeys (9:6-13); and a prophet who can speak much as the later classical prophets would (15:22-23); he is also found presiding over a band of ecstatic prophets (19:18-24).[5] None of these "portraits" necessarily excludes the others; part of the complication no doubt arises from the diversity of sources from which the books of Samuel are composed, sources that betray quite different attitudes toward Saul and the monarchy.[6] However, these uncertainties will not greatly affect our estimate of the ethical import of the narratives about the figure of Samuel.

Samuel began his career closely connected with the priesthood, at the sanctuary at Shiloh, ministering to Eli; later he is found detached from the priesthood and closely connected with a prophetic group,[7] he himself now being more a prophetic than a priestly figure. This "migration" may have had moral roots: on the one hand, the priesthood of Eli's family is presented as quite corrupt and, on the other hand, the prophetic movement now begins to emerge as a strong revitalizing factor in Israel.

The first commissioning of Samuel is said to have been for the denunciation of the priesthood of Eli's line as embodied in his corrupt sons, Hophni and Phinehas, and the promise of doom upon it. The principal crime alleged against Hophni and Phinehas was that of using the power and authority of the priesthood to seize, by force if need be, the priest's share, and more than his share, of the sacrifices before they had been properly offered.[8] This behavior involved contempt both for God and

---

[5] See the useful article by John L. McKenzie, "The Four Samuels," *Biblical Research* 7 (1962) 3–18; see also Blenkinsopp, *History of Prophecy,* 52–53.

[6] The composition of 1–2 Samuel is vastly more complicated than the formerly proposed "two-source theory" (variously called the "promonarchic" and "antimonarchic" or "early" and "late" sources); for a more adequate analysis see, e.g., Artur Weiser, *The Old Testament: Its Formation and Development,* tr. D. M. Barton (New York: Association Press, 1961) 157–70, or, more recently, J. Albert Soggin, *Introduction to the Old Testament: From Its Origin to the Closing of the Alexandrian Canon,* tr. John Bowden. OTL (3d ed. Louisville: Westminster John Knox, 1987) 210–18.

[7] 1 Samuel 10:3-13; 19:18-24. These passages are the earliest witnesses to the appearance of such prophetic bands in Israel.

[8] The text is not totally clear. Verses 13-14 of 1 Samuel 2 speak of the priest's servant taking for the priest all that a three-pronged fork would bring up from a boiling pot, suggesting perhaps that more was taken than was due the priest and certainly indicating a

for those who had come to worship, inseparably involved in the same act. This sort of denunciation of contempt for God in and through contempt for neighbor is something that will be found time and again in the prophets, and it is fitting that this first recorded revelation to Israel's first prophet (3:11-14) should be paradigmatic for so much that would follow in the history of prophetism. What appears somewhat untypical is that Samuel issues no ringing condemnation but simply repeats the revelation to Eli when pressed to do so. While the classical prophets often addressed the people as a whole, the early prophets generally were sent to individuals, usually the king or whoever was the responsible ruler, in this case Eli.

From Samuel we get two favorite phrases that express ready obedience, or the importance of obedience, to the Lord. The first is "Speak, LORD, for your servant is listening" (3:9), words Samuel uses on Eli's order. This is in the somewhat amusing scene in which Samuel has to be called repeatedly by the Lord because he thinks it is Eli who is addressing him. The other phrase is "obedience is better than sacrifice" (15:22), words spoken to Saul when he failed to carry out the ban against the Amalekites with the completeness Samuel had insisted on.[9]

Samuel was a kingmaker, though in some texts (especially ch. 8) he is presented as a very reluctant one. There are three accounts of Saul's

greedy impatience. (Both greed and appropriation of the choicest portions are indicated in v. 29.) Apparently a new example of wrongdoing is given in vv. 15-16, for they speak of the priest's servant demanding the meat raw, before the sacrifice had been properly offered, i.e., before the burning of the fat. Presumably this show of contempt for the Lord's sacrifice (v. 17) is what explains the reference to Hophni and Phinehas as "blaspheming" God in 3:13 (so *NAB* and *NRSV*). The matter is not made any easier by the variety of sources that tell of their sins: narrative in 2:12-17, words of an unnamed "man of God" in 2:29, and God's revelation to Samuel in 3:13. In addition, in 2:22 (missing in the Qumran and important Greek manuscripts) it is reported to Eli that they were having relations with the women who served at the sanctuary entrance.

[9] That Samuel, according to this account, believed that God willed what we would have to call genocide is troublesome to us and is one of the things that must be taken into account in any evaluation of early prophetism. We may note that this chapter is one that Weiser classifies as "later prophetic reflection on events." It may well reflect, rather than any historical action of Samuel and Saul, Deuteronomy's hostility to pagans and specifically its command "you shall blot out the memory of Amalek from under the heavens" (Deut 25:19); 1 Sam 15:2 cites Amalekite opposition to Israel at the time of the Exodus as the reason for destroying them, and in this also it echoes Deut 25:17-18. Thus the narrative may be simply a fictional "idealized" account of the fulfillment of the deuteronomic precept. However, the transfer of the responsibility for such an attitude from a character in a narrative to a lawgiver does not make it less troubling.

elevation to the kingship (1 Sam 9:15–10:8; 10:17-27; 11:5-15), and in each one Samuel plays a key role. When Saul disappointed him, Samuel attempted to depose him (13:13-14; 15:26-29). By then Saul's popularity was such that the attempt did not succeed, though it is likely that Samuel's rejection afflicted his spirit and played a part in the emotional instability that brought his world crashing down. We cannot be certain that Samuel actually anointed David as the text reports (16:1-13), but he does appear to have supported David even after Saul perceived him as a rival to the throne (19:18-24).

It is apparent that Samuel, to the extent that he agreed to the monarchy at all, wanted a limited kingship, one in which the king would be a military and political leader with none of the sacral aspects that were common in some ancient Near Eastern monarchies.[10] This is undoubtedly why he is presented as reacting so strongly to Saul's offering sacrifice before going into battle (13:8-15) and to Saul's deciding for himself how the ban was to be carried out against the Amalekites (ch. 15).

In all this Samuel was being jealous for the Lord's prerogatives. Yet he is pictured as believing that it was the Lord's will that Israel utterly exterminate the Amalekites and therefore as giving a different response to the question "What sort of God is Yhwh?" than some of the later prophets. We need always to keep in mind the progressive nature of revelation, most especially in the area of ethics. We can believe that God revealed himself to Samuel and at the same time realize that such revelation was refracted by the human nature that received it, a human nature that had been shaped by the attitudes, presuppositions, and circumstances prevalent in the culture in which Samuel lived. The gradual transformation of many of those attitudes and presuppositions is one of the fascinating aspects of the development of the Old Testament and its ethics.

EARLY ECSTATIC GROUPS

The dangers that specially threatened Israel at this point, according to William F. Albright, were military takeover by the Philistines and the temptation to apostasy from Yhwh through compromise with Baalism. As Albright expressed it: "At this dangerous moment in the history of

---

[10] This matter is dealt with in detail by Frank Moore Cross, *Canaanite Myth and Hebrew Epic* (Cambridge: Harvard University Press, 1973) 219–24. Cross gives substantial attention to the Northern Kingdom's attempt to preserve the tradition of a covenantal and limited kingship, along with preference for prophetic designation over dynastic succession (pp. 225–33 and *passim*).

Yahwism . . . came the prophetic movement like a refreshing west wind, blowing from the sea and dispersing the stagnant air of the sirocco." Aside from the figure of Samuel, which, as we have seen, takes its shape in part from later tradition, the earliest prophetic movement was embodied especially in the ecstatic groups that began to emerge about this time. Albright points out, as have many who have come after him, that this phenomenon is universal, both in antiquity and in modern times, in primitive as well as sophisticated societies. Such groups would sometimes arrive at an ecstatic state brought on through rhythmic singing and dancing. "In this state the subconscious may be abnormally active, and persons of a certain psychological type may have visions and mystic experiences which thereafter control, or at least affect, their entire life."[11]

While it is important to avoid falling into the error of confining ecstaticism to these early prophets, it is clear that it was more characteristic of them than of their later successors. Since it could be, and apparently often was, self-induced, the experience carried no guarantee of divine initiative and was open to the possibility of self-deception. There surely was a later deterioration, but at least in the beginning these prophets contributed to Israel's religious fervor.

The earliest references to such groups are found in stories about Samuel and Saul. In 1 Sam 10:5-11 an encounter with such a band is among the things Samuel foretells to Saul as a sign that Saul's anointing is from God. The description of the encounter speaks of the group's use of musical instruments (see above on singing and dancing), their connection with a "high place" (v. 5), i.e., a cult center, and the proximity of a Philistine outpost. The members of the group were "prophe[sying]," i.e., were caught up in the ecstatic prayer that had probably begun during worship at the high place. The account suggests something of the contagious nature of the experience, as "the spirit of God rushed upon [Saul], so that he joined them in their prophetic state" (1 Sam 10:10).[12] The experience, Samuel said, would change Saul "into another man" (1 Sam 10:6). The presence of such groups, with their ardent Yahwism, prayer, and contagious spirit undoubtedly did much to increase the fervor and

---

[11] William F. Albright, *From the Stone Age to Christianity* (Garden City, NY: Doubleday, 1957 [c1942]) 301–302. Johannes Lindblom, *Prophecy in Ancient Israel,* offers a detailed investigation into religious experience, and prophetic experience in particular. Lindblom reviews many examples of mystic experience but concludes that only the type he calls "concentration ecstasy" applies to the Old Testament prophets.

[12] The contagious nature is underlined even more strongly in 19:20-24, where all those who approach the ecstatic band are, willy-nilly, caught up into the same ecstatic state.

general level of devotion of the Israelite people and to confirm them in their loyalty to the Lord in the face of the temptations of pagan religion. It is no doubt a testimonial to their effectiveness that about a century and a half later Jezebel, in her zeal to promote the religion of the Tyrian Baal,[13] sought to suppress the movement by persecuting and killing the prophets (1 Kgs 18:4, 13).

Not much is said explicitly to relate these groups to the war against the Philistines, though the very fervor they excited would undoubtedly have provided an impetus in that direction. From a later period (again, about a century and a half later, in the days of Ahab) we find such prophets[14] in the field with the troops, encouraging them, advising their leaders, and buoying them with oracles of victory in their battles with Syria (1 Kgs 20:13-14, 22-25, 28). It was probably their Yahwistic zeal that led them to condemn the Israelite king for sparing Ben-hadad, the Syrian king, and for entering into covenant with him (1 Kgs 20:42), either because this was a breach of the Holy War discipline (cf. the case of Saul and Agag, 1 Sam 15:8-9, 32-33) or simply because they considered a covenant with a foreign power a betrayal.

Kings sought encouragement from such prophetic groups. The narrative about the campaign against Ramoth-gilead speaks of the king asking response from four hundred prophets (1 Kgs 22:5-7) and punishing the prophet who did not oblige with a favorable oracle (vv. 8-27). It is very possible that both Elijah and Elisha came from the line of such groups. Both manifest ecstatic behavior (1 Kgs 18:46; 2 Kgs 3:15), and Elisha had close contacts with one such group after the "assumption" of Elijah (2 Kgs 2:13-18; 4:1-7, 38-41, 42-44; 6:1-7; 9:1-3). As in the days of Samuel, such groups might be found near cult centers such as Bethel (2 Kgs 2:2-3), where they might impart some of their enthusiasm to those who came

---

[13] Jezebel was the daughter of Ittobaal (Ethbaal), king of Tyre and Sidon. She was, therefore, a Phoenician princess and it is generally held that the god she worshiped and whose worship she promoted was the Tyrian god, Baal Melqart, though some argue it was Baal-shamen. The worship of Baal Melqart had already spread far from Tyre.

[14] The texts here cited use the term "sons of the prophets" *(běnê hanněbîʾîm).* The expression "son(s) of . . ." is often a Hebrew idiom to express membership in a group, and that is undoubtedly what is intended here. (The *NAB* translates "guild prophets.") The designation occurs in 1 Kgs 20:35; 2 Kgs 2:3, 5, 7, 15; 4:1, 38; 5:22; 6:1; 9:1, all from around the middle of the ninth century in the Northern Kingdom (and cf. Amos 7:14). Whether the groups referred to in these texts differ substantially from the ones that appear in Samuel is disputed. Robert R. Wilson, *Prophecy and Society in Ancient Israel* (Philadelphia: Fortress, 1980), sees the "sons of the prophets" as more highly structured and finds no evidence they were ecstatics (p. 141).

there to worship. Some of them, at least, lived a community life of sorts (2 Kgs 4:38-44) and sometimes knew poverty (4:1-7). The group of four hundred mentioned above lived off the king's bounty at the royal court, so gravitating into the king's service may have been a way of meeting an economic necessity. Once there, their zeal for Israel would have led them to willingly offer oracles of victory for the king's undertaking, though the temptation to become "yes-men" to the king by underwriting royal policy must also have been present. As already noted, we find the whole group of four hundred in opposition to Micaiah ben Imlah, the only prophet willing to say what the king did not want to hear.

In conclusion, it can be said that such prophetic groups probably had a significant religious and ethical impact on Israel by inspiring the populace with zeal to remain faithful to the Lord, though it is not clear that they always avoided conceiving YHWH simply as a nationalistic deity.

NATHAN

Nathan, David's court prophet, appears on three different occasions: he delivered the dynastic oracle of 2 Sam 7:1-17, he rebuked David for his sin concerning Bathsheba and Uriah (12:1-15), and he helped assure the throne to Solomon near the end of David's life (1 Kgs 1:11-40).

Not all attribute the dynastic oracle to Nathan and David's time,[15] but I find no compelling argument against it. This oracle is studied most frequently because of its import for Old Testament messianism, but there are also strong political overtones to it, and this has to have an impact on how we see the role of Nathan as a prophet. Israel had accepted the monarchy only recently (David was the second king) and with some reluctance. Not all were in favor of the transition from tribal league to monarchy, in spite of the obvious need for greater political and military unity to repel the Philistine threat. There was also the fact that David's right to the throne was not unchallenged. Kingship had not passed to him peacefully and uncontested. After the death of Saul, Ishbaal, Saul's son, ruled for a time in the north, and even now a grandson of Saul, Meribbaal, might be considered a claimant to the throne. David, astute leader that he was, had united the two orders, the old tribal league and the new monarchy, by making Jerusalem his capital and then enshrining there the ark of the covenant; the ark embodied the spirit of the old tribal

---

[15] Cross, *Canaanite Myth*, for example, sees the oracle bringing a new unconditional character to the kingship of Solomon (pp. 241–61). The literature, pro and con, is immense, but pursuing the question here would not greatly advance the aims of this book.

league as well as any object could. The oracle of Nathan had the effect of legitimating both the monarchy for Israel and David's kingship within Israel: not only did it constitute a recognition of David as king in God's name but promised that his dynasty would always hold the throne. A comparison of the oracle as it appears in Samuel with the parallel versions of it in Ps 89:20-38 (*NRSV* 89:19-37) and 1 Chr 17:1-15 suggests that it is first of all David (and only after him each son in succession) who is adopted as God's son and that this is not simply a prophetic promise but a covenant God makes with David. In fact, it is an unconditioned covenant. No conditions are listed and it is explicitly said that sin will not annul it, even though sins will be punished.[16] This covenant seems to have had much more of an impact in the south, in Judah, especially after the division of the monarchy, than the Sinai covenant, with the strongly ethical demands that tradition early had associated with it.

In its original form (i.e., without v. 13a, which virtually all concede to be a later addition) the chapter expresses Nathan's (and the Lord's) rejection of David's plan to build a temple in favor of Israel's older tradition of a tent shrine. This tells us something of Nathan's attitude toward the Temple, an attitude apparently shared by other prophets as well.

In his confrontation with David over his adultery with Bathsheba and indirect murder of Uriah, Nathan is portrayed much like the best of the classical prophets, boldly rebuking the king for his sins. The use of a fictitious story to induce David to pass judgment on himself and the climactic "You are the man!" is one of the Old Testament masterpieces. It is important to note that the story Nathan tells, which evokes such a

---

[16] The comparison of the three versions of the oracle is made by John L. McKenzie, "The Dynastic Oracle: II Samuel 7," *TS* 8 (1947) 187–218. Psalm 89, although an expanded form of the oracle (probably originally in verse), preserves the original sense of David's adoption as God's son and explicit reference to a covenant. Cross' argument for the perdurance of a tradition of covenantal, conditional kingship is undoubtedly true for the north, but what he has to say about David's kingship is less persuasive. He believes the oracle to David was originally a conditional, covenantal one, and holds that the unity of 2 Samuel 7 is the work of the deuteronomistic historian (*Canaanite Myth*, 252). David's acceptance as king by the northern tribes was in fact inaugurated with a covenant (2 Sam 5:3), though whether its (unrecorded) conditions continued to be kept throughout his long reign, marked by two revolts, cannot be known. Nathan's oracle need not have signaled any difference in David's manner of rule, though it would have implications for his successors. That Jeroboam planned a revolt in the days of Solomon and that Rehoboam, Solomon's son, was rejected by the northern tribes when he refused to accede to limits on his power may signify a more dominating style of rule than the people were willing to accept.

strong response of condemnation from David, does not speak of murder and adultery but of a rich man using his power to abuse the rights of the weak (something that was *also* involved in David's crime). It would be difficult or impossible to point to any law that the rich man in the parable violated, so it is obvious that in Israel judgments could be based on broader ethical grounds than explicit law.[17] The punishments that Nathan proclaims are to come upon David correspond to the sins he has committed—certainly a case of letting the punishment fit the crime. We will see more of the same pattern in narratives about Elijah. The fourfold restitution of the lamb may seem like a small penalty for the egregious wrong done by the rich man, but the real reference is probably to the punishment visited on David in the loss of four of his sons: the child just now conceived by Bathsheba, Amnon, Absalom, and Adonijah.

If Nathan taxing David with his sin does not surprise us, it is no doubt because it is the sort of thing we expect, since we see the later prophets doing it constantly. Yet this is the first time, and there is something astounding about it. Why does a prophet suddenly accost the king? Obviously it is because God sent him, since he is God's spokesman. But this means that God is concerned about human behavior, about human righteousness, about the treatment of others. And it reveals that God is concerned about sinners because it is to the sinner that the prophet is sent, both to chastise him and to lead him to repentance.

In the third instance we find Nathan intervening (effectively) in a palace intrigue over the royal succession. So again (as in the case of Samuel) we find a prophet acting as a power broker. It is not clear why Nathan backed Solomon. Solomon dealt viciously with Adonijah, his rival to the throne, and with Adonijah's supporters. He built the Temple that Nathan had told David he was not to build, for reasons that would have been equally valid for Solomon. And he became an oppressive ruler who was in large part responsible for the revolt of the northern tribes. Ultimately he merits a severe judgment from the deuteronomic historian. Perhaps there was a lesson here for the later prophets.

AHIJAH

Ahijah is undoubtedly a historical figure, though the account about him in 1 Kgs 11:29-39 has been heavily overlaid by the deuteronomic historians and their special concerns. What would appear to be accurately

---

[17] On this, see further in Chapter Eight below.

recorded is that Ahijah was the one who instigated Jeroboam's revolt. The initial impulse was given during Solomon's lifetime through the symbolic act of tearing a new cloak into twelve pieces and giving Jeroboam ten of them, each piece representing a tribe; the words that go with the act ("I will tear away the kingdom from Solomon's grasp and will give you ten of the tribes," v. 31) are an open invitation to rebellion with prophetic sanction. The attempt was abortive and Jeroboam had to flee to Egypt, but after Solomon's death he returned. When Rehoboam, Solomon's designated successor, rejected the demands of the ten northern tribes for more lenient treatment the split took place and Jeroboam became the first king of the Northern Kingdom. The deuteronomic historians explain the "rending of the kingdom" from David's line as punishment for Solomon's apostasy, detailed as worshiping foreign gods, particularly those of his many wives. But the actual dispute between the northern tribes and the king of Judah had to do with matters of taxation and forced labor. Jeroboam, it is to be remembered, was in charge of the forced labor of "the house of Joseph"[18] in Solomon's administration (11:28) and it would not be far-fetched to suppose that it was the oppression of his kinsfolk that led him to accept the prophet's invitation to revolt or even that it played a role in Ahijah's action. If this is the case, Ahijah's concern in rejecting Solomon and his line could well be termed "social justice." No doubt he saw the irony of the situation in which the Israelites, who had cried out to the Lord in Egypt because they were state slaves, were reduced to forced labor in their own land and under their own king.

Ahijah is referred to as "the Shilonite," i.e., "man from Shiloh," the place of Israel's central shrine before its destruction by the Philistines. A major cause of his opposition to Solomon may well have been the building of the Jerusalem Temple, which, since it conformed in many ways to pagan models,[19] could have been judged a form of apostasy. This would be another indication of prophetic opposition to the Temple. In any case, while one prophet was instrumental in bringing Solomon to the throne, another prophet tried to bring him down.

The split that finally did take place under Solomon's successor was never healed. The situation we call the "divided monarchy" perdured for the two centuries until the destruction of the Northern Kingdom.

---

[18] Whether Judah also was subjected to taxation and forced labor is a disputed point.

[19] Cf. e.g., William G. Dever, *What Did the Biblical Authors Know, and When Did They Know It? What Archaeology Can Tell Us about the Reality of Ancient Israel* (Grand Rapids: Eerdmans, 2001) 144–57.

Isaiah saw the division as an example of the worst sort of thing that could befall a people (Isa 7:17), and a reunion of Judah and Israel is seen as a necessary element of any messianic future blessedness (Isa 11:13-14; Ezek 37:15-28). The division left two weak states in place of one strong one, a situation that made them more easily prey to the fate that finally overtook them, that of being swallowed up by more powerful nations. Yet it was a prophet who provoked it. This is an instance of something seen in other early prophets: namely, a willingness to bring rather terrible things upon the nation because of sin.

Ahijah appears again to condemn Jeroboam for setting up rival shrines to the Jerusalem Temple at Dan and Bethel and to foretell the total extinction of his line (1 Kgs 14:1-18). Again we can see the hands of the deuteronomic historians with their concern for unity of sanctuary, though here too there may be a historical basis for the report. Jeroboam's line does in fact come to an end. Nadab, his son, who succeeds to the throne after his death, is assassinated by Baasha, a usurper; Baasha then proceeds to kill off "the entire house of Jeroboam, not leaving a single soul to Jeroboam but destroying him utterly, according to the warning which the LORD had pronounced through his servant, Ahijah the Shilonite" (1 Kgs 15:29). Baasha's purpose would have been to protect his throne by eliminating all those who might have a claim to it as being descendants of the previous king, but it must necessarily be of some concern to us that prophetic words provided justification for this wholesale extermination, or at least so it was said. This is not the only time a usurper is reported to have wiped out all the male descendants of his predecessor and not the only time a prophet plays a role in the procedure.[20] While there is a certain idealism in the concept of prophetic designation rather than dynastic succession, which continued to have great influence in the north, in practice it led to instability and set the stage for anarchy.

ELIJAH

An abundance of material about Elijah and Elisha survives. The traditionary circle or circles responsible for these cycles of stories were probably the prophetic groups already described, with whom, as we have already noted, Elijah and Elisha had some connection. There is a sense in which the work of Elijah and Elisha cannot be separated in terms of the overall policy pursued by them, but we will take them in turn.

---

[20] The same happened to Baasha's line (1 Kgs 16:1-4, 8-13), the prophet being Jehu ben Hanani, and to Ahab's (1 Kgs 21:21; 2 Kgs 10:7-10), the prophet being Elijah.

Elijah was a prophet who obviously made a tremendous impact on the popular mind, a charismatic individual instinct with power; he could call down fire from heaven or be spirited away in a trice. The stories about him can be listed in five groups:

(1) 1 Kgs 17:1–18:46: a drought and the events at Mt. Carmel;
(2) 1 Kgs 19:1-21: trek to Mount Horeb and theophany there;
(3) 1 Kgs 21:1-29: Naboth's vineyard and doom pronounced on Ahab;
(4) 2 Kgs 1:1-17: doom on Ahaziah and fire from heaven;
(5) 2 Kgs 2:1-18: Elijah's departure.

This listing is in canonical order, but our treatment will depart from it for obvious chronological reasons: Elijah's slaughter of the prophets of Baal in the first of these narratives occasions Jezebel's threat against Elijah's life and his subsequent flight to Mount Horeb, where he receives a commission that should take him far afield. Given these circumstances, we would not expect to find him back in Israel or exposing himself again to Jezebel's wrath.[21] Chronologically, therefore, the Naboth story would seem to come first.

All but the last of the five stories relate in some sense to Israel's apostasy from the Lord, though we will look only at the first three in any detail. It would be a mistake to take lightly the struggle of the prophets against this sort of apostasy, as though the religious conflict over "Yhwh or Baal" were an esoteric thing, remote from our times and from us. It is far more than simply a question of what name one gives to the God one worships, for these two were radically different in character, in what they expected of their worshipers, and in every other way. We will look into this matter more closely when we discuss Hosea. At this point let us simply take note of the comment of Lindblom, who says, referring to the preexilic prophets in general, "in the view of these prophets moral depravation was a consequence of religious apostasy. If the people had kept to Yahweh, they would have understood what Yahweh's will was and would have obeyed His ethical demands."[22]

The Naboth Incident

In this narrative we see Elijah behaving much like the later classical prophets (and like Nathan confronting David over his behavior toward Bathsheba and Uriah), i.e., rebuking the ruler over the abuse

---

[21] One reason for the present location of the Naboth story is apparently the desire to place it, with Elijah's prediction of Ahab's death, between ch. 20, in which Ahab is victorious over the Syrians, and ch. 22, in which Ahab falls in battle against the Syrians.

[22] *Prophecy in Ancient Israel,* 348.

of his power to the injury of the weaker party; it is a matter of social justice that reaches (as in the case of David) the ultimate limits of oppression in murder. Francis Andersen notes that "commentators have rightly seen in the episode a clash of Israelite and Canaanite ideas of kingship, of citizenship, and of property."[23] That assertion is justified by the difference in the behavior of Ahab and Jezebel. The king's offer to Naboth was reasonable, but family property in Israel was inalienable and Naboth had the right to refuse to sell. The egalitarian concept was strong in early Israel. Ahab had to recognize Naboth's right to refuse, but being the kind of person he was, he sulked. Jezebel, without a background in Israel's sociology and covenant concept, thought that a king had better ways of dealing with the situation than to sulk.[24] In Israel, however, seizure of property by naked royal power would not do, so Jezebel uses the royal power to arrange a judicial murder.[25]

Elijah is promptly dispatched to the scene to denounce the deed and to pronounce judgment on Ahab. This judgment initially consisted, in all probability, of the statement that the dogs would lick up Ahab's blood in the same place where they had licked Naboth's (1 Kgs 21:19), another instance of the punishment fitting the crime. Other elements of the oracle as it now stands were probably added later: the extinction of Ahab's line (vv. 21-22), Jezebel's fearful end (v. 23), and the transfer of the enactment of the punishment pronounced on Ahab to the days of his grandson (vv. 27-29).[26] The last of these, at least, seems to be a later addition to deal with the apparent fact that Ahab did not perish where and in the manner the oracle suggested.[27] This is a reminder that the

---

[23] Francis I. Andersen, "The Socio-Judicial Background of the Naboth Incident," *JBL* 85 (1966) 46. Whether the initiative attributed to Jezebel is rightly labeled "Canaanite" is disputed by some.

[24] Andersen, "Naboth Incident," cites an Amarna letter to the effect that a king may act according to his fancy (p. 46). Waldemar Janzen, *Old Testament Ethics: A Paradigmatic Approach* (Louisville: Westminster John Knox, 1994) describes this as violating "Israel's royal paradigm by resorting to a Canaanite royal paradigm" (p. 19).

[25] Andersen, "Naboth Incident," believes that the false witnessing—and even the documents sent by Jezebel—were intended to establish that Naboth had in fact sold or agreed to sell the property to Ahab, to explain why Ahab could take possession after Naboth's death. Whether or not that position is accepted does not affect the present treatment.

[26] This in itself is rather difficult from an ethical point of view. Punishment remitted is intelligible, but not punishment deferred to another generation.

[27] In the narrative in 1 Kgs 22:1-38, in which the dogs lick up the blood from the chariot of the slain Israelite king, the location is not Jezreel (where Naboth was killed), but Samaria. However, there are those who doubt that this narrative is about Ahab at all, for

essence of prophetic teaching consists not so much in predicting this or that punishment as in the moral implication of the condemnation of the crime.[28] That Ahab recognized the wrong done is clear from the fact that Jezebel had to overcome his scruples and act herself and from the fact that he does not defend himself from Elijah's accusation. What kind of God Yhwh is, at least in his concern for the weak, has been revealed to Israel and is here proclaimed again by his prophet.

The Drought and Events at Mount Carmel

The story covers two chapters (with the interlude of Elijah's stay with the widow of Zeraphath), but the beginning and end are closely tied. The story is intelligible only against the circumstances prevailing in Ahab's reign, in particular his marriage to Jezebel and her attempts to promote Baal worship. This is seen, in part at least, from the royal support[29] given the prophets of Baal and Asherah (1 Kgs 18:19) and her persecution of the Yhwh prophets (18:4, 13), as well as in the Baal altar and asherah ("sacred pole") Ahab is said to have provided, no doubt at the behest of Jezebel (16:31-33). Although the very name Jezebel has come to stand for a wicked, bold, or abandoned woman, by her standards she was a very religious person.

It is in the context of the promotion of Baal worship that Elijah enters so abruptly upon the scene—so suddenly, in fact, that some think the opening of the story has been lost; we would expect at least a genealogical notice on Elijah.[30] The drought he proclaims relates to Baal's claim (more accurately,

---

various reasons. (1) The notice of Ahab's death in 1 Kgs 22:40, "Ahab rested with his ancestors," is taken to mean he died a peaceful death. (2) The narrative throughout refers regularly only to "the king of Israel," naming Ahab only in v. 20, though Jehoshaphat of Judah is named frequently, and so some suppose it could originally have told of some other Israelite king. (3) Ahab is known to have been an ally of Syria in 853, not long before his death in 850. For these reasons some authors believe the narrative tells of the defeat and death of another Israelite king and was secondarily applied to Ahab, but there is no agreement on this. Some authors reject the arguments offered and those who accept them come up with widely divergent ideas of whom the story originally applied to.

[28] So also, as will later be noted, the authentic truth in Jeremiah's words against Jehoiakim (Jer 22:13-19) is to be judged not on the accuracy of what was predicted of Jehoakim's burial but on the moral content of the condemnation of the king's behavior.

[29] 1 Kings 18:19 speaks of these prophets eating at Jezebel's table, which may be taken to mean that by such support she was attempting to make Baal worship the official cult of the court.

[30] The town of Tishbeh, from which "Tishbite" presumably comes, has not been located with certainty and other explanations are sometimes given for the word.

the claim of his worshipers) to be a god of fertility; as such Baal has also to be the giver of the rain and dew on which the fertility of the soil depends. Through Elijah, YHWH is now about to prove that he is the one who gives and withholds the rain and therefore is the God who controls fertility—even though he is not a fertility god in the sense that Baal was believed to be. Elijah proclaims the word of YHWH, that there will be a drought until he again speaks through Elijah (17:2)—and then Elijah departs the scene.

The drought already demonstrates something of Baal's ineffectiveness, but the denouement of the affair is to come in a way that will further bring home the point of YHWH's power over that of Baal. So we have the dramatic scene on Mount Carmel in which Baal and his prophets are unable to meet Elijah's challenge. YHWH, for his part, vindicates his prophet by answering with fire. Obviously the story has lost nothing in the telling, but some dramatic event no doubt lies behind the narrative;[31] Elijah did not have a reputation as a power-filled figure without reason.

We could wish that the story ended there, but Elijah now commands that the prophets of Baal be seized; he brings them down to the Wadi Kishon, where he slits their throats.[32] That business out of the way, the affair concludes with a drenching rainfall that puts an end to the drought.

Trek to Mount Horeb and Theophany

This event is closely tied to the preceding in that it is said that Jezebel's anger over the slaughter of her prophets and her threat against Elijah ("if this time tomorrow I have not done with your life what was done to . . . them," 19:2) is what motivates Elijah's timely pilgrimage to the mount of the covenant.[33] Elijah had the reputation of moving swiftly (18:12), and "by this time tomorrow" he was long gone. Elijah's

---

[31] The "fire of God" can easily be understood as lightning that preceding the storm that immediately follows. Lightning preceding rain is not uncommon especially at the time of the fall interchange, when the autumn rains begin to bring an end to the dry season. See Aloysius Fitzgerald, *The Lord of the East Wind*. CBQMS 34 (Washington, DC: Catholic Biblical Association of America, 2002) 109.

[32] There are various attempts to transfer this bloody act from Elijah to someone else. For example, it is said that in reality it recounts, and attributes to Elijah, the slaughter of Baal worshipers carried out by Jehu (2 Kgs 10:18-27). This suggestion can perhaps claim a basis in the fact that the anointing of Jehu is part of the commission Elijah receives on Mount Horeb (1 Kgs 19:16), but that would still implicate Elijah in what Jehu did. On the whole thorny question of Elijah's commission, see below.

[33] That is, Mount Horeb, which is the name given the mount of the covenant in the northern traditions preserved in E and D; as is well known, Judean traditions, as in J and P, call the mount of the covenant Mount Sinai.

destination was chosen, no doubt, both because it was a long way off and because there one might specially experience the presence of YHWH.[34] We might wish to think that the fact that YHWH is *not* present in the more violent elements of the theophany (wind, earthquake, fire), as compared to the one in which he *is* present (a still, small voice), commends a gentle approach over a violent one, but unfortunately the content of the oracle does not commend that interpretation.

Elijah's complaint is an indictment of the Israelites; he laments that he is the only faithful one left, and even his life is being sought. The Lord, in reply, instructs him to anoint Hazael to be king of Syria, Jehu to be king of Israel, and Elisha[35] as his own successor; the result will be that everyone will fall by the sword of one or the other of them, though a faithful remnant of seven thousand will be preserved. The purpose of this strange commission is the punishment of Israel for apostasy from YHWH by the destruction that will be visited upon them. Elisha encourages the ambitions of Hazael even though he foresees the havoc he will wreak ("because I know the evil that you will inflict upon the Israelites. You will burn their fortresses, you will slay their youth with the sword, you will dash their little children to pieces, you will rip open their pregnant women," 2 Kgs 8:12); the point of it all is expressed somewhat more clearly in the words spoken by the prophet who anoints Jehu: "You shall destroy the house of Ahab your master; thus will I avenge the blood of my servants the prophets, and the blood of all the other servants of the LORD shed by Jezebel, and by the rest of the family of Ahab" (2 Kgs 9:7-8). It is at this point that the Elijah and Elisha stories become inseparable and Elijah's career is seen stretching from his defeat and slaughter of Jezebel's Baal prophets on Mount Carmel through Jehu's extermination of Ahab's line and slaughter of Baal worshipers.

The divine commissioning is difficult to understand, quite apart from the ethical question of dealing with the problem of Baal worship by slaughtering its practitioners. Of the three Elijah is ordered to anoint, Elisha is the last named, though he is in fact the first one (and the only one) of the three that Elijah himself encounters. The commissioning could

---

[34] One might even argue that the cave Elijah seeks out is the very one Moses knew, for the Hebrew has the definite article (*"the* cave," 1 Kgs 19:9; my emphasis), but that argument cannot be pressed.

[35] Since the account of Elisha's call (1 Kgs 19:19-21) says nothing of anointing, the reference here is to be understood symbolically. Jehu was anointed by a prophet sent by Elisha (2 Kgs 9:1-10). Hazael was no doubt anointed soon after his accession to the kingship, but Elisha's role is restricted to instigating Hazael's murder of Ben-hadad and his usurpation of Ben-hadad's throne (2 Kgs 8:7-15).

be taken in the broader sense, as something to be carried out by Elisha, his successor; but then it is peculiar that the oracle begins by telling Elijah explicitly to head for Damascus and to anoint Hazael when he arrives there (1 Kgs 19:15). In fact, Elijah does not head for Damascus. The continuation of the narrative does tell of the call of Elisha, but he, not Elijah, becomes the instigator of the revolts of Hazael and Jehu. More strangely still, in one of the next stories the Lord himself removes Elijah from the scene (2 Kgs 2:1). It has been suggested that the mandate in the oracle really represents the policy of Elisha and that, being a questionable and unpopular policy for a variety of reasons, it has been placed under the aegis of a prophet of far greater reputation and prestige. No resolution of the problem seems possible. That it could have been Elijah's policy that Elisha carried out is not incredible, since Elijah is said to have prophesied the extermination of Ahab's line. On the other hand, it was Elisha who put it into effect. Both prophets have legends attributed to their names that make them seem less than careful about human life,[36] though we perhaps should not judge them on the basis of stories that can hardly be historical.

ELISHA

There is an extensive cycle of stories about Elisha: in addition to the Elijah narratives in which he figures (1 Kgs 19:19-21; 2 Kgs 2:1-18), almost all the material in 2 Kgs 2:19–9:3 relates to him. Many of these stories tell of his relations with the "sons of the prophets," of his miracles (e.g., the raising of a dead boy, the cure of Naaman the leper), and of his interventions in the battles between Israel and Syria.[37] The stories in which the miraculous element is so prominent were probably formulated and transmitted in prophetic circles and were intended to enhance his reputation as a man of God, whereas others, which relate historical events in which Elisha figures less prominently (e.g., the campaign against Moab in 2 Kgs 3:1-27), might come from a separate source.

---

[36] Elijah, besides the incident of the prophets of Baal, calls fire down upon two successive bands of fifty men whom the king sends to bring him in (2 Kgs 1:9-12), and Elisha curses some boys who taunted him so that two she-bears tore forty-two of them to pieces (2:23-24).

[37] It is no doubt this sort of activity that earned Elisha the title "Israel's chariots and horsemen" (2 Kgs 13:14), a title I would see bestowed secondarily on Elijah (2 Kgs 2:12). None of the stories of Elijah explain why he would have been called that, though his reputation as the greater prophet would easily attract the title to his figure from Elisha. Its use in 2:12 may even explain the appearance of the fiery chariot, since the narrative attributes his translation to a whirlwind, not the chariot (vv. 1, 11).

The miracle stories do not contribute much to our study, but the policy of Mount Horeb begins to be implemented in the anointing of Hazael (2 Kgs 8:7-15) and of Jehu (9:1-10). The first of these is much more difficult to explain than the latter. Elisha finds himself in Damascus at the time when the Syrian king Ben-hadad is gravely ill; in view of the commissioning of Elijah (cf. 1 Kgs 19:15), this is hardly by chance! He speaks words to Hazael that can only be understood as an incitement to do away with Ben-hadad and usurp his throne.[38] As mentioned earlier, this is done with the knowledge that Hazael would wreak terrible havoc against Israel and for that very purpose (1 Kgs 19:17; 2 Kgs 8:12), i.e., in order to punish Israel for their Baal worship.[39]

Elisha's role in the anointing of Jehu is intelligible if we assume that Elisha had a good idea of the sort of policy Jehu would pursue. After Jehu's anointing at the hand of one of the "sons of the prophets" and his acclamation as king by his fellow officers, Jehu drives his chariot hell-bent for Jezreel. Outside the town he kills Joram (Jehoram), Ahab's son, who is the reigning king of Israel; he also kills Ahaziah, king of Judah, who happens to be on hand. As he enters Jezreel he is contemptuously greeted by Jezebel as "Zimri, murderer of your master" (9:31). Zimri, of course, became king of Israel through the murder of Baasha, his predecessor (1 Kgs 16:15-20). He was not the only one to come to the kingship by that route, as we have had occasion to note, but Jezebel may have hoped that Jehu's reign would last only the seven days of Zimri's.

Jehu deals quickly with Jezebel, having her thrown from an upper window (9:30-37). He then arranges for the elimination of Ahab's seventy grandsons, thereby fulfilling Elijah's prediction concerning Ahab's line, and for the removal of other assorted supporters (10:1-11). Finally, he assembles the worshipers and priests of Baal in Baal's temple under pretext of celebrating a great sacrifice in his honor and then has all those assembled slaughtered (10:18-27). In the last of these acts Jehu has the company of Jonadab, the Rechabite, whom he invites with the words, "Come with me . . . and see my zeal for the LORD" (v. 16). If Jezebel hoped Jehu would share the fate of Zimri, she would have been disappointed, for he founded a relatively long-lived dynasty. The deuterono-

---

[38] Hazael (842–806) succeeded Ben-hadad II (870–842), though Syrian records do not say how he came to the throne.

[39] The fact that to Elisha is attributed both the bringing of misery upon Israel from Syria (by inciting Hazael to usurp the throne), *and* being Israel's firm support against Syria (as in 2 Kgs 6:8-23; 13:14-19) is difficult to explain.

mists provide him with a promise, presumably from prophetic lips, that "Because you have done well what I deem right, and have treated the house of Ahab as I desire, your sons to the fourth generation shall sit upon the throne of Israel" (v. 30). Later we will see that another prophet, Hosea, passed a different sort of judgment on him.

MICHAIAH BEN IMLAH

In spite of whatever unattractive aspects we might find in Elijah and Elisha, at least they were not nationalistic prophets, which was the overriding fault of many of the others. Neither was Michaiah ben Imlah. His story (in 1 Kings 22) intends mainly to show that the word of the Lord against Ahab would inexorably come to pass, even though it required a "lying spirit" (v. 22) in the mouths of Ahab's prophets so that he would proceed with his adventure against Ramoth-gilead; and even though he disguised himself, it was an arrow "shot at random" (v. 34) that found its mark between the joints of his breastplate.

A more advanced theological outlook finds it impossible to believe that Ahab's prophets were deceivers because the Lord had sent a "lying spirit" into their mouths. But the story does have value in illustrating the tension that must have arisen between prophet and prophet at various times.[40] Michaiah does not deny these men their status as prophets (and the Hebrew Old Testament never uses the term "false prophet"), but he does attempt to explain why their prophetic message is not true. We would say, rather, that a troop of nationalistic prophets gave the oracle of victory they wanted to give, impelled by wishful thinking and by the belief that their words had power to create victory, that men subservient to the king said what he wanted to hear. But the story also tells of a prophet who was more authentically attuned to the Lord's word and could speak only that, even though it brought down upon him the wrath of the king and other practical difficulties.

ASSESSMENT OF THE EARLY PROPHETS

We can conclude briefly. Much of the assessment is implicit, or even explicit, in what has already been said. We can see some very positive aspects in the life and works of these early prophets. They certainly

---

[40] This is seen most clearly in the head-to-head confrontation between Jeremiah and Hananiah (Jeremiah 28), but Isaiah, Micah, and Ezekiel (and Jeremiah outside the Hananiah incident) all complain about prophets who mislead.

exhibited zeal, enthusiasm, and fidelity to the Lord, as they saw their obligations. No doubt they did much to preserve Israel and its faith in very threatening circumstances. It may be that without them Israel and Yahwism would not have survived. It certainly would be wrong to judge them simply by our own lights.

Yet we can point out that their conception of their calling contrasted sharply on some points with the classical prophets. Samuel, Nathan, Ahijah, Elijah (probably), and Elisha (surely) often attempted to operate by power plays and coups, raising up kings and bringing them down, often being instigators of violence. Whether or not Elijah was involved in this sort of thing is not agreed upon by all. The opinion of some has already been noted: that the policy carried out by Elisha was not Elijah's policy at all but was attributed to him to make it more acceptable. If he was in fact responsible for the slaughter of the prophets of Baal, which is also disputed, he could just as easily have countenanced Jehu's bloody purge, even though he did not live to see it. Whoever originated the policy, there seems little doubt about what Elisha *did*. More will be said of this aspect of the early prophets in the next chapter, as we compare them with the classical prophets.

Chapter Five

CLASSICAL PROPHETS: DIFFERENTIA FROM EARLY PROPHETS

One objective difference between the earlier prophets and the so-called classical prophets, as mentioned earlier, is the existence of books composed of collections of oracles bearing the names of the latter. That alone can still leave the terminology somewhat arbitrary, but there are also discernible differences between the canonical/classical prophets and their predecessors that may be listed as three in number: (1) the sense of call or vocation, (2) a mission that is totally identified with being a bearer of God's word, and (3) the depth of the content of teaching.

SENSE OF VOCATION

Nothing is told of the call of early prophets except in the cases of Samuel and Elisha. In the case of Samuel we are no doubt dealing with a later literary composition intended to enhance Samuel's prophetic standing rather than a personal account of how he became a prophet, and in the case of Elisha there is simply an external action, namely, Elijah throwing his cloak over him—which relates more to his becoming the successor of Elijah than to a call from God as such.

Several of the classical prophets, on the other hand, give us circumstantial, first-person accounts of their call; that alone tells us it must have been important to them. The call narrative is intended as a legitimation of the prophet and his message. This was especially important if, as was often the case, the content of his message was unpopular or subject to challenge. So when Amos was ordered by Amaziah to be off to his native Judah and cease stirring up trouble at the Bethel sanctuary, Amos replied that he was/is no prophet,[1] but that the Lord took *(lāqaḥ)* him from his previous

---

[1] This raises the question of whether Amos and the other canonical prophets would have acknowledged the title *nābîʾ*. Joseph Blenkinsopp points out that the canonical

work and said, "Go, prophesy to my people Israel," which empowers him to say, "Now hear the word of the LORD" (Amos 7:15-16). Jeremiah, who is told he had been chosen to be a prophet before his birth, does not gladly receive the call and alleges his youth as a reason why he should not be sent, to which objection the Lord responds: "To whomever I send you, you shall go; / whatever I command you, you shall speak," and the Lord himself places his words in his mouth (Jer 1:7). Later there is a time when he is on the point of being put to death for giving out threats against Jerusalem and the Temple, and his defense is "I am in your hands; do with me what you think good and right. But mark well: if you put me to death, it is innocent blood you bring upon yourselves. . . . For in truth it was the LORD who sent me to you, to speak all these things for you to hear" (26:14-15). The need for such defense is clear from the account of his ministry and career: his message was unpopular and appeared to many to be both seditious and irreverent; because of it he was imprisoned, put in the stocks, left to die in an old cistern. Isaiah's account of his call (Isaiah 6) is undoubtedly formulated, in part at least, to vindicate a message that put him at odds with the rulers and the most influential people of the time; he was probably accused of conspiracy. Ezekiel's call is spread over three chapters (Ezekiel 1–3), and though conflict is not so dramatically clear in his career, he is warned of the resistance he will meet (2:3-8; 3:5-11), and the word of the Lord comes to him even more concretely than it did to Jere-miah, in the form of a scroll he is to eat (2:8–3:4). Even the story of Jonah, fictional though it is, provides a good insight into Israel's understanding of the inescapable nature of the Lord's call. Jonah, commanded by the Lord to go to Nineveh, boards a seagoing ship headed as far as possible in the other direction. But the Lord prepares a storm and then a fish to take Jonah back to his starting point. When "the word of the LORD came to Jonah a second time" (3:1), Jonah's obedience to it could no longer be in doubt.

It is hardly possible for us to explain exactly what lies behind these call narratives. Almost certainly there is a religious experience of some sort that, with no intention of denigrating ecstaticism, I would suggest is something quite different from that of the ecstatic prophets. It is partly on this basis that Albright distinguishes between "the age of the great

prophets refer "almost always disparagingly" to a class of people that call themselves *něbî'îm*, which leads us to wonder whether they would have wished to be known by that title. It has been suggested that the prophetic designation has been added to the canonical books at a later time (*A History of Prophecy* [Louisville: John Knox, 1996] 9). On Amos, see further in Chapter Six below.

natural prophets, which came to an end in the ninth century, and that of the literary prophets, which began several decades later," for, as he says, "except in very unusual cases, no prophet could emerge from an ecstatic experience to give a poetic address couched in such perfect literary form as are the best preserved oracles of Amos, Hosea, and Isaiah."[2] Two of those who have written extensively on this matter of religious experience, Lindblom and Heschel, have gone off in different directions. Lindblom gives much attention to the phenomenon of ecstasy. He rejects a distinction between classical and early prophets on the basis of the presence or absence of ecstasy, rightly noting that the classical prophets are not without ecstatic aspects. One can point out, for example, that Micah claims to be filled with the Spirit (Mic 3:8) and that Ezekiel manifests ecstatic traits. However, it is clear that he understands the term very broadly; any sort of vision or audition (or, I suppose, communication of the divine) he sees as evidence of ecstasy.[3]

Heschel's approach is very different. He does not start out with the broader phenomenon of religious experience as Lindblom does. Instead, after an introductory chapter, he begins at once to deal with individual (classical) prophets. Much later (Chapter 12) he explains their attunement to the divine in terms of their sharing in the pathos of God. In this chapter on "The Theology of Pathos" he asserts that "to the prophet, knowledge of God was fellowship with Him, not attained by syllogism or induction, but by living together"—though he explains that "the culmination of prophetic fellowship with God is insight and unanimity—not union." As a quasi-definition: "pathos denotes, not an idea of goodness, but a living care; not an immutable example, but an outgoing challenge, a dynamic relation between God and man; not mere feeling or passive affection, but an act or attitude composed of various spiritual elements; no mere contemplative survey of the world, but a passionate summons."[4] Here Heschel is speaking of *God's* pathos; the prophet comes into it, according to Heschel, in that he participates in God's pathos. In a later chapter he takes up the topic of ecstasy; more precisely, he distinguishes between ecstasy (which means being outside oneself—*ekstasis*) and enthusiasm (which means being possessed by a god—*entheos*). He investigates these

---

[2] William F. Albright, *From the Stone Age to Christianity* (Garden City, NY: Doubleday, 1957 [c1942]) 306.

[3] Johannes Lindblom, *Prophecy in Ancient Israel* (Philadelphia: Fortress, 1965): "A real vision is always based on ecstasy of one form or another" (p. 107).

[4] Abraham Joshua Heschel, *The Prophets* (New York: Harper & Row, 1962) 224.

phenomena especially in Greek and Roman sources and denies they are what we find in Israel's prophets.[5] Heschel's discussion is enlightening, though his rejection of ecstasy as an element of Israelite prophecy is at the expense of ignoring the early prophets (from whom, we insist, the classical prophets developed) and the evidence, mentioned above, with reference to Micah and Ezekiel. Nevertheless, his theory of pathos is important in pointing to a significant source of prophetic ethical teaching: the prophet who is in tune with God's outlook on the world, who enjoys fellowship with God, perceives right and wrong in a way not wholly dependent on existing laws and customs.

The religious experience of the classical prophets, at least of the sort described in their vocation narratives and in others they occasionally describe, is, in my view, something other than ecstaticism of the sort manifested in the charismatic groups. The ecstatic state can be induced in a number of ways; some groups, in addition to the singing and dancing referred to by Albright, use alcohol or narcotics. Thus there need be nothing supernatural about it or about "communications" received in such ecstacy. Lindblom wants to use the term "ecstasy" but is at pains to explain that it is not the sort "in which the *ego* fully loses consciousness of itself and becomes completely absorbed in the Divine, in the so-called *unio mystica*." He thinks of it rather as "denoting a mental state in which human consciousness is so concentrated on a particular idea or feeling that the normal current of thoughts and perceptions is broken off and the senses temporarily cease to function in a normal way." In rejecting the idea of *unio mystica* he is concerned to preserve the "personal character of prophetic religion" and says "they share in Yahweh's wrath and love and felt themselves bound to His will, because He has laid hold upon them."[6] In such an expression he is not far from the position in which Heschel speaks of the prophet sharing in the "pathos" of God, which sharing Heschel calls "sympathy." Heschel refers to "the inner personal identification of the prophet with the divine pathos," with a strong emphasis on the personal, emotional aspect: "he is convulsed by [the divine pathos] to the depths of his soul."[7] While there is little evidence in the prophets that would justify speaking of "mystical union," it may be

---

[5] *The Prophets*, chs. 19–21, pp. 324–66.

[6] *Prophecy in Ancient Israel*, 106. His concern about preserving the personal character of prophetic religion comes strongly to the fore in "Additional Note I" (pp. 423–24), where he discusses in detail scholars who are on one side or the other of the "ecstasy" question.

[7] *The Prophets*, 307–08.

asked whether the experiences of the great mystics such as Teresa of Avila or John of the Cross militate in any way against "personal religion"; the writings they have left us certainly do not favor that impression. Perhaps the experience of the classical prophets is comparable to that described by St. Paul when he was "caught up to the third heaven," not knowing whether in or out of the body, and received "visions and revelations of the Lord" (2 Cor 12:2, 1). The kind of experience we find in the great saints and mystics supposes a high level of prayer, attunement to God, union with God, ability to receive and communicate revelation, and neither requires nor rules out ecstatic aspects.

MISSION TO BE BEARERS OF GOD'S WORD

Although the early prophets certainly understood themselves to be bearers of God's word, they did not seem to think that was enough, and so we find them involved in revolts, coups d'état, harem intrigues, etc. Somehow they felt themselves compelled to take matters into their own hands, but by that same token they ran the risk of taking them out of God's hands. In the classical prophets, on the other hand, we find more emphasis on the word. Jeremiah is told that he has been set "over nations and over kingdoms" and that he is to "root up and to tear down, / to destroy and to demolish, / to build and to plant" (Jer 1:10), but the only means he is given for this ambitious program is the word of God that had been placed in his mouth, a word he compares to a fire and to a hammer shattering rocks (23:29). And Deutero-Isaiah speaks of the word of the Lord that stands (i.e., prevails, is effective) forever (Isa 40:8), which returns not empty but accomplishes all for which it is sent (55:11). The prophet's word may have political implications, he may attempt to influence policy by carrying the word before kings and people, and he may reinforce it with symbolic acts (as, e.g., in Isaiah 20; Jer 13:1-11; 19:1-13; 27:1-11; Ezekiel 4; 5; etc.), but he does not feel the need to engage in intrigues to bring it to pass. All that is to be done will be accomplished through the word, which, because it *is* the word of the Lord, is supremely efficacious.[8]

---

[8] Brevard S. Childs, *Biblical Theology in Crisis* (Philadelphia: Westminster, 1970) 101, warns of the danger of judging the prophet's experience by our own, of reducing the prophets to our own size by taking the prophet's "hear the word of the LORD" to mean (as we perhaps would mean, since we do not share their experience) "this is what I as a sensitive religious person think."

DEPTHS OF CONTENT OF TEACHING

Speaking of the early prophets, Albright says: "At first sight it is curious that practically no oracles have survived; what we have belongs to the category of Deuteronomic sermon, though it presumably rests on a traditional nucleus. The prophets of the ecstatic period were men of deeds, not men of words, and the ecstatic tradition was still too strong to be broken."[9] We may question the emphasis given to ecstaticism as the reason, but the fact is that we have nothing from the early prophets that can compare with the collections of oracles of the classical prophets; what we have are mainly threats against this or that king, usually fleshed out by the deuteronomists. If there had been oracles worth preserving, they would have been preserved. On the other hand, we often have extensive narratives about them; this is especially the case with Elijah and Elisha. With the classical prophets we may know very little of their lives and deeds (Jeremiah is by all means the exception), but it is clearly their words that count most. They form perhaps the most important part of the Old Testament and have profoundly influenced the history of the world and its literature (including the New Testament).

---

[9] *From the Stone Age to Christianity*, 306.

Chapter Six

AMOS

Amos was from Tekoa, a small village about twelve miles south of Jerusalem. He was, therefore, a Judean, but exercised his prophetic ministry in the north because, as he tells us, "the LORD took me . . . and said to me, 'Go, prophesy to my people Israel'" (Amos 7:15). Israel under the Omri dynasty[1] had been strong and prosperous. This was largely because of favorable trade relations with Phoenicia and peace with Judah, both of which Omri and Ahab promoted. Jehu's dynasty,[2] as we have seen, was inaugurated with a bloody purge that included not only Jezebel and Baal worshipers, but also all of the previous royal house; the king of Judah, too, was wantonly murdered. Such behavior naturally alienated Phoenicia and Judah and so left Israel without two valuable allies, and this at a time when Syria was a serious threat. Moreover, Assyria, which Ahab had fought against on the side of Syria and the rest of the anti-Assyrian coalition, was again on the move; in 841 Jehu submitted and paid tribute.[3] Syria, by now under Hazael, was in a stronger position, and after Assyria's withdrawal took most of northern Transjordan from Israel; in the days of Jehoahaz much more of Israel's territory fell to Syria. But a number of circumstances

---

[1] Although the deuteronomists give Omri (876–869) short shrift, he was one of the most important of Israel's kings. His dynasty continued through Ahab (869–850), Ahaziah (850–849), and Jehoram (849–842), and even during the dynasty of Jehu Assyrian records continue to refer to Israel as "the house of Omri." Ahab, too, while given much space in 1 Kings, is judged unfavorably, though he clearly was a strong king. Omri was able to take back much of the land Israel had lost after the separation from Judah and during the ensuing political instability. While pursuing friendly relations with Phoenicia and Judah, Omri acted vigorously against Syria; Ahab followed the same policies, though he entered into alliance with Syria for a while, probably in the interests of offering resistance to Assyrian expansion.

[2] It consisted of Jehu (842–815), Jehoahaz (815–801), Jehoash (801–786), Jeroboam II (786–735), and Zechariah (746–745).

[3] An act depicted on Shalmaneser III's famous Black Obelisk.

changed things dramatically shortly before the middle of the eighth century, when Amos appears on the scene. The threat from Syria was put on hold for the moment, as the vigorous Adad-nirari III ascended the throne of Assyria and turned attention to the Aramean states that had been in the forefront of resistance. Then for two generations both Israel and Judah were blessed with strong and able leaders.[4] Israel under both Jehoash and Jeroboam II had military successes against Syria and succeeded in retaking much of the territory Israel had lost since the division of the kingdom. Judah, too, had success, extending its control over Edom and other territories to the south. Together the two kingdoms controlled lands from Lebo-hamath (south of Kadesh on the Orontes River) in the north to the Gulf of Aqabah in the south. The rebuilding of the important port of Ezion-geber and consolidation of control over the caravan routes allowed the sister kingdoms, in friendly alliance under Jeroboam II and Uzziah, to tap the commercial wealth flowing through their borders.

Thus with Syria quelled, Assyria not threatening, and Judah an ally, the Israelite scene onto which Amos stepped was, on the surface at least, both peaceful and prosperous. This was a situation that should have made for good times for all, but that was not the case. That it was not is attributable, in large part at least, to the social evolution that had been taking place in Israel since its earliest days. The Naboth affair demonstrates the egalitarian ideal of early Israel; they thought of themselves as a society of small landholders, pastoral and agrarian. But times were changing. The settlement of the Israelite tribes in Canaan occasioned profound changes in their social and economic structures.[5] Some elements of tribal structure continued long after the settlement, but gradually they were replaced. Belonging to a village or city began to replace blood kinship as the primary bond. The appearance of the monarchy hastened the process immeasurably. This was partly because the very concept of "royalty" created a class consciousness that had not previously existed. The change was not so apparent under Saul and David, perhaps, but it certainly was by the time of Solomon. But it was also partly because a

---

[4] There is a surprisingly close coincidence of dates of these two tandem pairs: Jehoash (802–786) in Israel and Amaziah (800–783) in Judah; then Jeroboam II (786–746) in Israel and Uzziah (a.k.a. Azariah, 783–742) in Judah.

[5] See Johannes Lindblom, citing the studies of M. Weber, E. Meyer, A. Causse, A. Lods, J. Morgenstern, "and many others," *Prophecy in Ancient Israel* (Philadelphia: Fortress, 1965) 346–47. See Jo Ann Hackett, "There Was No King in Israel," in M. D. Coogan, ed., *The Oxford History of the Biblical World* (Oxford and New York: Oxford University Press, 1998) 132–34.

new class of royal officials was created. Furthermore, Solomon, as one of his measures for more efficiently organizing the populace for taxation and forced labor, divided the northern territories into twelve administrative districts and placed them under governors responsible to the crown (1 Kgs 4:7-19); the inevitable weakening of tribal organization and loyalty that resulted may well have been part of his intention. Another Solomonic innovation, the introduction of chariot forces, involved a feudalism of sorts: namely, the bestowal of land and favors from the royal bounty on those—the rich—who could own and maintain such expensive equipment and be ready to use it when called upon by the king.

In addition, many turned from the pastoral and agricultural life to practice crafts or engage in commerce. These activities often generated the sort of income that allowed its holders to amass property and other forms of wealth. The old egalitarianism was gone and this alone would have been disturbing to Amos and the prophets who followed him, but it is clear that things went much further. The distinction between rich and poor fed on itself when the rich were willing to use their wealth to exploit the weakness of the poor, even to the extent of foreclosing their property and enslaving them for debts they could not pay. Even worse, they might use their resources to bribe judges and other officials so as to obtain unjust judgments against the poor and strip them of their property and other rights. All of this was present and evident in the Israel into which Amos stepped.

SOURCES OF AMOS' TEACHING

What are the sources of Amos' teaching? Covenant, law, and wisdom have all been suggested, and each has some claim to truth, at least in the sense that there is every reason, in the case of Amos, to presuppose the first two, and valid arguments have been presented for the third.

There was a time when quite a number of scholars held that the covenant concept was late in Israel, arguing from the infrequency of references to it in the early prophets. Few would hold that now; even those (e.g., McCarthy) who reject Mendenhall's identification of the Decalogue with the treaty form (as I do) would nevertheless hold that covenant is early in Israel. The covenant concept does come up in Hosea, and he and Amos are practically contemporaries. Amos does not use the term, but given the time and place, namely, the eighth century in the northern kingdom, it was surely part of the thought world. He was aware of the Exodus tradition (2:10; 3:2; 9:7).[6] Even Martin Noth, who argues that Exodus and Sinai were

---

[6] Hans W. Wolff rejects the authenticity of some of these passages, but see below.

originally separate traditions, sees them as melded together (along with promises to the patriarchs, wilderness wandering, and entrance into the land) into the unified tradition of Israel's faith during the period of the tribal league.[7] As previously pointed out, however, covenant would not provide the content of moral teaching but only the context for recognizing Israel's obligation of obedience to Yhwh and to whatever laws may have been attached to the covenant.

There are, however, those who argue for the covenant concept in Amos (and other prophets) on inadequate or invalid grounds. A parade example might be Frank H. Seilhamer, who argues from the use of the terms *pešaʿ yādaʿ, tôrâ, ḥōq,* and *mišpāṭ* for a covenant background in Amos.[8] Part of the argumentation is based on the assertion that *pešaʿ* (or the verb *pšʿ*) refers to the violation of covenant or treaty obligations. In fact, *pešaʿ*, although it can and does occur in contexts where the crime involved amounts to an infringement of the covenant, is one of the most common Hebrew terms for transgression of almost any sort, and covenant violation is indicated in only a small percentage of the cases.[9] Somewhat surprisingly, Seilhamer and others point to the use of the term in Amos 2:6, where it refers to Israel, as an example of covenant terminology, and neglect to note that the same term is used of the pagan nations six times in the preceding verses.[10]

---

[7] Noth held that there was a G (= *Grundschrift*) on which both J and E depended (thereby explaining their similarities) and that necessarily existed before either of them.

[8] Frank H. Seilhamer, "The Role of Covenant in the Mission and Message of Amos," in Howard N. Bream, *et al.*, eds., *A Light unto My Path: Old Testament Studies in Honor of Jacob M. Myers*. Gettysburg Theological Studies IV (Philadelphia: Temple University Press, 1974) 435–51. Much the same position, with many of the same arguments, is taken by Richard V. Bergren, *The Prophets and the Law*. HUCAMS 4 (Cincinnati: Hebrew Union College, 1974).

[9] No covenant background is discernible, for example, in Gen 31:36; 50:17; 1 Sam 24:12; 25:28; Job 14:17; 35:6; Ps 32:1, 5; 36:2; 51:3, 5. Hardly one of the dozen occurrences in Proverbs suggests covenant transgression; cf. 10:12, 9; 12:13; 17:9, 19; 19:11; 28:13, 24; 29:6 (sense uncertain), 16, 22. Prov 28:2 *could* refer to treaty violation.

[10] The pagan nations did not have a covenant with Yhwh, though one might argue for reference to treaty with Israel. However, H. W. Wolff, *Joel and Amos*. Hermeneia (Philadelphia: Fortress, 1977) 146, holds that these uses of *pešaʿ* in Amos 1–2 are not presented as violations of Israel's political interests but of Yhwh's will. He notes that the *pšʿ* root is rare in the Pentateuch (where Israel's covenant and legal tradition are particularly to be found), and that its relative frequency in Amos is matched by its frequency in Proverbs. He believes that Amos' use reflects clan tradition and that the translation "crime" rather than "rebellion" is appropriate.

The case is a little different with *yādaʿ*, ("to know"), for there have been serious studies that relate this term to the treaty tradition,[11] where it is said to mean (1) "to recognize the legitimacy of a suzerain or a vassal," and (2) "to recognize treaty stipulations as binding." But it is a large and unjustified leap from saying that *yādaʿ* can be treaty/covenant terminology to saying that because *yādaʿ* is used in a text, the reference is to covenant.[12] So also *tôrâ* (in Amos only at 2:4, in a passage that almost all see as a later interpolation), *ḥōq*, and *mišpāṭ*, although they do frequently occur within a covenant context, occur also in many other contexts,[13] so that their mere occurrence cannot be used as proof.

As to law, the legitimate case is similar to that of covenant; there is little in Amos that proves he speaks from a background of Israelite law, but again there is a legitimate presupposition. But one needs to be critical. Reference to "law" here regards primarily the Code of the Covenant, which most authors see as a collection that existed from the period of the tribal league and was operative especially in the north. And we can point to one example that is unlikely to be a coincidence; Amos' criticism of those who "upon garments taken in pledge / they recline beside any altar" (2:8) would seem to reflect Exod 22:25-26, where it is enjoined that the garment taken in pledge must be returned before sunset. However, when parallels from later codes are cited, one can reasonably be skeptical. This caution does not necessarily extend to all instances taken from Deuteronomy, for its roots are in the north and are clearly older than the finished code as it appeared in the light of day in 622. As in the case of covenant, not all arguments are equally valid. The example of Bergren has already been discussed in Chapter Two.

Wisdom as a source of Amos' ethical teaching cannot be presupposed in the same fashion as covenant and law, but some persuasive arguments have been put forward by Wolff.[14] He points to the sayings in

---

[11] Most especially H. B. Huffmon, "The Treaty Background of Hebrew *Yādaʿ*," *BASOR* 181 (Feb. 1966) 31–37; H. B. Huffmon and S. B. Parker, "A Further Note on the Treaty Background of Hebrew *Yādaʿ*," *BASOR* 184 (December 1966) 36–38.

[12] For example, in Gen 4:1 "the man had relations with his wife Eve, and she conceived," would not be interpreted, we hope, as implying a suzerain-vassal relationship.

[13] Cf., e.g., the frequent use of *mišpāṭ* in Proverbs.

[14] Hans W. Wolff, *Amos the Prophet. The Man and His Background* (Philadelphia: Fortress, 1973). The title of the German original, *Amos' geistige Heimat*, is more expressive of the content. Wolff was preceded in his interest in wisdom in Amos by Reinhard Fey, *Amos und Jesaja*. WMANT 12 (Neukirchen-Vluyn: Neukirchener Verlag, 1963) and Samuel Terrien, "Amos and Wisdom," in Bernhard W. Anderson and Walter Harrelson, eds., *Israel's Prophetic Heritage* (New York: Harper & Row, 1962) 108–15.

Amos that involve a numerical sequence of n, n+1 ("for three crimes of __ and for four . . .") , which are popular in wisdom. Various numbers appear, though the 3, 4 sequence is the most frequent.[15] In the wisdom sayings the emphasis falls on the last in the series—which served chiefly to present or illuminate social phenomena. In Amos' use only the one to be emphasized is named; at least that is the case in the opening oracle against the surrounding nations.

Wolff also argues from Amos' use of didactic questions. The use of rhetorical questions as such would not be sufficient to demonstrate wisdom influence, but he means the building up of a series of them, as in 3:3-8, to make them a vehicle of instruction. He argues also on the basis of Amos' use of antithetical pairs (good-evil, love-hate). The use of antithetical parallelism is a procedure found especially in wisdom compositions.[16] He points to the term *nĕkōḥâ* in 3:10 (the "right" in "they know not how to do what is right"), which he says is very much at home in wisdom diction but is rare otherwise.

Wolff presents a great many other arguments, some of which have validity, while others may be questioned. In particular he argues that the use of "woe"[17] springs from a wisdom background, basing his position on an influential article by Erhard Gerstenberger.[18]

The wisdom background that Wolff sees in Amos is not that of professional courtly wisdom, but that of the clan: the admonitions, instruction, and values that are rooted there. James L. Crenshaw, among others, has

---

[15] For example, "three things are never satisfied, four never say 'enough'" (Prov 30:15-16); "under three things the earth trembles, yes, under four it cannot bear up" (30:21-23); "there are six things the LORD hates, yes, seven are an abomination to him" (6:16-19); "three things are too wonderful for me, yes, four I cannot understand" (30:18-19).

[16] Although antithetic parallelism is frequently named along with synonymous parallelism (and synthetic parallelism) in explaining Hebrew poetry, it is rather rare in the Psalter, being found mainly in psalms that are classified as wisdom compositions (cf. Psalm 37); but abundant examples will be found in Proverbs, beginning especially with the first Solomonic collection (Prov 10:1–22:16).

[17] The Hebrew *hôy*, commonly translated "woe" in the past, now more usually "Ah!" or "Alas!" is found in Amos at 5:18 and 6:1. It is generally supposed that it belongs also at 5:7. *NRSV* judges it should be repeated ("alas") at 6:4.

[18] Erhard Gerstenberger, "The Woe-Oracles of the Prophets," *JBL* 81 (1962) 249–63. For a critique of the position that *hôy*-oracles arise from wisdom see Joseph Jensen, *The Use of tôrâ in Isaiah: His Debate with the Wisdom Tradition*. CBQMS 3 (Washington, DC: The Catholic Biblical Association, 1973) 101–02. A far better presentation of the origins of the *hôy*-oracle than Gerstenberger is that of Richard Clifford, "The Use of *HÔY* in the Prophets," *CBQ* 28 (1966) 458–64; Waldemar Janzen, *Mourning Cry and Woe Oracle*. BZAW 125 (Berlin: de Gruyter, 1972) presents roughly the same position as Clifford.

critically examined Wolff's arguments and finds many of them weak and inconclusive but attributes validity to others. His conclusion is that "in essence, an affirmative answer has been given to the question about Amos' dependence upon the wisdom tradition, although this may be explained on the basis of the rootedness of wisdom in experience."[19] In another article he again finds some indications that Amos and wisdom are to be linked together; he sees this especially in the theophanic language in Amos ("I will [not] pass through your midst," cf. 5:17; 7:8; 8:2; "prepare to meet your God, O Israel," 4:12; "I will set my eyes upon them," cf. 9:4, 8, as well as others) and in this sees a link with the wisdom tradition, especially the theophanic language of Job.[20] Mays points out that Amos "was especially adept at the employment of forms of speech that appear in the riddles, comparisons, and popular proverbs of folk wisdom" and goes on to speak of his use of graduated numbers-sayings and of comparisons and riddles to make his point.[21]

The conclusion from all this is that content for moral teaching can come from a variety of backgrounds, including those of the more general human impulse toward right conduct that is found in wisdom teaching.

PROPHET OF GOD'S JUSTICE?

Amos is sometimes called the prophet of God's justice. If we are using the ancient Hebrew concept of justice, however, as would seem only right, the assessment is correct only in an indirect, somewhat convoluted sense. It would be more accurate to say that he is the prophet who presents God's demand for justice or to call him the prophet of God's wrath. That wrath is explained, in fact, by the lack of Israel's "justice" in terms of the Hebrew ṣĕdāqâ, or, more accurately, the various forms of the Hebrew root ṣdq.[22] We are usually confined to giving English equivalents (normally "justice" or "righteousness") that do not really express the Hebrew concept, and it is important to understand it if we are to understand Amos and the rest of the prophets. As Gerhard von Rad expresses it, "There is absolutely no concept in the Old Testament with

---

[19] James L. Crenshaw, "The Influence of the Wise upon Amos: The 'Doxologies of Amos' and Job 5:9-16; 9:5-10," *ZAW* 79 (1967) 42–52.

[20] James L. Crenshaw, "Amos and the Theophanic Tradition," *ZAW* 80 (1968) 203–15.

[21] James Luther Mays, *Amos: A Commentary.* OTL (London: SCM, 1969) 6.

[22] The verb, in the qal, means "to be in the right, to have a just cause," and in the hiphil "to do justice toward, to justify, to pronounce a person guiltless." The adjective ṣaddîq means "guiltless, correct, just," etc.

so central a significance for all the relationships of human life as that of ṣdqh. . . . ṣdqh can be described without more ado as the highest value in life, that upon which all life rests when it is properly ordered."[23] "Justice" in modern western culture is "rendering to each one his/her due" and implies conformity to a specific norm, often the legal norm of law. It is objective, impersonal, and impartial; we represent justice as a blindfolded goddess with scales to symbolize this. The Hebrew ṣĕdāqâ differs from this on almost every point. As Pedersen has it, "Righteousness does not imply neutral, unconditioned justice on all hands; the ethics of the Israelite acknowledged neither neutral nor unconditioned acts. Justice is the mental quality on the strength of which peace is maintained; therefore it is at the same time the kernel of peace and blessing."[24] Pedersen, in the context, is speaking of covenant, and he goes on to say that "justice and truth both denote the maintenance of covenant. . . . He who maintains the covenant maintains himself, because he forms a totality with those with whom he has a covenant";[25] however, in a broader context the term "relationship" could just as well be substituted for covenant.[26] The understanding of what is involved here gives insight into the connection between the people forsaking justice and the prophet's threat of destruction. Further: "Justice is more frequently a claim on the stronger, the claim implying that he receives the weaker into his will and self-maintenance. Therefore righteousness is a kingly virtue. . . . Justice demands that equilibrium shall be reestablished between the wronged and him who commits the breach, for thereby the covenant is healed. To re-establish this relation is to *justify* a man."[27] Much the same position is presented by Katherine Doob Sakenfeld when she says that righteousness[28] in the Old Testament does not refer to some abstract ethical standard but rather "righteousness has to do with living and acting in a way appropriate to

---

[23] Gerhard von Rad, *Old Testament Theology* (New York: Harper & Row, 1962) 1:370; he deals with the topic especially through pp. 370–83.

[24] Johannes Pedersen, *Israel, Its Life and Culture*, I–II (London: Oxford University Press, 1926) 336.

[25] Ibid. 342.

[26] Cf. von Rad, *Old Testament Theology* I, quoting Hermann Cremer (*Die paulinsiche Rechtfertigungslehre im Zusammenhang ihrer geschichtlichen Voraussetzungen* [Gütersloh: Bertelsmann, 1901]): "The way in which it is used shows that ṣdq is out and out a term denoting relationship, and that it does this in the sense of referring to a real relationship between two parties . . . " (p. 371).

[27] Pedersen, *Israel*, 344–45.

[28] I am preserving here her use of "righteousness" for what I have been calling "justice." (On terminology see further in n. 30 below.)

a relationship. For individuals righteousness is a function of their many and changing interconnections with others. . . ." When she goes on to say that righteousness "provides a way of speaking of the entire fabric of the society itself, its warp and woof,"[29] we are forced to ask what will then happen to a society when righteousness disappears or is perverted. All of Amos' efforts are bent toward answering that question for the Israel of his day.

One may further consult Klaus Koch's treatment of ṣdq, in which he points out that a relationship of this root to a specific norm or divine command is never attested in preexilic times and is excluded. He relates it to intra-community relationship and behavior—"intra-community" taken in a broad sense that can include just two individuals, such as master and servant.[30]

Thus ṣĕdāqâ, far from being that which demands its pound of flesh, is a quality that will often incline toward mercy and generosity.[31] In the Old Testament šidqôt yhwh, the "righteous deeds of the LORD" (cf. Judg 5:11; 1 Sam 12:7; Mic 6:5; Dan 9:16; cf. Ps 103:6) were precisely God's acts of liberation in Israel's salvation history.[32] The significance of all this for our study of Amos is that, in a sense, the whole book is about justice (understood in this way)—not so much about God's justice as about Israel's lack of justice, which is a demand God lays upon Israel, and about the consequences of this lack.

---

[29] Katherine Doob Sakenfeld, *Faithfulness in Action: Loyalty in Biblical Perspective* (Philadelphia: Fortress, 1985) 119–20. She lays out her understanding of the relationship between *mišpāṭ* and *ṣĕdāqâ*: "The concept of justice (Hebrew *mišpāṭ*) . . . is integral to righteousness (Hebrew *ṣĕdāqâ*) in that justice is especially concerned for the mechanisms by which righteousness is maintained in community" (p. 120). From this we can conclude that *mišpāṭ* partakes somewhat of the same sort of fluidity as *ṣĕdāqâ*. In general I translate *mišpāṭ* as "judgment" and *ṣĕdāqâ* as "justice."

[30] In *Handwörterbuch zum Alten Testament*, ed. Ernst Jenni (Munich: C. Kaiser, 1971–1976) vol. 2, s.v. It is noteworthy that after the Hebrew title of the article, ṣdq, Koch gives *gemeinschaftstreu/heilvoll sein* as the German title, which would mean "faithful to community/healing, making whole").

[31] Again from von Rad, *Old Testament Theology* I: ". . . conduct loyal to a relationship includes far more than mere correctness or legality. . . . Such dependence upon one another demanded the showing of kindness, faithfulness, and, as circumstances arose, helpful compassion to the poor or the suffering" (pp. 373–74).

[32] Thus the development of Paul's argument in the epistle to the Romans is easier to understand when we remember that the contrast Paul draws is not between God's mercy and justice but between God's wrath (1:18), which inclines to judgment and punishment, and God's justice/righteousness (in the sense we have been explaining it here), which leads him to send Jesus for our justification.

Much of this can be seen already from a somewhat simplified[33] division of the material in the book.

> Opening oracle against the nations and Israel: 1:3–2:16
> Three words and three *hôy*-oracles: 3:1–6:14
> Three visions: 7:1–9:8(15)

The first of these sections climaxes in a judgment upon Israel; each of the "words" involves a similar kind of judgment; the term *hôy*[34] almost always suggests calamity, and all of these oracles are directed against Israel or particular groups or classes in Israel (those who turn justice to wormwood, those who yearn for the day of the Lord, the complacent/overconfident) and each of the visions (at 7:1; 8:1; 9:1) speaks of what sounds like final, irrevocable judgment.

AMOS' TEACHING

Although the Hebrew text of Amos is in good shape compared to many of the other Old Testament books, scholars discern a number of additions, some more, some fewer. For example, virtually all would admit a later "messianic perspective" at the end of the book that would encompass 9:11-15 or at least vv. 13-15; many would also so judge vv. 8c-10, though a case can be made for their authenticity. Wolff postulates a rather complex redactional history and distinguishes additions that pertain to "the old school of Amos," the "Bethel-exposition of the Josianic age," the deuteronomistic redaction, and postexilic eschatology of salvation. One may be skeptical about many points of the theory and in particular of his judgment on individual passages.[35] Francis I. Andersen and David N. Freedman come to a very different assessment.[36]

The opening oracle (1:3–2:16), consisting of eight condemnations of specific peoples, indicates something of the pains Amos took to get his message across. We have to think of it as delivered at a place where many people came together, probably an important cult center. The opening

---

[33] Not all the materials in the designated sections in fact fall into the categories suggested; however, the division is useful for the point being made here.

[34] For the sense of the term, see n. 17 above.

[35] The question of authenticity, of course, is important for establishing what a particular prophet taught. But there is a sense in which, in a discussion of "ethical dimensions," the question of authenticity is secondary; the text as we have it now is the canonical text and bears whatever authority we are willing to attribute to Scripture.

[36] Francis I. Andersen and David N. Freedman, *Amos: A New Translation with Introduction and Commentary*. AB 24A (New York and London: Doubleday, 1989) 141–44.

pronouncements against surrounding pagan nations serve the double function of winning a friendly hearing from those addressed (it is a popular human vice to enjoy hearing our enemies condemned) and of laying a basis on which Israel's own condemnation could rest. Almost all agree that the oracle against Judah comes from a later time, added at some point in order to make his words relevant to the southern kingdom when they had been brought there after the fall of the north. That would leave the good biblical number of seven and suggests that Amos' hearers would be waiting expectantly to hear who would come in the climactic seventh place, thus giving the oracle against Israel a special impact. However, the oracles against Tyre and Edom are frequently judged to be secondary, the one against Tyre because it repeats the charge against the Philistines of the previous verses and the one against Edom because the charge seems to reflect what the Edomites did to Judah after the fall of Jerusalem rather than anything from Amos' day. Even if these arguments be accepted, it is still possible that these two oracles replaced others and that the original number was indeed seven.

The mere fact that Amos directs these judgments against pagan nations tells us much about his conception of God. While Amos believes in Israel's election, the Lord is not a narrowly nationalistic God but one who is Lord of all the earth, the one who judges and punishes even the pagan nations.[37] But the crimes with which he charges them are of special interest: Aram, "because they threshed Gilead / with sledges of iron" (1:3); Philistia, "because they took captive whole groups to hand over to Edom" (v. 6); Tyre, "because they delivered whole groups / captive to Edom, / and did not remember the pact of brotherhood" (v. 9); Edom, "because he pursued his brother with the sword, / choking up all pity" (v. 11); Ammon, "because they ripped open expectant mothers in Gilead" in a war of expansion (v. 13); and Moab "because [they] he burned to ashes / the bones of Edom's king" (2:1).[38] The last named, at least, was not a crime against Israel nor any injury to them, but Amos sees it as a sin

---

[37] For Amos, the Lord is also the only operative force in the history of other nations, the one who brought the Philistines from Caphtor and the Arameans from Kir, just as he had brought Israel from Egypt (9:7). Some scholars argue that the nations named in this opening oracle may have been part of the ideal empire of David and Solomon and as such were expected to meet certain standards of conduct.

[38] Various emendations of the text have been proposed to produce widely divergent meanings without generating any consensus; the translation given above seems to be the meaning of the text. The cruelty involved would be to deprive the king of rest in the netherworld by making proper burial impossible.

against the Lord and one he will punish. Basically, then, we have a series of crimes—mainly, but not exclusively, directed against Israel—that are considered sins Yнwн will punish. They represent behavior that is cruel, oppressive, and often of the strong against the weak.

If Amos' audience assents to such judgments, as presumably they do, they then have no defense when, in the final oracle, Amos turns his fire on them. His references to Tyre's crime against "brotherhood" (apparently recalling the covenant of David and Solomon with Hiram, king of Tyre) and to Edom's crime against "brotherhood" (a reminiscence of Esau's hatred of Jacob in Gen 27:41) are especially telling because the crimes practiced by Israel are crimes against a more immediate kind of brotherhood, against members of the covenant community. Amos begins: "For three crimes of *Israel,* and for four . . ." (2:6; emphasis mine). Interestingly enough, the crimes listed here can indeed be counted as four if we take into account the parallelism that describes the same crime in different terms:

> (1) they sell the poor for a paltry sum;
> (2) they trample upon the weak/lowly;
> (3) son and father go to the same maid;
> (4) they recline upon garments taken in pledge.

At any rate, whether that number is indeed intended, Amos' indictments are indicative of his message.

In the very first item it is the *ṣaddîq* who is named (so we are immediately in material relevant to justice/righteousness), and in parallel to the poor. There is no obvious connection between being poor and being righteous, but here the poor person is righteous as over against the rich person who oppresses the poor; the term, in all probability, indicates that the poor person is one who ought to be declared in the right in judgment "at the gate" (5:10). When it is said that he is sold for "silver" we get into the sort of effects of sociological changes that may not always be unjust (in the legal sense of the word) but are deplored by the prophets. Small landowners would live from harvest to harvest. If there were a crop failure from drought or locust plague or blight they would either have to borrow, even for seed to plant, or face starvation. As security for the loan they would have only their property to put up; if there were another poor harvest they would have only their children or their own persons to sell.[39] Thus it could happen that the rich could come to pos-

---

[39] 2 Kings 4:1 attests to the taking of children as slaves to satisfy a debt, but legislation such as Exod 21:7-11, designed to protect certain rights of a daughter sold into slavery, undoubtedly supposes the same sort of desperate situation. And cf. Lev 25:39; Deut 15:12.

sess first the land and then the very persons of those less fortunate than themselves. All of this might be done in a perfectly *legal* way (it was, in fact, regulated by law), but for Amos and the Old Testament in general this was not ṣĕdāqâ. In some cases, as when bribery and corruption of judges were involved, not even the legal niceties were preserved (see below on 5:12).[40]

The second item listed does not appear to be anything new and specific but suggests an attitude of disregard and contempt, which says much about Amos' sensitivity.[41]

The third item relates to neither cultic nor secular prostitution, as some translations would suggest (*NAB*: "son and father go to the same prostitute," 2:7). Hebrew has vocabulary for both types, but the term used here is simply that for a young woman, naʿărâ (the feminine of naʿar, "young man"). It is a matter of the exploitation of the weak, the maid or slave girl (naʿărâ can mean either) who is unable to reject the advances of the males, young or old, in whose home she works. This interpretation, not followed by all,[42] places the third item in line with the others in this series, another example of the oppression of the weak and helpless. The text is powerful: such an act is a profanation of YHWH's holy name.

The fourth item is a condemnation of mistreatment of the poor by keeping garments taken in pledge that should be returned before nightfall (Exod 22:25-26) or, in the case of a widow, should not be taken at all (assuming that Deut 24:17 is an old law). The text includes condemnation of religious hypocrisy in that this is done in proximity to the altar,

---

[40] The phrase "and the poor man for a pair of sandals" may be simply a parallel expression to "they sell the just man for silver" (2:6) and indicate a paltry sum, but more probably this is an idiomatic way of indicating a bribe. The prophets, including Amos, often inveigh against this way of perverting justice; cf. Amos 5:12; also Isa 1:23; 33:15; Micah 3:1. It is also condemned in Israel's legislation (Exod 23:8; Deut 16:19) and wisdom tradition (Prov 17:23; Eccl 7:7).

[41] In spite of the designation of Amos as a shepherd (1:1; 7:14), he was no unlettered rustic; his Hebrew has been described as the purest in the Old Testament and his control of historical and contemporary events has been commented on. It has often been pointed out that the Hebrew term for "shepherd" in 1:1 (nōqēd), is the same as that applied to Mesha, king of Moab, in 2 Kgs 3:4, whose annual tribute to the king of Israel was 100,000 lambs and the wool of 100,000 rams. See also Richard C. Steiner, *Stockmen from Tekoa, Sycamores from Sheba: A Study of Amos' Occupations.* CBQMS 36 (Washington, DC: Catholic Biblical Association of America, 2003).

[42] Wolff, for example, thinks there is no reason to speak of maid or slave; rather "the . . . father has intruded upon his [the son's] love affair, and by so doing has turned a young woman into an object of gratification of forbidden lusts."

in relation to a service of worship and sacrifice.[43] A lengthy exegesis would be required to plumb the depths of the irony contained in these few words of Amos. They are in line with other texts in which Amos expresses or implies criticism of the cult hypocritically offered by those who oppress the weak (3:14; 4:4-5; 5:21-25; 9:1).[44]

Thus each of these four items has to do with offenses of the rich and powerful against the poor and weak. It is instructive to note that the first two terms in the fourfold indictment are *ṣaddîq* and *ʾebyôn* (2:6) and that they are in parallel. Amos' use of the *ṣdq* root is not that frequent, even though it is characteristic of his concerns: *ṣaddîq* is found here and at 5:12, *ṣĕdāqâ* at 5:7, 24 and 6:12, in each case parallel to *mišpāṭ* (see further below). This first use of *ṣaddîq* gives no clear indication of illegal procedure, but it is otherwise at 5:12.[45] The term *ʾebyôn* is also characteristic of his concerns; it is used here (2:6) and at 4:1; 5:12; and 8:4, 6; *ʿānāw* is used at 2:7, parallel to *dal,* and a related form at 8:4, parallel to *ʾebyôn; dal* is found, in addition to 2:7, at 4:1; 5:11; and 8:6.[46]

In this opening oracle Israel is put on a par with pagan nations; in either case there is cruelty and oppression that calls for Yhwh's judgment. But with Israel it is a matter of "how much worse," given the community and covenant context, the obligation of *ṣĕdāqâ.*

In what immediately follows (2:8), Amos gives further point to what has already been said: in bringing Israel into the land, Yhwh had championed Israel, then weak and needy, against the powerful inhabitants, here called Amorites, just as he had against the powerful Egyptian oppressors at the time of the exodus. Yhwh continues to champion the weak

---

[43] Wolff, again, would excise the reference to "altar" and "house of their god." But there is no doubt about Amos' condemnation of religious hypocrisy from other texts.

[44] In this connection we might think also of the manner in which Amos uses phrases probably taken from the cult to suggest destruction rather than (as they were originally intended) salvation: "Prepare to meet your God, O Israel" (4:12); "I will not pass it by again" (cf. 7:8; 8:2). The cultic claim that "the Lord is with us" will be verified only when they "hate evil and love good" (5:15).

[45] Arvid Kapelrud, "New Ideas in Amos," Congress of the International Organization for the Study of the Old Testament, *Congress Volume 1965.* VTSup 15 (Leiden: Brill, 1966), points out that since it was assumed that the *ṣaddîqîm* would have success in life (as asserted in many psalms), and since society normally identified such with the leaders, Amos turns this whole assumption upside down by identifying the *ṣaddîq* with the *ʾebyôn,* the poor man.

[46] These terms are roughly synonymous to designate the weak, poor, and helpless members of society; more exactly, *dal* conveys the idea of being weak and helpless, *ʿānāw* suggests being humble and meek, and *ʾebyôn* being needy and poor.

and needy, but now the oppressors are found among his own people. No matter; Amos depicts bluntly how they will be treated (2:13-16). The catalog of what YHWH has done for Israel, given now as a basis for condemnation, means that they were expected to learn how to behave from the divine example. Thus we here touch indirectly on the theme of the imitation of God with its basis in the narrative tradition (see above, Chapter One).

THE WORDS OF AMOS

The first of the "words of Amos" (3:1-2) continues the same theme. YHWH had shown special favor[47] to Israel, but if the proper response is not forthcoming, Israel's election becomes the occasion for greater punishment. To think that YHWH is a God who bestows gifts on favorites because they are favorites is an immature understanding of his nature, but one that seems to have been held by those Amos is here warning. Those whom the Lord has favored ought not to be guilty of crimes that provoke his wrath.

The "crimes" of which Israel is guilty, not specified in this passage, are probably to be understood in terms of the sorts of things said in the opening oracle and in the collection generally. In 3:9-11 we have again an indictment of Israel for oppression. Amos' great literary skill in the use of surprise and irony shapes this into a powerful oracle. Pagan peoples[48] are invited to observe what is going on in Israel's capital city; those whom Israel despised for their abominable ways are invited to be aghast at the disorders and oppression rampant among the chosen people. "They know not how to do what is right" (3:10) is a blanket judgment that is then specified in the strongest terms. Amos says they have stored up violence and robbery, though of course it is the fruit of these wrongful deeds that they have treasured away. The wrongdoers shall themselves become the victims of violence, and their ill-gotten goods will be snatched away. Let the punishment fit the crime. The unnamed "enemy" is a foreign power that will reduce and pillage the strongholds in which they trusted.

Amos' second "word" (4:1-3) proves that his interests are "inclusive" in that the female members of society are not neglected. Bashan, in

---

[47] *NAB*'s "you alone have I favored" renders the sense of the literal meaning of the text, "you alone have I known." See further on "to know" in Chapter Seven on Hosea.

[48] The Hebrew has "Ashdod" as the first name, but the LXX has "Assyria" and this reading is adopted by some translations. Whether Ashdod or Assyria, it is a matter of a pagan people that, in parallel with Egypt, Israel disdained as sinful and unclean.

Transjordan, was proverbial for its lush pasturelands and sleek cattle; to call the women "cows of Bashan" was intended to shock, as were so many other of Amos' words. Again Amos' concern is with the weak *(dal)* and the needy *(ʾebyôn)*. Although women in Israel could sometimes hold and administer substantial fortunes and so be in a position to abuse the poor by their own actions, Amos here designates the role they play in driving their husbands to unjust practices by the demand for luxurious lifestyles. Again the punishment Amos proclaims points to a foreign enemy, and here the reference is to exile; the fine ladies will be dragged off through the mire to a fate he does not further describe but that may easily be imagined.

Among the other passages the editor has appended to this second "word" is a polemic against the cult, something common in Amos. We have already seen his sarcastic reference to hypocritical worship in 2:8, and a major assault is to come in 5:21-24. In 4:6-12 Amos details a series of afflictions the Lord had sent against Israel to persuade them to return to him, none of which had the desired effect. As elsewhere (7:1-9), the conclusion is that the Lord's patience is exhausted and only punishment now awaits the sinful people. With dreadful irony an expression from the theophanic tradition, "prepare to meet your God" (4:12), signifies now not a cultic encounter of blessing but terrible judgment.

The third "word" (5:1-2) is rather poignant, accusing Israel of no sins but simply announcing the end in what we would call a dirge (in the mournful *qînâ* meter). "Fallen, to rise no more . . . abandoned" are all expressions suggesting the hopelessness of the situation, just as "virgin Israel" suggests vulnerability. But the intention is not to evoke pity but to express the finality of judgment on one who is already as good as dead. Israel is morally dead through sin and as good as destroyed by reason of the inevitability of the punishment the Lord has decreed.

After a brief reference to the almost total destruction Israel can expect to suffer in battle (v. 3),[49] Amos provides a major exhortation and invitation to reform (vv. 4-6). There is really very little of this from Amos, who seems not to expect anything other than the conduct that assures judgment. But here he offers at least the possibility of deliverance and lays down the condition: "seek me, that you may live" (v. 4). From all that Amos has said, the manner of seeking God is clear. The verb used

---

[49] Amos speaks of the loss of nine-tenths, whereas "decimation," loss of one-tenth, is already calamitous; thus there is little reason to see here, as some do, a hopeful remnant theme.

(*dāraš*) is sometimes employed in a cultic context, but here that manner of "seeking" God is explicitly excluded. More will be said about the proper manner of seeking in vv. 14-15.

THE *HÔY* ORACLES

Although it appears that the editor wished to collect in 5:7–6:14 three *hôy*-oracles, there is some disorder in the text. Verse 7 of chapter 5 is usually designated as a "woe," even though *hôy* does not appear in the text.[50] Furthermore, the doxology that comprises vv. 8-9 almost certainly does not belong after v. 7, but after v. 6 (where the *NAB* has transposed it).

With these adjustments, the first *hôy*-oracle consists of vv. 7, 10-11. It is perhaps the most powerful indictment in a book full of powerful indictments, the corruption (turning judgment into wormwood) of something of so high a value as *mišpāṭ* and casting to the ground something so precious as *ṣĕdāqâ*.[51] The two images that go with "judgment" and "justice," turning into wormwood and casting to the ground, are very different, but in each case it is a matter of perverting or setting at nought. Verse 10 clearly addresses those who would see justice perverted ("the gate" being the open plaza at the city gate, the place of judgment). The one who speaks the truth is the witness, or possibly even the defendant or plaintiff who had right on his side, as opposed to the one attempting to defraud him. The one who reproves is the one who strives to see justice done, perhaps even the prophet; that he is hated means that those present do not wish to see justice done. Job 31:21 suggests that having "supporters at the gate" could determine the outcome of a trial regardless of innocence or guilt.

The short passages that follow this indictment (i.e., vv. 12-17) may come from different contexts, but they relate to the same theme. The literal import of "trampling upon the poor" is not clear, but the second member refers to exactions the poor cannot afford and to which they should not be subject. As in earlier passages we have seen, the threat that the oppressors will not be able to enjoy the fruit of their oppression suggests death or exile.

---

[50] The construction is that which is normal for a *hôy*-oracle, namely, the plural participle that designates the kind of wrongdoing whose consequence is described (cf. 5:18-20; in 6:1-7, however, *hôy* is followed by an adjective rather than a participle).

[51] Wolff points out that this word pair is completely unknown in Israel's ancient legal collections in the Pentateuch; it is frequent, however, in Proverbs and is taken up by Isaiah and later writers.

The blanket accusation of v. 12a (many crimes, grievous sins) receives specification in v. 12b. Again it is a matter of action "at the gate," and the *ṣaddîq* terminology is particularly to the point because here it must have the technical sense of the one who is legally in the right in his suit; he can be oppressed, no doubt, because, as the parallel term suggests, he is an *ʾebyôn*. The phrase between these two expressions explains specifically how this is accomplished, namely, by the perversion of the judicial system through bribes.

Verses 14-15 expand on or specify some points raised in earlier verses in this chapter and have the effect of changing threat into exhortation. Here is told what must be done to avoid the threatened destruction. To seek/love good, to avoid/hate evil is the sort of behavior required; the expressions relate to the whole conduct of life, but specifically this can be manifested by the exercise of justice "at the gate." The consequence, that "the LORD . . . [will] be with you" (v. 14), reflects the claim, made especially in the context of the Holy War, "the LORD is with us"—a false claim in the present circumstances. For the Lord *not* to be with Israel is the greatest evil imaginable for a believing Israelite, good or bad, a formula for disaster. But this passage explains the only circumstances under which he will be with them. Even so, only a conditional hope is held out for the Lord's pity on "the remnant of Joseph," the reference being, of course, to the northern kingdom.

The original conclusion to the first *hôy*-oracle is probably to be found in vv. 16-17. It is a scene of general consternation and lament; here it is not a matter of enemy action but of the Lord's own action, for "I [will] pass through your midst" (v. 17). For the Lord to pass through Israel's midst can have a favorable or an unfavorable sense, depending on his intention; in the case at hand that intention has been specified by the kind of behavior that has been described and that occasions the Lord's advent.

The second *hôy*-oracle, 5:18-20, contains the earliest Old Testament reference to the "day of the LORD" (v. 18). Amos did not invent the idea but is here alluding to what is clearly a popular expectation. Where the expectation of "the day of the LORD" originated is debated, though von Rad's argument for an origin in the Holy War tradition has much to commend it.[52] Amos does not reject the idea, but he demolishes it as a basis for any sort of hope or security; he reinterprets it and indicates it is something they should fear rather than long for. It will be a day of

---

[52] See his *Holy War in Ancient Israel*, tr. M. J. Dawn (Grand Rapids: Eerdmans, 1991); *Old Testament Theology* (New York: Harper & Row, 1965) 2:119–25.

destruction for them, the sort of day on which one who manages to escape one danger inevitably encounters a worse one. It is indeed YHWH's day, the day of the Lord's special triumph and justice. Those who share in the Lord's justice can hope to share its triumph. But there is nothing automatic about Israel's privilege; Israel in its present condition will find itself among the Lord's enemies. This reinterpretation of the day of the Lord is of a piece with Amos' other efforts to cut off hope in every source of false security: election, the cult, the riches they have amassed, and now the day of the Lord.

Verses 21-24 are not part of the *hôy*-oracle but are a vigorous expression of an important Amos theme we have touched on before, namely, that sacrifice and other cultic worship is unacceptable to the Lord in the present circumstances. The terms used are very strong (I hate, spurn, will not accept, will not listen, away with!). It is human nature to want to be right with God, and participation in religious rites is one way of persuading ourselves that we are right with God. There is a cultic worship that consists in acknowledging our sins and begging forgiveness (the Old Testament knew sin and guilt offerings and penitential rites of various kinds), and these are always acceptable ("a heart contrite and humbled, O God, you will not spurn"—Ps 51:19; 1986 *NAB*). But cultic worship necessarily supposes sincere dispositions on the part of the worshiper, contrition for sins, if nothing else. In the present circumstances it was being offered by those who were unrighteous, perhaps consciously as a sop to substitute for lack of righteousness, without contrition, without right dispositions. This is what draws the harsh words. What Amos tells us, in effect, is that without loving concern for others, no worship rites are acceptable. Indeed, because they project an outward show of righteousness where none exists within, they are hypocritical and detestable. Because the Lord is assumed to accept such worship, he might seem to be accepting those who offer it; Amos says clearly that he does not. In terms of what was said above of the implications of the covenant, we could express it by saying that no vertical dimension is possible without the horizontal dimension. What the Lord does demand is expressed in v. 24, namely, *mišpāṭ* and *ṣĕdāqâ*; the imagery of rolling, flowing waters suggests an abundance of these qualities, perhaps even fertility and cleansing.[53]

---

[53] Verse 22a, in its present form, presents a difficulty. The *NAB* has transposed it to the beginning of v. 24 and interprets it to mean that justice and judgment represent a precondition for acceptable sacrifice ("But if you would offer me holocausts, then . . .").

Amos' third *hôy*, 6:1-7,[54] is more fully developed than the first two, with its introductory *hôy*, designation of the group addressed, elaboration of their crimes, and then the statement of punishment (v. 7, introduced by "therefore"). He paints a picture of wealth and luxury, damnable because it is obtained by taking from the poor and because of the want of concern for the poor. Unrighteousness shreds the fabric of society (see above on *ṣĕdāqâ*), and so such behavior "hasten[s] the reign of violence" (v. 3). Amos, in speaking of exile, relates the punishment to enemy attack, and indeed a people is especially vulnerable to invasion from without when the social structure within has become rotten. Amos' description of the luxuries[55] enjoyed by the rich could easily be paralleled in any number of ways from our culture, as could the lack of concern by the more fortunate for those in their midst who are hungry, homeless, and ill-clothed. Again, the punishment will fit the crime. The situation of these insouciants will be violently reversed, and Amos emphasizes the reversal with an ironic play on words about these leaders of the foremost (*rēʾšît*) among the nations being the first (*bĕrōʾš*) to go into exile.

One of the sayings appended to this *hôy*, that in v. 12, again relates importantly to the matter of justice. The rhetorical questions here used by Amos manifest the perversity of the situation and reveal the frustration of the speaker. Pointless, irrational things (such as plowing the sea) are not done even when only animals are involved. To "turn judgment into [poison]" is worse than irrational; it is perverse and wicked. Again the parallel is *mišpāṭ* and *ṣĕdāqâ*. In the present arrangement of the text, vv. 13-14 give a preview of the punishment to come. Although Israel has exulted boastfully over recent victories (v. 13), even now YHWH is raising against them an adversary (unnamed) who will oppress them from northernmost to southernmost boundaries.

THE VISIONS OF AMOS

A series of visions, placed near the end of the book, indicates the inevitability, the finality of the judgment to come. Some scholars see these

---

[54] *NRSV* provides an additional "Alas" at v. 4, Wolff an additional "woe" at v. 3, though neither is in the Hebrew text; Wolff sees v. 2 and v. 6b as later additions.

[55] Since material goods were looked upon as God's blessings and since very little that is puritanical is found in the Old Testament, one must understand that the drinking and feasting Amos here condemns are truly excessive. On "wine from bowls" (v. 6) see Philip J. King, *Amos, Hosea, Micah—An Archaeological Commentary* (Philadelphia: Westminster, 1988) 157–59.

visions as the starting point of Amos' prophetic career, the experience by which he was constituted a prophet and which shaped his message that Yʜᴡʜ was about to bring Israel to an end. This is possible but by no means certain.

It is fairly clear that five visions are being recounted, but the first three are so closely related, and indeed convey but a single message—the first two visions acting as a foil for the third—that they could almost be treated as one.[56] The message is clear, however the visions are counted.

The first three visions (7:1-3, 4-6, 7-9), then, can be taken in close conjunction. The first two depict grave danger in the making; in each case Amos intercedes, successfully. But on the third occasion Amos is given no opportunity to intercede; the Lord simply announces his intention unconditionally. The plumb line could be used to determine whether an edifice was straight or leaning, apparently a step in deciding whether it was to be demolished or allowed to stand; here the image relates to Israel's viability. In Isa 28:16-17 similar imagery (but different terminology) shows us the Lord laying a "cornerstone as a sure foundation" and in the process making "of right *(mišpāṭ)* a measuring line *(qāw)*, / of justice *(ṣĕdāqâ)* a level *(mišqālêt)*." And in 2 Kgs 21:13 the Lord says, referring to the destruction of Jerusalem (and using the same terminology as in the Isaiah passage), "I will measure Jerusalem with the same cord as I did Samaria, and with the plummet I used for the house of Ahab." The final phrase of v. 8, "I will never pass him (it) by again," is interpreted in various ways. For example, *NRSV* apparently takes it to mean the abandonment or destruction of Israel ("I will never again pass them by"), the *NAB* sees a refusal to forgive ("I will forgive them no longer"). Crenshaw, however, doubts the "non-forgiveness" interpretation and argues convincingly that these two passages (7:8 and 8:2) belong to the theophanic tradition and that what we have here is a final theophany for judgment, after which the Lord will cease to deal with Israel.[57]

---

[56] Wolff, in fact, not only treats the three together but also adds the fourth one as originally forming a single literary unit. Mays, on the other hand, sees the first four visions as constituting two pairs; in the first two (7:1-3 and 4-6) Amos "watches in the supranormal experience of charismatic perception," while in the second pair (7:7-9 and 8:1-3) mundane objects are shown him whose significance is then explained. (In the latter pair there is also the identical declaration that the Lord will no longer pass through Israel.)

[57] Crenshaw, "Amos and the Theophanic Tradition," 206–07. Wolff says that the phrase "to pass by" means "not to intervene (with punishment) against someone," and he translates, "I will no longer (benignly) pass him by."

Thus these first three visions would indicate that after two threatened destructions in which the Lord relented, there is a third from which there will be no relenting. In all this Israel's guilt is taken to be obvious—and indeed Amos never seems to argue about it, but does no more than specify wherein it consists. *If* we take v. 9 with the preceding (against Wolff), we have something specified about the manner of the judgment to come.[58]

The fourth vision (8:1-3) features a well-known play on words between "ripe fruit" *(qāyiṣ)* and "end" *(qēṣ)*. The vision of the summer fruit itself seems to have no purpose except to occasion the question from the Lord, "What do you see?" and Amos' response: *qāyiṣ*—which then opens the way for the Lord's word of judgment: *qēṣ.* The inconsequential nature of what is seen, a basket of fruit, coupled with the brevity of the exchange, seems to emphasize the lack of need for any further explanation of Israel's fate and to leave open no space for any adjustment in it. The scene of judgment itself is described briefly but very evocatively—i.e., only a couple of details are alluded to, which leaves room for much more to be imagined.

The fact that the vision does not detail any of Israel's sins gives occasion for the insertion here of vv. 4-7, which depict the merchants as being hardly able to wait for the end of the holy days (New Moon, Sabbath) so that they can resume defrauding the poor with crooked weights and measures. The merchants perhaps had little enough piety, adequate only

---

[58] Perhaps not at all inappropriately the account of Amos' vocation (7:10-17) is sandwiched in after this first vision (or series of three visions) and occasioned by the threat he has just uttered against the nation and the ruling dynasty. The exchange between Amos and Amaziah demonstrates the conflict that can now be seen between the prophet and the royal (and priestly) establishment. Walther Eichrodt (*Man in the Old Testament.* SBT 1/4 [Chicago: Regnery, 1951] 42–43) comments on this conflict: "Here true service of the people involved a bitter struggle with the natural representatives of the national will—the king and his officials, the priests and prophets of the State religion. As a result of the prophets' efforts this struggle led to the utter surrender of the national life, which had been untrue to its real destiny. From Elijah onwards—with whom we see the first indications of this terrible result [making reference to 1 Kgs 19:14ff.]—the end of the nation appears ever more clearly to the great messengers of God as the inevitable result of failure to serve him, as we may see in the writings of Amos and his successors." Whether Amos here claims to be prophet is not agreed upon by all. Literally he says "No prophet I and no son of a prophet I" *(lō᾽ nābî᾽ ᾽ānōkî wĕlō᾽ ben-nābî᾽ ᾽ānōkî),* which has been variously understood to mean "I *am* no prophet or son of a prophet" or "I *was* no prophet or son of a prophet" (i.e., before the Lord called me). Probably he is rejecting the idea that he has been connected with a professional group (the "sons of the prophets" or "guild prophets" referred to in Chapter 4). Since he immediately adds "the LORD said to me, 'Go, prophesy *(hinnābē᾽)* to my people Israel,'" there is a question as to whether he rejects the title of prophet; and cf. 2:11; 3:7.

for refraining from business on the holy days, but there is nevertheless an ironic reference to the religious observance that is so quickly replaced by dishonest practices. The terminology here is *ᵓebyôn* and *dallîm*. The climax is in the oath of the Lord, words that express the degree to which his anger has been provoked ("Never will I forget a thing they have done," v. 7)—and we have to suppose that Amos was familiar with Israel's traditions and experience of the Lord's merciful and forgiving nature.

The final vision (9:1-4) is the most dramatic and chilling of the series. It is a picture of annihilation, and it begins at the sanctuary itself—not surprising in view of what has already been said or implied about the cult: sacrifice from unjust hands was hypocritical and designed to bring wrath rather than security. There is, however, a special irony in the worshipers being destroyed by the roof caving in on them; again it is a matter of letting the punishment fit the crime. There is no escape for any who might survive; all possible hiding places are considered, even the most improbable (the nether world, the depths of the sea), only to be relentlessly ruled out as routes to safety. The finality seems total: "I will fix my gaze upon them / for evil, and not for good, / I, the Lord GOD of hosts" (vv. 4-5). A very similar statement is found at the end of the fragmentary utterance in v. 8: "The eyes of the Lord GOD are on this sinful kingdom: I will destroy it from off the face of the earth."[59]

CONCLUSION

Thus it is possible to speak of a basic simplicity to the ethical teaching of Amos. With great singlemindedness he indicts Israel for their want of "justice" (*ṣĕdāqâ*), especially as seen in their mistreatment of the poor, including crimes against the legal system (bribery, dishonest weights and measures), but certainly not restricted to them. He has a special polemic against the cult because it allows its practitioners to convince themselves that they stand in a right relationship to God and so encourages them to continue evil practices. He cuts off every path to false security, including the cult, riches, election, and hope in the day of the Lord.

---

[59] In spite of such grim statements, it does not seem that Amos totally ruled out the possibility of deliverance for Israel, as can be seen in certain passages in which he lays down conditions for obtaining pity (5:15) or acceptance (5:23-24). And while it is almost universally agreed that the optimistic promises for the future of 9:11-15 are postexilic additions, a case can be made for seeing in 9:8c-10 the expectation of salvation for a righteous remnant; words such as "By the sword shall all sinners among my people die" (v. 10) are not the stuff of optimistic exilic promises.

Most surprisingly, Amos foretells, hardly as a threat or conditionally, the end of Israel. Obviously Amos is no nationalistic prophet. Amos' God (to begin to answer the question, "what kind of God . . .?") is not cruel or merciless; quite the contrary. If Amos threatens a punishment that amounts to destruction, it is an indication of how grave he saw the sins of the people to be. What God is, what God has done for Israel, demands a response. Different prophets judge Israel's failure to respond in different ways; Amos (and almost all the others, at least in part, but Amos almost totally) sees it in oppression of the weak. *What God has done for Israel* is known to Amos, but because of what Israel has done, the nation is placed on the same level as the others (1:3–2:8; 3:2; 9:7).

Amos sees the Lord as a God who has treated Israel with *ṣĕdāqâ*, vindicating it over against those who were more powerful (2:9-10). As a consequence God expected, or rather demanded, that Israel imitate the divine example, but this they did not do. Note that, as we said at the beginning of the chapter, Amos does not speak of God's justice, but only of God's demand that Israel manifest justice (= righteousness, = *ṣĕdāqâ*). Amos implies God's *ṣĕdāqâ* in what God has done for Israel in the past, but he implies it even more in setting forth how God wants Israel to behave toward the weak and poor. In this sense Amos' God is a God of mercy and compassion. Because of Israel's failure in this matter, God's wrath is revealed through Amos. In a sense this shows that God takes us seriously. Implied in all this is the idea that God wants us to treat others as he treats us. In a positive sense this is the "imitation of God" referred to earlier (Chapter One, p. 13). In a negative sense it means that God will treat us as we treat others, and we can remember the correspondences noted above between the crimes Amos denounced and the punishments he threatened. In this Amos is in line with what we find later in the teaching of Sirach and later still in that of Jesus. In the former we can refer to Sir 27:30–28:7, a passage in which the sage sees the vengeance or forgiveness we can expect from God to correspond to the vengeance or forgiveness we extend to others. The same position is expressed by Jesus in the parable of the unforgiving servant (Matt 18:23-35), especially "so will my heavenly Father do to you, unless each of you forgives his brother from his heart" (v. 35), and more briefly in the Lord's Prayer, "forgive us our debts as we forgive our debtors" (Matt 6:12) and the expansion, "if you forgive others their transgressions . . . If you do not forgive others . . . " (vv. 14-15). The New Testament threatens judgment, too, and it is there, in the epistle to the Hebrews, that the most chilling phrase of all is found: "It is a fearful thing to fall into the hands of the living God" (Heb 10:31). So Amos continues to be relevant and perhaps never more so than to the culture of the twenty-first century.

Chapter Seven

HOSEA

There is a good deal of contrast between Hosea and Amos, though not as much as some have suggested. It would be wrong to think of Amos, who was obviously much involved, as unemotional, so the contrast is not precisely there. But these two prophets do differ markedly in temperament; Amos is single-minded and unrelenting, whereas Hosea manifests rapid, sometimes even mind-boggling changes of mood. There is a sentimental aspect to Hosea we do not see in Amos, though it would certainly be an oversimplification to label Hosea (as is sometimes done) "the prophet of God's mercy." The recognition of God's mercy may be there, but much, much more. And terminologically the designation would be somewhat misleading.

HISTORICAL BACKGROUND

The beginning of Hosea's ministry is to be dated shortly after that of Amos but, on the evidence of 1:4, still during the reign of Jeroboam II or at least during the brief reign of his son Zechariah (a scant six months, according to 2 Kgs 15:8). The length of his ministry is uncertain; some would see it terminating before the fall of Samaria in 722/1 and the end of the Northern Kingdom, though a few would extend it beyond that time. In any case, it is obvious that his ministry reflects a radically different situation from the prosperous, stable times of Jeroboam II; the anarchy of the latter years of Israel is reflected in some of his oracles.

An important factor in this change is the close coincidence between the end of the reign of Jeroboam II (786–746) and the rise of the vigorous Assyrian king Tiglath-pileser III (745–727). Jeroboam had been a power that for a generation had helped to bring stability to Israel, but now the threat posed by Assyria would demand policy decisions that would divide and factionalize the country. In earlier periods when Assyria was strong its kings had conducted campaigns to the west, but mainly for the purpose of gathering tribute and plunder, not for conquering and holding territory.

Tiglath-pileser, the real founder of Assyria's empire, changed all this. He took land, annexed territories, and the countries he did not take over outright he subjected to Assyria through vassal treaties. As Israel faced this threat, the inner corruption, especially of the ruling class, began to be revealed; it was seen in a vacillation that began with internal weakness and ended in disintegration. Israel had the choice of either submitting to the Assyrians, with the crushing obligations that entailed, or of joining the anti-Assyrian coalition with its attendant dangers. While arguments could be given for and against either course, strong and wise leaders would have selected one course and adhered to it. In Israel, however, the course of policy was changed 180 degrees with almost every one of the new leaders who came to the throne in rapid succession. Jehu's dynasty ended with the death of Zechariah, who was assassinated by Shallum. Shallum then ruled as king for one month. He was in turn assassinated by Menahem, who replaced him as king (745–737). Menahem was the only king in these closing decades to be succeeded by his son. That son, Pekahiah, ruled only briefly (737–736). He was assassinated by Pekah, who became king for another short reign (736–732). Hoshea, the last king of Israel (732–724), came to the throne by murdering Pekah. And most of this royal carnage had to do with Israel's policy toward Assyria. Of the kings just named, it is clear that Menahem submitted to Assyria and paid tribute (2 Kgs 15:19-20), that Pekah, along with Syria, was active in the anti-Assyrian coalition (see below, Chapter Eight, on the Syro-Ephraimitic War), and that Hoshea became an Assyrian vassal but later revolted, thus precipitating his own deposition (724) and the end of the nation three years later (2 Kgs 17:3-6). Thus it is probable that these changes of "dynasty" were motivated by alternating stances toward Assyria. Meanwhile, however, conditions in the country were chaotic and violent. Hosea's revulsion toward the rulers and this state of affairs in general is obvious in his oracles.

THE BOOK

This is probably the most poorly preserved book in the Hebrew Bible, with the result that the text is uncertain in many places. This will not be obvious in a translation, though it explains why reliable translations may differ widely from each other in places.[1]

The book falls into two main parts: chapters 1–3 relate to Hosea's marriage and the allegory of the Lord's marriage to Israel; chapters 4–14 constitute "the rest of the book," with little discernible organization. Though some scholars hold that there is a rough chronological arrangement in this material, Francis I. Andersen and David Noel Freedman assert that "it is impossible to date any parts of the discourse, and organization of the material along historical lines involves too much guesswork to lead to firm interpretation." These authors do not find it possible to trace a logical development from section to section; they do find three major divisions (chs. 4–7 outline the state of the nation, chs. 8–11 rehearse the spiritual history of Israel, and chs. 12–14 present both retrospect and prospect), but their conclusion is that "the whole is a congeries of brief oracles, assembled without any recognizable principles of order."[2]

THE MESSAGE

The interpretation of Hosea is by no means undisputed, even with reference to the fundamental question of whether the prophet brings a message of hope to Israel. This matter is relevant to our investigation at least in the sense that it will have some bearing on the answer, in Hosea, to the question "What kind of God does he conceive the Lord to be?" And to the extent that we are called to the *imitatio Dei* it has a bearing on what is required of us. While most commentators, including Hans Walter Wolff and James L. Mays, see God's forgiveness triumphing to deliver Israel from the destruction Hosea threatens, there are others who

---

[1] The comparison of translations—or even citation by chapter and verse—is complicated by the variant methods of numbering chapters and verses. The *NAB* follows the numbering of the Hebrew text throughout, as does the *JPS*, but *RSV* and *NRSV* and some other translations follow the Vulgate. This problem relates especially to chs. 1 and 2. Citations will be given by both systems for passages in which there is a difference. The following chart will help:

Hebrew	*(NAB)*	*NRSV*
	1:1-9	1:1-9
	2:1-3*	1:10–2:1
	2:4-25	2:2-23

*This passage, considered a later interpolation, the *NAB* editors have placed at the end of ch. 3.

[2] Francis I. Andersen and David N. Freedman, *Hosea*. AB 24 (Garden City, NY: Doubleday, 1980) 313–14.

find Hosea to be as totally a prophet of doom as Amos. But this is possible only by labeling all the passages that speak of future hope as later interpolations. William Stinespring, for example, in an article published in 1974 refers to his 1950 article (entitled "Hosea, Prophet of Doom") and then surveys some of the literature that has appeared in the meantime. In order to sustain the position implied in the title of the 1950 article he had had to argue that the "happy endings" in chapters 1, 2, 11, and 14 had all been added by Judean editors after the book had migrated from Israel to Judah; his view is that Hosea came to feel that Israel would not repent.[3] In the course of his review of writings composed after that article the reader has the feeling he/she is being told when to cheer and when to boo.[4] The point of his survey is not very clear, for he is not able to point to much support that has emerged for his position in the almost twenty-five years intervening, and his judgment on the authors who do not agree with him is that "sentimentality and romantic illusions die hard."[5] It is not good methodology, however, to argue a position that can stand only by rejecting all the passages that would contradict it, unless there is very strong evidence against authenticity from the textual tradition or from the content of the passages themselves. Stinespring's main argument seems to be that Israel did in fact fall and so if Hosea had foretold mercy he would have been a poor prophet.[6] But this is what I would call *interpretatio ex eventu:* because something did not happen according to the prophet's recorded words, the prophet could not have said it.[7] The approach creates many problems. What of those who, on

[3] William F. Stinespring, "A Problem of Theological Ethics in Hosea," in James L. Crenshaw and John T. Willis, eds., *Essays in Old Testament Ethics* (New York: Ktav, 1974) 131–44.

[4] Cf. comments such as "Snaith has read Hosea more carefully than most, and has consequently arrived at some clear insights. . . . And on p. 50, I read this, with surprise and approval: 'We think that the whole of ch. 3 is late and not from Hosea.' . . . But by retaining . . . he manages to present a picture very similar to that of most other interpreters" (p. 135). Referring to W. R. Harper's volume on Amos and Hosea in ICC (1905) he says: "Thus he rejects the happy endings of chs. 1; 2; 11; and 14 and deals with ch. 3 (minus v. 5) as Lindblom did later, by putting it in the early period of Hosea's career. For an interpretation done nearly seventy years ago, this is very good. It is a pity that Harper did not have more followers" (p. 142).

[5] Ibid. 142.

[6] "But Israel fell forever, and the Ten Lost Tribes are really lost. Snaith's Hosea was indeed a poor predictor, who failed utterly in discerning the will of God for Israel" (ibid. 136).

[7] See my criticisms of this manner of dealing with Isa 7:15 in my "The Age of Immanuel," *CBQ* 41 (1979) 221–22.

this hypothesis, added the promises *after* the fall of Israel? Is it easier to believe that such words could have been penned after the fall of the kingdom, when Israel could no longer have been saved, than that Hosea spoke them at a time when survival was possible?

Beyond that, we should beware of confusing the deeper content of a teaching with a historical detail with which it is joined. For example, the truth value of Jeremiah's oracle against Jehoiakim (Jer 22:13-19) depends much less on whether Jehoiakim in fact received "the burial of an ass" than on the condemnation of the oppressive measures he was guilty of. So also, Hosea could be teaching us some very valid and important things about God's forgiveness even if he had failed to discern what God intended for Israel in those particular circumstances. Finally, it is probably not correct simply to identify Hosea's addressees with the political entity of the Northern Kingdom, as Stinespring does. The entity Hosea addresses is what he conceives to be the Lord's bride/covenant partner, and something much deeper than the survival of a political or national entity (whose leaders, at least, were the object of his scorn) and the integrity of its territory is involved. Many people from the north survived the calamity of 722 and retained their faith; some came to Judah to worship even after the destruction of the Temple (Jer 41:4-5), whereas others, probably including the bearers of the deuteronomic traditions, migrated to Judah, possibly much earlier. Nor would it be illegitimate to think of Judah, as all that remained of the original Israel, as the heir of all that the YHWH/Israel relationship meant. In the end very much the same thing happened to the *kingdom* of Judah as had happened to the *kingdom* of Israel. Yet much of the message of forgiveness of Hosea must be true, or there would be no Jewish people, no Christian people, and no one would today be studying Hosea![8]

---

[8] The Andersen-Freedman commentary, one of the relatively recent scholarly examinations, has this to say: "This theme—that beyond the menacing judgment of the present age, there would be a new age of beginnings to catch up the old beginnings of peoplehood and nation state [sic]—while challenged by many scholars, and awkward on the face of it, is so persistent in the surviving texts of the prophetic books that we must attribute it either to the prophets themselves, including Hosea, or to some master editors who were determined to reverse the message of the prophets whom they held in awe and turn them one and all into mediators of a doctrine of overarching divine grace. Since we find this paradox of irreversible judgment and irresistible redemption in the undoubted teaching of Ezekiel, who could hardly be accused of modifying his message to mollify his audience, and something approaching the same view in Jeremiah, it seems the better part of valor as well as common sense to acknowledge this peculiarity in other prophets as well, including Hosea" (*Hosea*, 48).

PROPHET OF GOD'S MERCY?

Yet what was said earlier in cautioning about thinking of Hosea as the prophet of God's mercy remains true. Just as Amos was a prophet who put forward God's demand for Israel's justice, so Hosea is the prophet who puts forward God's plea for Israel's *ḥesed*. This term has a range of nuances and, though often translated "mercy," it more accurately suggests "loyalty," "love," "steadfast love," sometimes "pity." This important term occurs six times in Hosea, where it always has Israel, not God, as its subject. This is in itself quite a paradox. An early study of *ḥesed* by Nelson Glueck (originally in Hebrew, 1927) had shown that *ḥesed* is received or shown "only by those among whom a definite relationship exists"; it can be practiced only between persons who share an ethically binding relationship, "the relationship among people who formed a fellowship which required the fulfillment of mutual responsibilities."[9] Katherine Doob Sakenfeld has in many ways modified and gone beyond Glueck's position. She acknowledges a debt to Sidney Hills, who, she says, performed a great service for the study of *ḥesed* in his recognition that *ḥesed* is done by the situationally superior party for one who is completely lacking in present resources or future prospects.[10] Sakenfeld distinguishes three different sorts of *ḥesed*, depending on the sphere in which it is exercised: secular (humans toward humans), theological (God toward humans), and religious (humans toward God). From analysis of early texts on secular *ḥesed* she concludes to four characteristics of the particular situations in which *ḥesed* is appropriate: (1) the individual making the request cannot do what is needed for himself or herself; (2) the assistance requested is completely necessary; (3) the need is such that one particular person is uniquely in a position to fulfill the need; and (4) the circumstances are such that the person in need can have no control over the response of the person of whom assistance is asked.[11] Theological *ḥesed* is that exercised by God and, of course, since it can be attributed to God only by analogy, necessarily rests on the understanding gleaned from secular *ḥesed*. Referring to the *ḥesed* of God (or theological *ḥesed*) in preexilic prose, she says that it

---

[9] From the English translation, *Ḥesed in the Bible* (Cincinnati: Hebrew Union College Press, 1967) 37, 48.

[10] Katherine Doob Sakenfeld, *The Meaning of ḥesed in the Hebrew Bible: A New Inquiry.* HMS 17 (Missoula: Scholars, 1978) 12. The reference to Hills is from an unpublished paper, "The *ḥesed* of Man in the Old Testament" and Part II, "The *ḥesed* of God," delivered before the Biblical Colloquium, Pittsburgh, Nov. 29, 1957.

[11] Sakenfeld, *Meaning of ḥesed,* from the summary on p. 44.

was a particularly useful word for speaking of God's relationship to his people . . . because it held together in a single expression an emphasis on divine freedom on the one hand and divine commitment on the other, an emphasis on human need and weakness on the one hand and human responsibility to trust in God alone on the other. By a stretching of the secular usage for delivering and protective action and concern to embrace even forgiveness, the term came to express the uniqueness of God's *hesed* as the basis for a relationship stronger than any human bond.[12]

It now begins to be clear why the use of the term in Hosea, and the few other prophetic passages that use it in its "religious" sense, to describe something Israel is called to manifest toward God, can be called paradoxical. Given the explanation of human *hesed* outlined above, God's *hesed* toward Israel (theological *hesed*) is easy to see; but Israel's toward God? In this usage we find a good example of what is often labeled "divine condescension." Sakenfeld explains the anomaly:

> Israel can never be in a position of power with respect to Yahweh so that she would be free from reprisal if she failed to meet her treaty obligations. . . . Israel always had freedom of choice, if not freedom from reprisal. Yahweh could not force her to worship him alone and to establish a just society. He could threaten to bring the relationship to an end . . . but this action would be counter to his ultimate concern for the people. From the perspective of his genuine love and concern for Israel as his chosen, the people's action could be a source of pain and anguish for him—and herein lay the strength of the familial imagery.[13]

In other words, although Yhwh is always the stronger vis-à-vis Israel, there is something God wants that only Israel can give, namely, a love and response that cannot be forced, and this helps explain why the prophets can speak of Israel's *hesed* toward God.

But there is also another way in which the sense of *hesed* has been stretched. In "secular" usage it was restricted to those with whom one is in a particular relationship (e.g., covenant, family, marriage), but included in Hosea's use is proper behavior in the broader social context. Sakenfeld explains that this extension of *hesed* can be readily understood when it is recognized that it is always spoken of within Israelite society, not to the world of humans as a whole. The basis for responsibility, therefore, is the membership of all Israelites in the covenant community.[14] Thus one of

[12] Ibid. 149–50.
[13] Ibid. 175–76.
[14] Ibid. 174.

the particularly important aspects of Hosea's use of the term, and one of the strong points of his teaching, is that it ties together Israel's obligation to YHWH and to members of the community—all part of the same package, so to speak. This helps to show where our obligation toward others comes from and at the same time gives it its religious character.

THE TEXT: CHAPTERS 4–14

Although the account and allegory of Hosea's marriage (chs. 1–3) do help to illumine the chapters that follow, so that starting there offers a legitimate approach, it seems better to let chapters 4–14 speak for themselves; the marriage account will be looked into later.

4:1-3

This opening oracle of "the rest of the book" is often identified as a "covenant lawsuit."[15] I am not convinced that the form even exists. Ronald E. Clements has argued that where the diction of such pieces is legal diction it is sufficient to suppose the prophet is using the imagery of the courtroom, without bringing in the covenant.[16] In the case at hand it is not even clear that legal diction is being used. The Hebrew word translated "grievance" or "controversy" in 4:1, *rîb*, means just that and is used also in non-legal contexts.[17] This is not to deny that the covenant is found in Hosea; there are two specific references to it (6:7 and 8:1, though not

---

[15] Works frequently cited in favor of the existence of a "covenant lawsuit" among the prophets are Herbert Huffmon, "The Covenant Lawsuit in the Prophets," *JBL* 78 (1959) 285–95; Julien Harvey, *Le plaidoyer prophétique contra Israël après la rupture de l'alliance* (Montreal: Les éditions Bellarmin, 1967); idem, "Le 'Rib-Pattern', requisitoire prophétique sur la rupture de l'alliance," *Bib* 43 (1962) 172–96.

[16] Ronald E. Clements, *Prophecy and Tradition* (Atlanta: John Knox, 1975) 20. See also Joseph Jensen, "Eighth-Century Prophets and Apodictic Law," in *To Touch the Text: Biblical and Related Studies in Honor of Joseph A. Fitzmyer, s.j.* (New York: Crossroad, 1989) 103–17; M. de Roche, "Yahweh's *Rîb* Against Israel: A Reassessment of the So-Called 'Prophetic Lawsuit' in the Preexilic Prophets," *JBL* 102 (1983) 563–74; Dwight R. Daniels, "Is There a 'Prophetic Lawsuit' Genre?" *ZAW* 99 (1987) 339–60. And see Andersen and Freedman, *Hosea:* "Since the forms of that supposed genre of prophetic speech have never been defined with adequate precision, we may prescind from explaining the absence of a true judicial interchange" (p. 336).

[17] For example, Exod 17:7: at Massa and Meribah (the latter name derived from *rîb*), where we have the "faultfinding" of Israel; Judg 12:2, where Jephthah and his followers have a great *rîb* with the Ammonites; Ps 18:44, where David thanks God for having delivered him from the *rîb* of the peoples.

all concede their authenticity) and it is the supposition for the marriage analogy, which is so important a part of his thought.

In these three verses God declares: (1) what is lacking to the "inhabitants of the land" to explain the Lord's *rîb* against them; (2) what their crimes are, though no doubt those listed are intended only as a sampling; and (3) the effects of their crimes. The things the people are lacking, in addition to *ḥesed*, are fidelity (*ʾemet*)[18] and knowledge of God. "Knowledge" in the Old Testament is not normally abstract; it is usually quite concrete, often intensely personal. "The man had relations with his wife Eve, and she conceived" (Gen 4:1) is sometimes referred to as a euphemism; it could be said, more accurately, to reflect the concrete reference of "to know" in Scripture. It can denote a special relationship, as in Amos 3:2 ("You alone have I favored, / more than all the families of the earth"). The terminology frequently denotes the response to God that is expected of Israel: "to know God" would mean to respond in fidelity, obedience, devotion, etc.

The fact that two of these qualities (*ʾemet* and *ḥesed*) are frequently attributed to God and that the third describes what would normally be human response to God puts us, we would suppose, into the context of divine-human relations. Yet what follows relates to behavior toward other people, and this indicates how closely Hosea perceives the two types of relation/behavior to be connected. These three, say Andersen and Freedman, are "qualities of people whose dedication to God finds expression in relations with their neighbors."[19] In general, what is deplored in these terms in not in doubt. As mentioned earlier (Chapter Two, pp. 20–21), the conjunction of "murder, stealing and adultery" (v. 2) are taken by many to be a reference to the Decalogue, and while that is indeed possible, it is far from certain. In any case, the list of these crimes tells us something of the moral state of the people as seen by Hosea. Whether there is reference to the covenant or not, the things listed are crimes, are damnable, and call for judgment. Although v. 3 can be interpreted otherwise, it may refer to punishment to come. "The land mourns" can relate to drought, and this would fit in well with Hosea's concern about the fertility cult. A drought would, of course, affect all dwellers in the land, but the naming of beasts, birds, and fish (!) hints at the cosmic scope of sin and of the judgment it merits.

---

[18] The word *ʾĕmêt* comes from the verbal root *ʾāman* (from which we also have our word "Amen"), from which comes *ʾĕmûnâ*, virtually synonymous with *ʾemet*. Both words are important and are encountered frequently in the prophets, as we will see.

[19] Andersen and Freedman, *Hosea*, 336.

4:4-19

The rest of the chapter is of great importance for the understanding of Hosea, though it also presents many difficulties: these relate especially to the Hebrew text, which appears in places to be corrupt, and to the division of the material.[20] Although it is not unlikely that we are dealing with more than one composition here, the content seems to relate to the same general matters, with one part throwing light upon another, so we will take these verses together.

The references to "priest" and "prophet" (vv. 4-5) are sometimes taken as collectives and translated as plurals, but even if one takes them as referring to particular individuals the basic thrust of the accusations remain much the same. The editor wanted these verses to be taken in close connection with vv. 1-3, even if they did not originally belong with them. Although vv. 4-19 give the appearance of a further setting forth of the *rîb* of v. 1, in fact v. 4 represents a more restricted group.

The accusation being made, apparently, is that the priests have not exercised their office so as to lead the people in the ways of fidelity to the Lord, but rather, through that very office, have led them into the idolatry of Baal worship. Hosea is often tantalizingly allusive, but here the sense seems to be clearly enough indicated. The people "perish for want of knowledge" (v. 6) through the fault of the priest. This would suggest that YHWH-worship is no longer the vehicle for instruction[21] concerning YHWH's saving deeds and moral demands, as in fact it should be—for example, in covenant renewal ceremonies and even in the psalms

---

[20] For example, although some commentators take this passage as one oracle, James L. Mays, *Hosea* (London: SCM, 1969), divides it into "God's case against the priests" (vv. 4-10), "God's indictment of the cult" (vv. 11-14), and "the liturgy of the lost" (vv. 15-19).

[21] The "*tôrâ* of your God" in v. 6 has to be understood as "instruction" in a more general sense rather than "law," as it is sometimes translated. Barnabas Lindars, "Torah in Deuteronomy," in Peter R. Ackroyd and Barnabas Lindars, eds., *Words and Meanings* (Cambridge: Cambridge University Press, 1968) 117–36, has shown that *tôrâ* does not come to be a generalized term to cover the whole corpus of laws (often summed up in the plural terms *mišpāṭîm, ḥuqqîm,* and *miṣwôt*) until the time of Deuteronomy, where its meaning is much closer to the notion of the "instruction" of the wisdom literature than to priestly regulation. In Deuteronomy "the choice of this term is dictated by the fact that the code is regarded as a single and complete entity, given by God through the mediation of Moses for people to ponder and lay to heart. . . . This can even be expressed in specifically wisdom terminology, as if the code is the instruction of a father to his sons." (This point is important also for the understanding of Isaiah, as we shall see.) In both the early and later period *tôrâ* can designate a single provision and is therefore frequently used also in the plural, as in Hos 8:12.

and prayers that would normally accompany Israel's worship. Instead of this kind of instruction, the cult appears to have been used to foster the fertility cult, the rites of Baal. That the fertility cult is one of Hosea's chief complaints is clear not only from chapters 1–3 (see below), but also from many other passages (e.g., 9:1-4). Here it is indicated especially by accusations such as that in vv. 10-11, that they have abandoned the Lord to practice harlotry *(zĕnût)*. So also the references to "the spirit of harlotry" and "commit harlotry" in v. 12 and "you yourselves consort with harlots, / and with prostitutes you offer sacrifice" in v. 14. The last reference would seem to be clear, since the phrase, in addition to the common term for harlot *(zônâ)*, uses what many consider a technical term for a cult prostitute[22] *(qĕdēšâ)*. More properly the word (which means literally "holy one") was the title of the goddess of fertility but was then applied to the devotees who were her surrogates in the cult. It appears that the crime condemned here is the substitution of the cult of Baal for that of YHWH, apparently by the very priests of the YHWH shrines.[23] This would involve the substitution of fertility rites, considered both pagan and immoral, for those that pertain to the YHWH covenant, thus also omitting the instructional dimension that went with them.

If this is the case, as it appears to be, a great deal more was involved than simply the matter of what one calls God (YHWH or Baal). The two represented totally different concepts of divinity, of the relationship between God and the cosmos, of the sort of demands that issue from the divinity, and of the sort of salvation that is offered to the worshiper. All this, of course, impinges importantly on the questions "what kind of God does Israel perceive YHWH to be?" and "how does Israel perceive its relations with YHWH?"

The fertility cult, basically a nature cult, was widespread in the ancient Near East, the god of fertility being known under different titles in different areas. In Palestine, Phoenicia, and elsewhere it was Baal. With him

---

[22] However, many now challenge this understanding of *qĕdēšâ*. The term could come in simply as parallel in this text with *zônâ,* though the reference to the related behavior of daughters and daughters-in-law in the same verse suggests sexual activity. In Genesis 38, Juda has relations with Tamar in the belief she is a *zônâ* (v. 15), whom Hiram, in searching her out in order to pay her and recover Judah's pledges, seeks for the *qĕdēšâ* he thought should be at the roadside (vv. 10-22). But the *qĕdēšôt* had other functions and may not always have been prostitutes.

[23] This could be what is meant by "exchanging their glory for shame" in v. 7. *RSV* has "I will change . . ." but this is not the better reading; *NRSV* now has "they changed their glory into shame."

goes his consort, again known by different titles (Ishtar, Anath; in the Old Testament we encounter especially the names Asherah and Astarte). The fertility god was understood to be so closely connected with nature that the cycle of the seasons was thought to be a reflection of his adventures. If nature languishes for part of the year it is because the god is resident in the nether world for that time.[24] In a similar fashion fertility in nature—the fields, the flock, the family—was thought to be the effect of the god and goddess of fertility coming together in fruitful sexual union. Along with this goes the belief that it is possible to manipulate the divine by "sympathetic magic," in this case by intercourse under cultic auspices. Initially this was carried out in a rather official manner, with the king representing the god and a temple priestess representing the goddess. In Mesopotamia this was done as part of the New Year's festival. The role the couple played was understood to bring them into contact with the divine, but it was also a question of manipulating the divine, i.e., the bringing together, by this sympathetic or imitative magic, of the god and goddess of fertility so that their union would assure fertility to family, flocks, and fields. Later the process became more "democratized," with cult prostitutes who could be approached by men who held no cultic office.

The practice itself would have been objectionable from the point of view of Israel's strict morality, and it may have generated promiscuity on a purely secular level—at least that is what 4:13b-14a would seem to indicate. In addition, it was in effect a denial of Israel's monotheism as well as a denial of the nature of Israel's God as Israel had always conceived YHWH, i.e., as a creator who stands quite above and quite apart from creation, able to cause it to give or withhold its fertility (cf. the story of Elijah in 1 Kings 17–18), in no way sharing its vicissitudes, and in no way able to be manipulated by creatures. Above all, there was the question of moral demands. The fertility deities did not make any,[25] but YHWH did.

---

[24] The story of "Inanna's Descent to the Nether World" (*ANET*, 52–57) and the closely parallel "The Descent of Ishtar to the Nether World" (*ANET*, 106–09) tell very dramatically how the goddess of fertility escapes from the realm of the dead, how her consort is made to be her substitute, but how his sister unselfishly takes his place for half the year.

[25] This would go along with their characters as presented in the stories about them. On one occasion Gilgamesh, in rejecting Ishtar's proposal, recounts a whole string of amours in each of which she had treated her lover cruelly, so that Ishtar complains to her father that "Gilgamesh has recounted my stinking deeds, my stench, and my foulness," and her father suggests that she had invited the insults (*ANET*, 84). In Ugaritic literature Anath is depicted as deriving sadistic pleasure from visiting bloody destruction upon soldiers and then, apparently not quite sated, reliving the experience in fantasy after she had returned home (*ANET*, 136).

Hosea and Amos are as one in perceiving Yhwh as a God who calls on Israel to manifest *ṣĕdāqâ* in their dealings with one another. Amos roots this call, it seems, in Yhwh's gracious deeds for Israel, whereas Hosea looks more directly to the close relationship he sees existing between Yhwh and Israel—a point to which we must return.

It is not clear whether Israel's crime in this matter of the fertility cult was out and out apostasy, i.e., openly worshiping Baal, or was rather a matter of syncretism. In the latter case Israel might continue in apparent fidelity to Yhwh, invoking the name of Yhwh but in fact worshiping with the rites of Baal. Some ambiguity was built into the system in that the word *baʿal*, before it became the proper name of a god, was first of all a common noun that might be applied to any "lord," such as to a woman's husband (cf. Hos 2:18 [*NRSV* 2:16]), the owner of a field, a slave's owner, and even more or less adjectivally, as when Joseph is called a "*baʿal* of dreams" by his brothers (Gen 37:19). In this sense it was often applied to Yhwh, apparently even as a name, so that it was possible, e.g., for Saul and Jonathan, loyal Yahwists though they were, to have sons named Ishbaal ("man of Baal") and Meri(b)baal (perhaps "beloved by Baal") respectively. That sort of ambiguity could make syncretism considerably easier. Whichever was the case, Hosea makes no bones about the situation, but simply accuses Israel of apostasy, of worshiping Baal.

Hosea's use of "harlotry" to describe such apostasy adds a whole new dimension to prophetic teaching. On the one hand it was quite apt, since the fertility rites did include ritual intercourse. On the other, however, at least to the extent that such "harlotry" is equated with adultery, Hosea is using sexual imagery to equate Israel's apostasy from the Lord with marital infidelity. Presupposed in such imagery is a likening of the relationship between Israel and Yhwh to that between husband and wife. This is a new thing and a bold step, especially since in the fertility rites Baal had a female consort with whom he was on terms of sexual intimacy. A more timid soul would have considered this sort of imagery the very last sort to be used. But it had the advantage of presenting Israel's crimes in a very personal framework, in terms of loyalty owed, in terms of hurt wrongfully visited on one who loves, in terms of *challenging* Israel.

The impulse toward depicting Israel's crime in these terms no doubt came from Hosea's own marriage experience with a woman who was unfaithful to him (see below on Hosea 1–3). It is because of the concept of this intimate sort of relationship between Israel and Yhwh that Hosea can introduce the call for *ḥesed* in a way that is so unexpected (as pointed out above), namely, Israel, the weaker partner, being called to render *ḥesed* to Yhwh. It is Yhwh's love for Israel that occasions the divine anguish at Israel's infidelity and that makes it possible to say that God wants something only Israel can give, namely, their loyalty. And it is something that cannot be compelled. It is in this sort of presentation of Yhwh that Heschel's words about God's pathos are most fully justified, as is his explanation of the prophet's message as stemming from his experience of God's pathos.

Yet although it may be the infidelity of the fertility cult that first occasions the marriage/adultery imagery, and while it may occasion the use of *ḥesed* terminology, *ḥesed* does not remain restricted to that kind of loyalty. We have seen that lack of *ḥesed* is deplored in 4:1, where the specific crimes condemned turn out to be social in nature. In that text it is used as a parallel term to "knowledge of God," which can have a very broad reference (i.e., to designate the proper response to God in a general sense, including right social behavior—cf. Jer 22:15-16). It is used in parallel with "knowledge of God" also in 6:6 (cf. 6:4). This is a key passage in the area of prophetic ethics because it says something about what the Lord desires and compares this with acts of cultic worship. What is required is loyalty and knowing God, much more so than sacrifice. Again it is not a matter of repudiating sacrifice *per se* but of indicating that it is unacceptable where these qualities are lacking. We find *ḥesed* used also in 10:12, along with *ṣĕdāqâ* and *ṣedeq*. This is one of Hosea's many exhortations to repentance and amendment. The agricultural imagery (sow, reap, plow, rain) obviously fits in with that used in a number of other places, and the conjunction of *ḥesed* with words such as *ṣĕdāqâ* and *ṣedeq* again indicates that the term has, for Hosea, a horizontal dimension in addition to its vertical dimension. Finally (apart from 2:21[19]—see below) *ḥesed* occurs in 12:7 (*NRSV* 12:6), now in conjunction with *mišpāṭ*, and again it is in the context of an exhortation to return *(šûb)*. The expression "to keep *ḥesed ûmišpāṭ*," if we understand the latter term to be "especially concerned for the mechanisms by which righteousness is maintained in community,"[26] again relates to the horizontal dimension. For Hosea the two dimensions are inseparable; ethics and religion are intimately bound up with each other.[27] Religion is a great concern to Hosea, but clearly he sees it as something far deeper than cultic worship.

---

[26] Katharine Doob Sakenfeld, *Faithfulness in Action: Loyalty in Biblical Perspective* (Philadelphia: Fortress, 1985) 120.

[27] As Sakenfeld, *Faithfulness in Action*, discussing 4:1-3, says, "the two categories of worship and justice are not really separable in Hosea's view. Faithfulness, loyalty, and knowledge of God are missing because of syncretism; and it is their absence which leads to violation of the other commandments of the Decalogue" (p. 108).

There are a number of additional areas in which Hosea has harsh words of criticism. In 5:13-14 he heaps scorn on Israel's attempts to find help from Assyria in its need. For Hosea this too is a kind of apostasy because it is looking to someone else for what they should seek from the Lord alone; we shall see more of this attitude in Isaiah. The same point comes up elsewhere in Hosea (e.g., 7:8), and in 8:7-10 he depicts this behavior in terms of "hiring lovers," so it seems that this too can be thought of as "harlotry"; thus he is quick to put Israel's sins in very personal terms, that is, to see them as affronts to the Lord in a personal sense.

In a number of passages he has sharp words of criticism for the king and other leaders, much of this no doubt reflecting the violent coups and foolish policies we referred to above. See 5:1-2; 7:3-7; 8:4; 10:3-4; and 13:9-11. Although we will not pause to discuss these texts here, there are obvious ethical implications in a number of them.

Hosea returns time and again to the matter of conversion and repentance, usually to find Israel wholly deficient. Thus in 5:4, "Their deeds do not allow them / to return to their God; / For the spirit of harlotry is in them / and they do not recognize the LORD," and in v. 6, "With their flocks and their herds they shall go / to seek the LORD, but they shall not find him: / he has withdrawn himself from them." Best known of all is 5:15–6:7. Israel's repentance here is too easy, too assured that reconciliation will certainly—almost automatically—be effected: it is as certain as the coming of the dawn and of the seasonal rains. They say all the right words ("strive to know the LORD," 6:3, etc.), but there is no substance or staying power ("*ḥesed* like a morning cloud"—it is almost a contradiction in terms). The Lord does not easily forget their guilt, but they do not realize this (7:1-2). The Lord's good intentions are frustrated by continual sin; their repentance was prompted only by self-interest (7:13-14). They offer sacrifice for sin, but to no avail (8:11-14; cf. 6:6).

From all this it is easy to understand the position of those who would see no hope offered by Hosea, and yet there are the "other" passages, and it is not legitimate to eliminate them in the interests of consistent doom (see the discussion above). This is perhaps a good time to turn to the point at which the book and many treatments of it begin.

HOSEA'S MARRIAGE

The material found in the first three chapters is not interpreted in the same way by all. Harold H. Rowley, for example, takes literally the call to knowingly marry an immoral woman.[28] More likely the formulation is proleptic, an anticipation of what in fact came to pass but formulated after the event. Each of the three chapters could stand alone: chapter 1 is a third-person account that describes the taking of the wife, the begetting of the children, and their naming; chapter 2 is in the form of a YHWH-speech, though it is not obvious at once that it is the Lord speaking; and chapter 3 is Hosea's first person account. Chapter 1 immediately explains the import of his relationship with this unfaithful woman ("for the land gives itself to harlotry, / turning away from the LORD," v. 2), and its message is totally negative,[29] found primarily in the names of unfavorable significance that are given to the children.

In chapter 2 there is struggle and development, as the husband calls on the children to *rîb* against the mother and expresses his outrage against the unfaithful wife, threatening many dire punishments. In this monologue the real situation emerges, i.e., that it is the Lord accusing Israel, no longer Hosea accusing Gomer. The parallelism between the Hosea-Gomer and YHWH-Israel situations is so obvious that there is still a strong sense of identification between the two "marriages," but the switch to YHWH-Israel is clear in the references to the Baals (as lovers), to the gifts (of fertility and abundance) that only the Lord can give, and to the punishments (putting an end to religious celebration and devastation of the land). The struggle within the Lord's heart and the development become clear as it is revealed that the punishments are intended to call Israel back in fidelity.[30] With bold anthropomorphism the poet speaks of the Lord erecting a wall to prevent the errant wife from following her "lovers." Affliction and deprivation are intended to lead to conversion and repentance *(šûb:* "I will go back . . . ," v. 9). Then all is tenderness as the Lord leads her back to the conditions and fidelity of the Exodus, conceived of as a kind of honeymoon,[31] and promises better times for the future.

---

[28] Harold H. Rowley, "The Marriage of Hosea," in idem, *Men of God; Studies in Old Testament History and Prophecy* (London and New York: Nelson, 1963) 66–97.

[29] That is, following chapter and verse as in the Hebrew text (see n. 1). The early verses of ch. 2, according to the Hebrew, are 1:10–2:1 in *NRSV* and some other English versions; they are, in any case, a later addition intended to reverse the unfavorable significance of the names given to the children.

[30] This development is clearer still if, with the *NAB,* vv. 8-9 are placed after v. 15; in *NRSV* enumeration this would be vv. 6-7 after v. 13.

[31] This concept of Israel as faithful during the Exodus and wilderness wandering contrasts with the Pentateuchal narratives (and with some passages in Hosea—cf. 9:10; 11:1-2), though it is found also in Jeremiah (Jer 2:2).

The interpretation of chapter 3 is again not undisputed, but it seems best to take it as a sequel to chapter 1, i.e., as a new phase in the Hosea-Gomer relationship rather than as a new marriage.[32] The fact that Hosea has to buy her back indicates to some that in the meantime she had been dedicated to service in a shrine of the fertility cult. In any case he sets for her a time of testing, the meaning of which is explained in terms of what God is about to do to Israel, namely, to end the present order, leaving them without rulers or cult; after this there will be a conversion (*šûb*) and restoration.

Thus the message of chapters 2 and 3 is more or less the same, though expressed in very different terms. The hope or promise of restoration is held out, but it is understood that this is no easy, ephemeral thing (à la 6:1-3); it will be attained only through great trial. What can be stressed is the persistence of the Lord's love, which in the end will overcome all obstacles—not by wiping them away, but by leading Israel along difficult paths. The theme of restoration after exile (therefore after the destruction of the present order) is found also in the famous chapter 11. Much is made of the Lord's emotional struggle depicted here, and some take it to mean that God has decided to forgive in spite of uncorrected infidelity (i.e., as though repentance and conversion could be dispensed with), but that is far from clear. It should be legitimate to read this passage against chapters 2 and 3, especially since in each case there is reference to exile and restoration. So much attention is given in chapter 11 to the struggle in the Lord's heart that little is said of Israel's dispositions. In chapter 14,[33] another restoration passage, conversion is much in the forefront. In v. 2 the call to conversion ("return," *šûb*) is made, and in the following two verses there is renunciation of two specific sins on the part of Ephraim, trust in other nations and idolatry.

It is worth looking a little more explicitly at the restoration promised near the end of chapter 2 (vv. 18-20, 21-22 in *NAB*, vv. 16-18, 19-20 in *NRSV*). The first section speaks of conversion from Baal worship and then promises a new messianic order. The second concentrates on the dispositions to be given the new Israel, expressed in terms we have already encountered: *ṣedeq*, *mišpāṭ*, *ḥesed*, *ʾĕmûnâ*, and "you shall know

---

[32] This is true whether *ʿôd*, "again," is taken with the "said to me" or with the "go, love." In either case it suggests a new action. The same conclusion follows from the parallelism between Hosea and Yнwн, who continues to love Israel "though they turn to other gods"; if Hosea were not dealing with the same woman, the reference would be unintelligible.

[33] In the Hebrew (and *NAB*) text. *NRSV* begins the ten verses of this chapter at 13:16, and each verse in ch. 14 is one number less than in the references given here in the text.

the LORD" (v. 22). Obviously these are the dispositions Israel has been lacking (cf. especially 4:1-2). The fact that they are given as gift (or as bridal price, as some insist) does not alter the fact that Israel must have them as the condition for any restoration.

Thus Hosea gives us ample material to answer the questions "what kind of God does he conceive YHWH to be?" and "how does he conceive Israel's relationship to YHWH?" The Lord is a God who calls upon Israel to manifest the qualities we have just referred to; these qualities relate to Israel's relationship to the Lord, but also to intra-Israelite relationships in such a manner that these two aspects of obligation are inseparable. The Israelite's obligation to others in the community (something Amos insisted on so strongly) finds its basis in God and is one expression, though not the only one, of fidelity to God. But loyalty is owed directly to God, and to such an extent are they connected that with the abandonment of God, social sins will almost surely follow. Although God's *hesed* toward Israel is not mentioned (so that Sakenfeld speaks of "skewed" usage in Hosea), it is implied in God's continued love for Israel and attempts to bring Israel back. We learn that there can be no return without conversion and that conversion may not be an easy thing. Where conversion does not materialize, God may step in to create conditions that can promote it. In any case it remains God's gift, God's grace.

Chapter Eight

ISAIAH

Here we are speaking only of chapters 1–39 of the book of Isaiah, the material attributed to Isaiah of Jerusalem of the eighth century; attention will be given later to Deutero-Isaiah (chs. 40–55) and to Trito-Isaiah (chs. 56–66). Not all of the material in chapters 1–39, by any means, is attributable to Isaiah. The collection had a very complicated history that we will not attempt to detail here. The following breakdown into smaller collections is vastly oversimplified but will serve as an aid to discussion.

Chapters 1–12: early oracles of Isaiah (mainly under Ahaz)
Chapters 13–23: oracles against the nations
Chapters 24–27: the "Isaiah Apocalypse"
Chapters 28–33: later oracles of Isaiah (mainly under Hezekiah)
Chapters 34–35: songs of Zion
Chapters 36–39: historical appendix (from 2 Kgs 18:13–20:19)

The so-called "Isaiah Apocalypse" and the "songs of Zion" are conceded by virtually all critical scholars to come from periods long after Isaiah. The "oracles against the nations" are somewhat mixed, consisting largely of later material into which many authentic compositions of Isaiah have been incorporated; in this collection the judgment of Isian authenticity has to be rendered on each piece individually. The "historical appendix" is found also in 2 Kings, but some scholars have suggested that the three stories of which it consists (Sennacherib's assault on Jerusalem and its deliverance, Hezekiah's illness and recovery, and the visit of the Babylonian envoys) were originally composed in the circle of Isaiah's followers, were utilized by the editors of 2 Kings, and were later taken into the Isaiah collection. This may be true, but then it is surprising that the first two accounts feature Hezekiah far more than Isaiah. The section may preserve some authentic words of Isaiah, but the stories have been overlaid with legend. Even chapters 1–12 and 28–33 have complicated histories and contain later additions. In this chapter we intend to deal with what Isaiah himself taught, though since the judgments of various scholars on what is original and what is not often do not agree, it is impossible to escape controversy on this point.[1]

HISTORICAL BACKGROUND SKETCH

Isaiah's ministry is dated, at least to an extent, in terms of the kings under whom he prophesied (e.g., his call came in "the year that king Uzziah died," generally taken to be 742). However, the chronology of the kings of Judah, especially for this period, is disputed; some of the difficulty stems from the biblical text itself.[2]

Isaiah's ministry was overshadowed from beginning to end by the overwhelming power of Assyria and its ambitions for world domination. During this period Assyria was blessed (if that is the proper word) with a succession of vigorous and able kings: Tiglath-pileser III (745–727), Shalmaneser V (726–722), Sargon II (721–705), and Sennacherib (704–681). Assyria itself and the question of how Judah ought to conduct itself vis-à-vis Assyria come prominently into many of Isaiah's oracles, including a number of those important for understanding his ethical teaching. His words relating to political events are mainly clustered around three important events: the Syro-Ephraimitic War (735–732), the revolt of Ashdod (714–711), and Hezekiah's revolt (705–701).

SOURCES OF ISAIAH'S MORAL TEACHING

Amos and Hosea both preached in the northern kingdom; the background that can be presupposed for their teaching is somewhat different from that of the Judah of Isaiah's day. In the authentic oracles of Isaiah there is no reference to covenant, to Sinai, to Moses, to Mosaic law, and

---

[1] The value of a scriptural teaching does not hinge on the question of whether or not a given oracle is rightly attributed to the prophet in whose collection it is found, of course. Some of the passages passed over here may be dealt with as authentic prophetic teaching in a later chapter.

[2] For example, we are told that Sennacherib's invasion (which from Assyrian records can be dated to 701) was in the fourteenth year of Hezekiah (2 Kgs 18:13 // Isa 36:1); but 2 Kgs 18:1 dates Hezekiah's accession to the throne in the third year of Hoshea of Israel (which, again from Assyrian records, can be dated to about 732). Thus one datum would begin Hezekiah's reign in 715, the other in 728. There are other complicating factors, too, but since they will not greatly affect the matters we will be discussing, it will be sufficient to have alluded to the problem.

only one (indirect) reference to the Exodus tradition. Many authors assume without discussion that this was all part of the general background of any prophet and so speak quite confidently about law and covenant in Isaiah, but this is a methodologically dubious procedure. The Decalogue, as we have noted (above, Chapter Two) *may* be late, the Covenant Code seems to have been mainly a northern collection, and Deuteronomy surfaced only during the reign of Josiah (in 622), so there is very little that can be pointed to as legislation that was definitely current in the Judah of Isaiah's day.[3] Certainly there were some general norms of morality that were recognized by all in both the north and the south. There were some things that were "not done in Israel"[4] or were stigmatized as "foolishness."[5]

But in Isaiah we probably have to recognize a fairly strong influence of the wisdom tradition, as has been pointed out by quite a number of authors. The foundational study, in the strict sense of that term, was that of Johannes Fichtner.[6] He noted that on the one hand Isaiah turned sharply against a human wisdom that overvalued itself and went the way of its own political choices without (and therefore against) God. But on the other hand, Isaiah himself stood to some extent in the wisdom tradition and demonstrated multiple relations to, and even literary dependence on the wisdom tradition and its forms and procedures. Fichtner has pointed to Isaiah's love of comparisons and wordplays and to his use of a whole host of wisdom terms; many of Isaiah's sayings he tried to relate directly to individual sayings in the Book of Proverbs. Attempting to explain this love-hate relationship, Fichtner postulated that Isaiah himself had been a sage, i.e., a professional wise man, before his prophetic vocation, but

---

[3] John Barton, "Ethics in Isaiah of Jerusalem," *JTS* 32 (1981), in an article that is generally excellent, claims that Isaiah appeals to law in something like the form it has in the Book of the Covenant, referring to condemnation of murder, theft, oppression of widows and orphans, bribery and corruption in the courts, etc. (p. 5), but the references in Isaiah are too general to relate to any specific law or body of law.

[4] See Tamar's words to Amnon in her attempt to dissuade him from rape in 2 Sam 13:12.

[5] "Foolishness" would be a literal translation of *nĕbālâ*, but the contexts in which it is used show that something much stronger is intended: so in the rape of Dinah (Gen 34:7), again in the rape of Tamar (2 Sam 13:12), the rape of the Levite's concubine (Judg 20:10), the unnatural desire of the men of Gibeah for the male guest from Ephraim (Judg 19:23-24), the woman found not to be virgin at the time of marriage (Deut 22:21), Achan's violation of the ban (Jos 7:15), and false prophets (Jer 29:23). Thus it is normally translated "crime," "wanton folly," or some such expression.

[6] Johannes Fichtner, "Jesaja unter den Weisen," *TLZ* 74 (1949) 75–80.

after his call he found himself the bearer of a message that people in their (human) wisdom would not grasp. Although not many have accepted the "converted sage" hypothesis, there is now widespread recognition of the importance of wisdom in Isaiah.[7] Isaiah's relation to the wisdom tradition is not a key to unlock all the mysteries of his book, but it does help to explain a lot and appears to provide important elements of the content of his ethical teaching.

WISDOM AND ETHICAL TEACHING IN ISAIAH

Isaiah was probably not a converted sage, but he almost certainly had attended the school that without doubt existed in Jerusalem, just as had the leaders and rulers to whom most of his words are addressed.

Although there is no direct reference to such a school during this early period, its existence from the time of Solomon on can be inferred with a great deal of certainty. One of the better articles on this topic is that of J.P.J. Olivier,[8] who argues from the widespread evidence for such schools in Mesopotamia, Egypt, and the Levant (i.e., the Mediterranean region) and their functions. He speaks of the need for scribes to administer the empire, organize forced labor, record taxes, etc. Israel, which had very much the same needs and had multiple contacts with these countries, would have filled them in much the same way; more positively, we see the same officials in Israel as those who emerged from the schools in these other places.[9] The "scribe" in all these countries held a prominent public office, the equivalent of our Secretary of State; he was a central figure in his culture and was held in high esteem. Olivier draws attention to the connection between the schools and wisdom literature, which

---

[7] Most recent commentaries give the topic the attention it deserves, especially the voluminous one of Hans Wildberger, originally published in BKAT, now available in English as *Isaiah 1–12: A Commentary; Isaiah 13–27: A Continental Commentary;* and *Isaiah 28–39: A Continental Commentary,* tr. Thomas H. Trapp (Minneapolis: Fortress, 1991, 1997, 2002); and there have been other full-scale works, especially William McKane, *Prophets and Wise Men.* SBT1/44 (Naperville, IL: Allenson, 1970), which, while not restricted to Isaiah, gives him major attention; James William Whedbee, *Isaiah & Wisdom* (Nashville: Abingdon, 1971), and Reinhard Fey, *Amos und Jesaja.* WMANT 12 (Neukirchen-Vluyn: Neukirchener Verlag, 1963); Joseph Jensen, *The Use of tôrâ by Isaiah: His Debate with the Wisdom Tradition.* CBQMS 3 (Washington, DC: The Catholic Biblical Association of America, 1973).

[8] J.P.J. Olivier, "Schools and Wisdom Literature," *JNWSL* 4 (1975) 49–60.

[9] On this point Olivier cites Tryggve N. D. Mettinger, *Solomonic State Officials: A Study of the Civil Government Officials of the Israelite Monarchy.* Coniectanea Biblica, OT Series 5 (Lund: Gleerup, 1971) 149–50, saying that he "has also shown that the school in Old Israel was the channel by which Egyptian wisdom literature found its way into Israel" (p. 49).

apparently constituted a major part of the curriculum.[10] He mentions that at Ugarit the trainees in the scribal school were classified as *lmdm,* "learners," a term that can be related to what Isaiah calls his disciples at 8:16.[11] Turning to Israel, Olivier refers to evidence that quite a number of scribes were employed in the public administration and became attached to the royal household. The chief scribe, who acted as Secretary of State (2 Sam 8:16), was also, of course, a royal adviser (1 Chr 27:32). He cites Wolfgang Richter's study[12] and says it has shown that schools did exist in Israel and that wisdom literature belonged to the schools.

We need this background to understand the import of much of what Isaiah has to say. There are ample reasons for believing that he had attended the school in Jerusalem, which was not simply for the professionals but also for the education of the children of the upper class.[13] "The wise" to whom Isaiah refers or alludes at various places are those who had gone through the school and were now applying this wisdom professionally as court officials who (1) administered justice and (2) advised the king.[14] Isaiah's polemic against "the wise" is directed now to one, now to the other of these functions.

In the first of these two areas his complaint would have been that they did not live up to the lofty ethical notions their training had imparted to them. It is particularly in wisdom that we find a great deal of concern for

---

[10] "It seems evident that one cannot deny the strong connection between education and wisdom literature" (p. 54). "In Egypt all education can be related to scribal schools. . . . The development of education into an institution can be traced back as far as the Old Kingdom with its royal school for the education of princes. . . . During the Middle Kingdom a kind of government secretarial training school was formed at court. This school served to further the aim of forming a friendship between crown-prince and those who would later hold high positions as state officials" (p. 55).

[11] Which would be *limmûdîm,* except that it carries the first person possessive pronoun and so appears as "my disciples" *(limmûdāy).*

[12] Wolfgang Richter, *Recht und Ethos: Versuch einer Ortung des weisheitlichen Mahnspruches.* STANT 15 (Munich: Kösel, 1966). See above, Chapter Two, n. 31.

[13] James L. Crenshaw, "Education in Ancient Israel," *JBL* 104 (1985) 601–15, has expressed doubts about some of the arguments reviewed above (without mentioning the article by Olivier, however). But his emphasis has to do with a somewhat different question; he does not appear to dispute the existence of a scribal school in early Israel but asks rather about where the child normally received its education and says that this is in the home. Obviously this would not cover the case of the professional destined for a career in the royal court; whether it would cover the case of the children of noble families is unclear. In any case, Crenshaw admits he is being "minimalist" in interpreting the evidence.

[14] A vivid example of the procedure is found in the story of Hushai and Achitophel in 2 Sam 15:31–17:23.

right judgment on the part of judges, avoiding everything that would pervert it (bribes and drunkenness, for example) and for righteousness (*ṣĕdāqâ*) in dealing with the disadvantaged.[15] Here it would help to recall some of the high ideals of the wisdom tradition, both within and outside Israel. The Egyptian composition "The Protests of the Eloquent Peasant" (*ANET*, 407–10) is instructive on at least three points: (1) it demonstrates how an official might use his authority to the disadvantage of a poorer member of society; (2) it shows the tendency of other officials to side with one of their own (cronyism); and (3) it points to the high ideals that were supposedly recognized, as seen both in the peasant's words and in the treatment ultimately accorded him. Passing over many other examples that might be given from Egyptian wisdom, we find in "The Instruction of Amen-em-opet" exhortations to preserve the widow's right to her property (*ANET*, 422), not to covet a poor man's property, to remit two-thirds of the debt a poor person cannot repay (*ANET*, 423), not to accept a bribe from the powerful, not to oppress the disabled, not to be harsh to a widow found in your field (*ANET*, 424). All of this corresponds very well with what we find in Israelite wisdom literature. For example:

On the poor: Prov 14:31: "He who oppresses the poor blasphemes his Maker, / but he who is kind to the needy glorifies him."

19:17: "He who has compassion on the poor lends to the LORD, / and he will repay him for his good deed."

21:13: "He who shuts his ear to the cry of the poor / will himself also call and not be heard."

22:16: "He who oppresses the poor to enrich himself / will yield up his gains to the rich as sheer loss."

22:22-23: "Injure not the poor because they are poor, / nor crush the needy at the gate; / For the LORD will defend their cause, / and will plunder the lives of those who plunder them."

On sacrifice: 15:8: "The sacrifice of the wicked is an abomination to the LORD, / but the prayer of the upright is his delight."

---

[15] Such concerns play a role in Israel's legislation, of course, but the distribution of the root *ṣdq*, if it is at all a test case, is rather impressive. Klaus Koch's article on *ṣdq* in *Theologisches Handwörterbuch zum Alten Testament*, ed. Ernst Jenni, vol. 2 (Munich: Kaiser, 1976), shows only 42 occurrences in the Pentateuch (of which only nine are found in Exodus and Leviticus), but 94 in Proverbs, second only to the Psalter (139 occurrences), with Isaiah in third place (81 occurrences). If one restricts the listing to *ṣĕdāqâ*, the distribution is as follows: Isaiah 1–66, 36 times, Psalms 34 times, Proverbs 18 times, and the Pentateuch nine times (three times in Genesis and six times in Deuteronomy).

On justice in judgment: 17:15: "He who condones the wicked, he who condemns the just, / are both an abomination to the LORD."

19:5: "The false witness will not go unpunished, / and he who utters lies will not escape."

On sobriety in judgment: 31:4-5: "It is not for kings, O Lemuel, / not for kings to drink wine; / . . . / Lest in drinking they forget what the law decrees / and violate the rights of all who are in need."

To these examples could be added many others that have to do with honest weights and measures, honesty in speech, etc. These all resemble prophetic accusations in the crimes they condemn, and many also in depicting the offense given to God by them and the punishment merited by them.

If we keep all this in mind we may be able to understand better three key passages in which Isaiah points to Israel's failure to know or understand as the main problem. The first is that programmatic passage at the beginning of the book, 1:2-3. Here an animal proverb is employed to emphasize Israel's stupidity. These animals are proverbial (in the strict sense!) for being stupid or stubborn or both. Israel, it is implied, is even worse, for these animals are here said to have a perception and docility that is lacking in God's children. The verbs used in v. 3b to designate Israel's lack of perception have wisdom overtones.[16] Both are used absolutely; i.e., no object is given and no object is to be supplied from the context: Israel does not know, has not understood.

The second passage, 6:9-10, is found in Isaiah's vocation narrative. Once we are aware of Isaiah's conflict with the wise, especially in the area of foreign policy, these difficult words become more intelligible. Many authors have emphasized that the primary purpose of a prophet's vocation narrative is to justify the message he proclaims, a message frequently unpopular and sometimes considered even sacrilegious and seditious. If Isaiah's preaching was characterized by opposition to the policies adopted by the kings under whom he prophesied and by opposition to the counsel of the circle of the king's royal advisers—those who were held in esteem by all for their wisdom, prudence, and insight—as was in fact the case, this would call for some justification. In light of this we can note that the message of destruction in vv. 11-12 is preceded by the command to deafen, blind, and harden. In v. 9 it is said that they are to hear but not understand *(byn)*, to see but not know *(yādaʿ)*, the same verbs found in the passage just

---

[16] *lōʾ yādaʿ . . . lōʾ hitbônān.* The first of the two is, of course, a very common verb, but the latter, the hithpolel of *byn,* is found most frequently in wisdom compositions.

discussed (1:2-3). Just as there, they are here used absolutely, without an object. The action affects the whole people ("say to this people," 6:9), but it is not surprising if it touches first and primarily those within the people who had the special office of understanding and knowing. However we answer the difficult question of what is in fact intended by the command to harden, there is every reason to think that these verses deal with the problem of the opposition Isaiah experienced from the wise on the question of policy. If this is really the same God whom Israel has known throughout its history, we can hardly take it as his will that they *not* be converted so that God can heal them.[17] In order to understand this Isaiah passage, what we need to do is translate the sequence into the process that *should* take place: seeing and hearing *should* lead to understanding, and understanding to return (conversion), while return (conversion) is the condition for being healed (restored). Thus is seen the tragedy of the hardening, which makes the whole sequence impossible by squelching it at the outset.

The third passage is 5:11-13, the only one in Isaiah's authentic oracles that speaks explicitly of exile. Note the close connection between v. 12 and v. 13; it is the failure of the leaders to *see* YHWH's work (v. 12) that explains the lack of knowledge that leads to disaster (v. 13), giving us the same sequence we found in 6:9-10. The culpable ones here are not the priests, as in Hos 4:6, but probably the royal counselors and ruling class, and it would seem that it is not a matter of their failing to impart knowledge to others (as was the case of the priests in Hosea), but rather of being without it themselves and therefore adopting the disastrous policies that result in the people being sent into exile.

We need to look at some specific passages in each of the two areas referred to above, namely, social justice and policy, to see what insights Isaiah offers in each. In some of these passages the usefulness of recognizing the wisdom background will become apparent.

SOCIAL JUSTICE

A good starting point will be 1:10-17. This passage begins with a call to attention very much of the sort we find in wisdom literature.[18] This

---

[17] Similarly Jesus, in a saying that in part echoes this passage, says, "I came into this world for judgment, so that those who do not see might see, and those who do see might become blind" (John 9:39), and again we do not take this as literally expressing what was his intention.

[18] There are many varieties of the call to attention (*Aufmerkruf*) in the Old Testament, beginning with the prophet's simple "hear this word." But the one in Isa 1:10 closely

kind of call to attention is the "invocation of the teacher." What it communicates is *tôrâ*, instruction in the wisdom sense,[19] and it is immediately followed by a rhetorical question. The basic content is that YHWH does not find their sacrifices (or even their prayer!) acceptable because of the violence they are guilty of. When this is specified (v. 17), it has to do with oppression and neglecting justice to the widow and orphan.

All of this relates nicely to the wisdom tradition. The idea that sacrifice is not acceptable without justice goes back at least to early Egyptian wisdom, where we learn that "more acceptable is the character of one upright of heart than the ox of the evildoer."[20] Closer, especially since v. 17 uses both the substantive *mišpāṭ*[21] and the verb *šāpaṭ*, is Prov 21:3: "To do what is right and just (*ṣĕdāqâ ûmišpāṭ*) / is more acceptable to the LORD than sacrifice." Even more to the point is Isaiah's use of "abomination" (*tôʿēbâ*) in this context (1:13 [*NAB*: "loathsome"]).[22] The expression "abomination to [or of] the god" is found often in Egyptian wisdom. For example, various kinds of deceit are characterized as "abomination of the god" in Amen-em-opet.[23] It would seem that this is the sort of background from which it comes into Proverbs. In Proverbs, for example, we find:

> Lying lips are an abomination to the LORD,
>   but those who are truthful are his delight (12:22).

> The sacrifice of the wicked is an abomination to the LORD,
>   but the prayer of the upright is his delight (15:8).

> The sacrifice of the wicked is an abomination,
>   the more so when they offer it with a bad intention (21:27).

resembles those we find in the wisdom instruction form: it has the double address in parallel, verbs to listen/give ear, specification of the one(s) addressed (usually son, children, though sometimes, as here, rulers), and what they are to hear (instruction, etc.). These elements designate it as the "invocation of the teacher" (*Lehreröffnungsformel*), found frequently in Proverbs. It is very ancient in the wisdom tradition and is represented in one of the earliest pieces of writing in existence, the "Instruction of Shurrupak" (*ANET*, 594–95).

[19] See what is said about the dating of *tôrâ* as law and as instruction above, Chapter Seven, n. 21.

[20] From the "Instruction of Meri-ka-Re," *ANET*, 417.

[21] A useful study on *mišpāṭ* throughout the whole Book of Isaiah is Thomas L. Leclerc, *Yahweh is Exalted in Justice: Solidarity and Conflict in Isaiah* (Minneapolis: Fortress, 2001).

[22] This is especially clear if we recognize that the *tôʿēbâ . . . lî* of v. 13 is the equivalent of *tôʿăbat . . . yhwh*, which is found elsewhere in the Old Testament only in Proverbs and in Deuteronomy, and the persuasion is that it came to Deuteronomy through the wisdom tradition.

[23] "The Instruction of Amen-em-opet," xiii, 15–16; xiv, 2–3; xv, 20–21 (*ANET*, 423).

And Prov 6:16 characterizes seven sins as "an abomination to [his the LORD's soul]" (*tô'ăbat* [following the Qere] *napšô);* the emphasis falls on the seventh, the false witness, but the foundation is laid with references to six parts of the body, including "a lying tongue" and "hands that shed innocent blood."

Thus it is not at all clear that in 1:10-17 we are dealing with any *law* Isaiah wants to see enforced; rather, the general moral norms that rulers have been taught are here proposed and sanctioned with the full authority of YHWH, whose instruction *(tôrâ)* it is said to be. The import is that the *source* of the content is not so important as the fact that its goodness creates an obligation to act accordingly, because that is the kind of God YHWH is and this is the sort of thing YHWH demands.

The same sort of thing may be seen in 5:20-23. Here we have several antithetical pairs, a series of accusations against those who obviously think themselves wise ("in their own sight," v. 21), and have the reputation of being so, who are guilty of perverted judgment—accepting bribes and doing wrong to the innocent—which accusation is joined to that of excessive drinking. The obligation of judging justly does come up in the law codes, but the conjunction of all those elements (especially the linking of drinking and judgment—cf. Prov 31:4-5 above) points to wisdom. It is what they have learned in the school; *because* it is good it is sanctioned by the Lord (cf. v. 24, which, however, is a culminating judgment to the whole series of "woes"). In this series of "woes" the accusation of perverted judgment is closely joined to others that relate to policy (see below).

Relevant to the matter of social justice is 10:1-4. This is another "woe" *(hôy),* which, in the opinion of most commentators, originally was part of the series of "woes" we find in chapter 5 (which would then comprise a total of seven). Again the words are leveled against the rulers and administrators, though here it is not a question of withholding justice from the poor or simply of failure to properly administer justice (through, e.g., unjust judgment, accepting of bribes) but of defrauding them by enacting unjust decrees. Israelite law was notably "slanted" in favor of the disadvantaged; here it is a question of making laws that do just the opposite. Thus we are dealing with the ruling class, those who have the authority both to enact laws and to administer them. All the familiar terms (*mišpāṭ*, poor *[dal]*, widow, orphan) show up here. But punishment is to be leveled, apparently in the form of plundering at the hands of foreign armies (vv. 3-4). We are reminded of Prov 22:22-23:

Injure not the poor because they are poor,
    nor crush the needy at the gate;
For the LORD will defend their cause,
    and will plunder the lives of those who plunder them.

Like Amos, Isaiah spoke out against those who acquired large estates at the expense of the poor. Note the irony of the "woe" in 5:8-10: the rich live in splendid isolation on spacious lands because they have dispossessed the poor of the property they formerly owned. As in the case of Amos, it is not a question of asking whether this had been done by means that were strictly legal or not. In fact, as 10:1-4 (which, as we have indicated, may be a part of this series) indicates, in some cases the distinction would be meaningless, since laws could be designed to despoil the poor.

A final example of what Isaiah has to say on social justice, though far from exhausting the list, can be taken from 5:1-7, the so-called "parable of the vineyard." This piece also provides a good example of the skill with which Isaiah presented his message.[24] We tend to think of parables simply as homely stories intended to teach religious truths, but often they have a strongly polemical bent; the hearers are called upon to make a judgment and so the point of the parable is borne home, often impaling those to whom it is spoken. Thus Isaiah refrains at the outset from speaking of YHWH's vineyard, referring to the owner as "my friend" (v. 1) in order to avoid tipping his hand. After he has described all the care lavished on the field and the bitter fruit it has produced he asks for a judgment: "What more . . . ? Why . . . ?" (v. 4). The implied answers to those questions justify the judgment of destruction to be visited on the vineyard. It is only in v. 7b, by way of a play on words, that the nature of the crimes is exposed:

He looked for judgment *(mišpāṭ)*, but see, bloodshed *(miśpāḥ)!*
    for justice *(ṣĕdāqâ)*, but hark, the outcry *(ṣĕʿāqâ)!*

The outcry of the poor is heard in YHWH's city because they are deprived of judgment and justice precisely by those whose calling it was to be guardians and defenders of the disadvantaged members of society. The theme of *imitatio Dei* is subtly introduced in the references to the care YHWH has lavished on his inheritance; clearly it was to be a means of showing the "inhabitants of Jerusalem and the men of Judah" something

---

[24] This passage, so skillfully composed, is sufficient demonstration that Isaiah did not understand literally as a command the Lord's words, spoken during his call narrative, about dulling the ears and closing the eyes of his hearers (6:10).

of the concern they were to show. The threatened punishments spring not so much from the wrath of a vindictive God as from the disappointment of a Father who has tried to show by example how his children should behave (cf. 1:2-3).

POLICY

Isaiah's debate with "the wise" is probably the best starting point also for the other principal point, referred to above, that of policy. Much of chapters 28–33 concerns Hezekiah's revolt against the Assyrians, under whom Judah now stood as vassal. Isaiah's oracles from this period demonstrate his bitter opposition to the planned revolt. The arguments of Hezekiah's advisers prevailed, however, and Isaiah has some choice words of condemnation for the royal counselors. In 29:13-14, 15-16 he says that their "wisdom" (v. 14) shall perish,[25] pronounces a "woe" on them, and ridicules their attempt to "hide their plans / too deep for the LORD" (v. 15), likening it to an attempt of clay to renounce the potter who shapes it.

This struggle between Isaiah and the royal advisers reflects the one that took place earlier, in the days of Ahaz, when the prophet attempted to prevent the initial submission to the Assyrians. Isaiah based his message relevant to such matters in part, at least, on his conviction that YHWH has his own "plan" (*ʿēṣâ*), which he pursues, and against which no other "plan" can prevail. It is clear from 5:19 that Isaiah spoke of the "plan" (or purpose or policy)[26] of YHWH, a term that can be paralleled to his "work" (*maʿăśeh*); the taunt of his critics is occasioned by the apparent failure of the "plan" to materialize. The certainty that what YHWH has planned will come to pass is stressed in 14:24-27. This passage begins with YHWH's oath that "as I have proposed, / so it shall stand *(tāqûm)*" (v. 24) and ends with the (rhetorical) question, "the LORD of hosts has planned, who can thwart him?" (v. 27). On this point of certainty, YHWH's purpose is very

---

[25] Verse 13. The phrase *miṣwat ʾănāšîm mělummādâ* (*NRSV:* "human commandment learned by rote"; *NAB:* "routine observance of the precepts of men"), is most often taken as a condemnation of external observances and as directed at priests, but v. 14, introduced by *lākēn* and directed against the wise, does not favor this understanding. It is preferable to understand v. 13 as referring to the teaching of the wise (which also can be designated as *miṣwâ*), as opposed to what YHWH teaches. See Jensen, *Use of tôrâ,* 67–68.

[26] No English translation is totally suitable for *ʿēṣâ.* It means "counsel" or "advice" (cf. the verb *yāʿaṣ*), but since it is counsel intended to lead to action, "plan" or "policy" is often more appropriate. "Plan" may suggest something too concrete and limited, and so "policy" or "purpose" may often seem preferable. See further Joseph Jensen, "Yahweh's Plan in Isaiah and the Rest of the Old Testament," *CBQ* 48 (1986) 443–55.

different from the plans of the nations; the contrast is clear in 8:9-10, where it is said that the plan they form shall be thwarted, shall not stand *(lōʾ yāqûm)*. This comes in the context of the Syro-Ephraimitic war and helps us to understand what Isaiah means when he tells Ahaz, concerning the plan the coalition has formed against him (note the verb *yāʿaṣ,* 7:5), that "this shall not stand *(lōʾ tāqûm)*, it shall not be" (7:7).

Thus Isaiah's teaching on what we would call "foreign policy" becomes more intelligible when we recognize that he sees YHWH as having a plan or policy and that in the face of it no human plan or policy can stand.[27] The only safe, the only viable way, the only way that is not a road to destruction, is to align oneself with YHWH's policy. This is what Isaiah means by "faith," and this is the challenge he offers to Ahaz and Hezekiah. "Faith," therefore, is not some vague belief, but a concrete call for action. No doubt he bases his stance on the revelation he as a prophet has received, but he can also point to elements of Judah's faith that the rulers and people should be able to accept: for example, the Zion tradition, the Davidic tradition, and the Holy War tradition. And if this is not enough, he can also offer the ruler a sign (7:11). On this matter of faith Lindblom has this to say:

> The profoundest expression for Israel's relation to Yahweh in the pre-exilic prophets is belief, trust, confidence in Yahweh *(heʾĕmîn, bāṭaḥ)*. Isaiah is the first to have presented belief and confidence in Yahweh as a central religious demand. In his teaching this notion has a very concrete significance. In every concrete situation in the political life of the people he ventured to make resolute confidence in Yahweh the only sure way of deliverance. . . . This implied a condemnation of all human expedients. There seems to be something paradoxical, something utopian about this saying [the reference is to 7:9], uttered in a critically dangerous political situation; but it is entirely credible in the mouth of a great prophet. Later, when Judah was menaced by the armies of Sennacherib, Isaiah repeated the same appeal [reference to 30:15]. Neither alliance with the Egyptians, nor the strengthening of their own defensive forces could help. The true meaning of words such as these is not that quietness and confidence in itself would help, but that confidence would create the condition in which alone Yahweh could intervene as a helping power in the distress of the people.[28]

---

[27] We may note that *ʿēṣâ* (noun) and *yāʿaṣ* (verb) terminology, when used of human agents, regularly have an unfavorable sense for Isaiah. In addition to 7:5 and 8:10, mentioned above, which come from the time of Ahaz, see 29:15 and 30:1, from the time of Hezekiah and the 705 revolt against Assyria.

[28] Johannes Lindblom, *Prophecy in Ancient Israel* (Philadelphia: Fortress, 1965) 342.

He speaks of the people rejecting Isaiah's admonition but goes on to say that there was a group who listened and obeyed, and these embodied the true religion. He says:

> This pure and unadulterated religion is what Isaiah describes in metaphorical language in the saying on the cornerstone [here he quotes 28:16-17]. The prophet here presents Yahweh as a builder erecting a house. The house has a foundation stone and walls raised by means of measuring-line and plummet. The text itself gives the true interpretation. The foundation-stone means confidence in Yahweh, the walls mean justice and righteousness. These are the marks of the true Yahweh religion. Those who understood and practiced this religion would be saved from ruin, while the "scoffers," those who made lies their refuge, would perish.[29]

Eichrodt says something very similar in fewer words: "In Isaiah's prophetic influence the decisive point is reached when with a grave warning he turns away from the unrepentant people, who are on the brink of disaster, and a circle of disciples appears. Here is Israel *kata pneuma*, the people of God living not by common blood but by faith in the word, the people that God will use as the cornerstone for the new building of his kingdom."[30]

PRIDE AS THE CAPITAL SIN

John Barton provides a listing of the various crimes condemned by Isaiah[31] that is very useful for two reasons. The first is that he gives a rather full accounting of the various crimes Isaiah touches on (including many that are not mentioned in the present study). The second is that Barton groups the relevant passages into three levels or categories that attempt to ascend from the concrete and specific to the abstract and general.[32] Barton's third

---

[29] Lindblom, *Prophecy in Ancient Israel,* 342–43.

[30] Walther Eichrodt, *Man in the Old Testament.* SBT 1/4 (Chicago: Henry Regnery, 1951) 43. Bernhard Anderson, *Understanding the Old Testament* (4th ed. Englewood Cliffs, NJ: Prentice-Hall, 1986) 336, also lays emphasis on this "faithful community," which he refers to as a "prophetic remnant."

[31] John Barton, "Ethics in Isaiah of Jerusalem," *JTS* 32 (1981) 6–8.

[32] (1) Isaiah condemns specific crimes, sins, and errors:
—In the sphere of social relations (treatment of widows and orphans, theft, murder, perversion of justice, expropriation of land, drunkenness, luxury);
—In the political sphere (preparations for war, foreign alliances, boasting of conquests);
—In the religious sphere (idolatry, misuse of sacrificial cultus, mocking God, skepticism of God's power to act and direct events);

level is what he considers the "organizing principles for ethics in Isaiah." In this understanding, which I think is a correct one, it boils down to pride being the ultimate sin or, more accurately, "an attitude producing sin." He understands the texts he lists to relate to pride in some sense. After discussing these texts he concludes:

> Isaiah, then, begins with a picture of the world in which God is the creator and preserver of all things, and occupies by right the supreme position over all that he has made. The essence of morality is cooperation in maintaining the ordered structure which prevails, under God's guidance, in the natural order of things, and the keynote of the whole system is order, a proper submission to one's assigned place in the scheme of things and avoidance of any action that would challenge the supremacy of God or seek to subvert the orders he has established.[33]

There is much truth in this, though the formulation is rather abstract, and Barton goes on to reduce this "maintaining of the orders" to a natural law ethic, something I have already commented on.[34] But there is much truth in seeing pride as the ultimate sin in Isaiah. This fits in with his seeing YHWH as king of all the earth while considering the mighty world powers as simply instruments of YHWH's will (5:26-29; 7:18-20; 10:5-15), and with the demand that human policy be totally subservient to YHWH's policy.

    Among the texts Barton lists in his third category (see n. 32) is 2:6-22. This text contains not a few critical problems, most of which we need not go into, but three points are of some importance for us: (1) as the text stands it is not directed specifically to Judah, at least not after v. 8,[35] but to the whole earth (cf. the references to "human being" "humankind"—*ʾîš*, *ʾādām*—in vv. 9, 11, 17, 20, 21, 22);[36] (2) the "day," in this text, is not eschatological but relates to YHWH's action in history; (3) Isaiah does not

---

(2) Isaiah denounces culpable attitudes and states of minds (pride of the "wise" and powerful, delight in prestige, failure to trust in God alone, contempt of rulers toward legitimate claims made on them, folly or stupidity which moves to sin);

(3) Isaiah attempts to encapsulate what is the essence of sinful actions and wrong attitudes. (The texts he lists for this last point are 2:6-22; 3:1-2; 5:8-10, 20; 19:15-16.)

[33] Barton, "Ethics in Isaiah," 11.

[34] See above, Chapter One, p. 3.

[35] Among the "critical problems" referred to is the question of the unity of this almost certainly composite piece. Some argue that vv. 10-17 originally formed an independent composition, and most of what is asserted here finds its justification in these verses.

[36] The mysterious v. 22 quite certainly does not belong to the original composition, but it accords well in depicting humankind as fragile and not to be reckoned highly.

speak of the destruction of humankind, but rather of its humbling. The ultimate effects are that all that is high and lofty will be brought low and that YHWH alone will be exalted on that day.

It is of interest to note that here, too, we seem to be close to the wisdom tradition, the only place pride itself invites humiliation. This assertion has elsewhere been detailed at length,[37] but here we will simply call attention to the relevance of Prov 25:6-7:

> Claim no honor in the king's presence,
> nor occupy the place of great men;
> For it is better that you be told, "Come up closer!"
> than that you be humbled before the prince.

Consider also Prov 29:23:

> Man's pride causes his humiliation,
> but he who is humble of spirit obtains honor.

These sentiments are also strongly echoed in Sir 10:6-18, which speaks of pride being a reservoir of sin, because of which "God sends unheard-of afflictions / and brings men to utter ruin" (v. 13), overturning the thrones of the arrogant, plucking up the roots of the proud, and includes the line:

> The traces of the proud God sweeps away
> and effaces the memory of them from the earth (v. 17).

SOME POSITIVE ASPECTS

The fact that 2:6-22 does not refer to humankind's destruction but rather to the humbling of pride leaves the way open to understanding it in a more favorable sense. Since pride is the principal form of rebellion against YHWH,[38] the humbling of it leaves the way open for conversion and the reception of YHWH's blessings. That this sort of restoration is YHWH's will and that it will come to pass through a purgation can be seen in 1:21-26. That passage describes the present sinful state of Jerusalem, promises that YHWH "will turn my hand against you" (v. 25) but also that he will restore its judges and counselors "as in the beginning" (v. 26) with the result:

> After that you shall be called
> city of justice, faithful city (v. 26).

---

[37] See Hans Wildberger, *Isaiah 1–12*, 110–11, 115; for a shorter account see Joseph Jensen, "Weal and Woe in Isaiah: Consistency and Continuity," *CBQ* 43 (1981) 183.

[38] Rather than the texts given by Barton (see above, n. 32), I would prefer to list 2:11-12, 17; 3:16; 5:15-16; 9:8-9; 10:7-16, 33-34; 28:1-4, 22; 29:5.

So also it is worth noting that Assyria, as sent for the punishment of Judah, is referred to as Yhwh's "rod" and "staff" (10:5), instruments apt for correction but not for inflicting death. In the wisdom tradition there are repeated references to the use of rod and staff, especially to the chastisement that the loving parent, the one intent on raising the child wisely, employs.[39] Such passages remind us, in turn, of Isa 1:4-6, which, after depicting the nation as "corrupt children" (v. 4) personifies it as having been struck so often that there is no longer place for fresh blows.

Isaiah does hold out hope for the future and what he has to say on this subject is also a source for his moral teaching. The best example of this is 2:2-4, which is most instructive if read in the light of 30:8-14. In the latter text Isaiah excoriates the people as "children who will not listen to the *tôrâ* of Yhwh" (v. 9)[40] and sees total destruction as the consequence of this rejection (vv. 13-14).[41] But the former text, looking to a better future, sees a time when not only Judah but all the nations will deliberately seek out Yhwh on his holy mountain "that he may instruct[42] us in his ways,"

> For from Zion shall go forth *tôrâ,*
>   and the word of the Lord from Jerusalem (v. 3).

Because all peoples will accept Yhwh's instruction and his judgments, the result will be universal peace. The difference between the two scenarios is striking, but it relates primarily to different human responses to Yhwh's instruction: rejection of it leads to destruction; acceptance is the way to peace. That this should be so is not surprising, given faith in the wisdom and goodness of God. The real mystery has to do with the reason for the difference in the human response. If Isaiah looks forward to a time when this response will be so totally different from that

---

[39] Prov 10:13 (MT, not *NAB*); 13:24; 22:15; 23:13, 14; 26:3; 29:15.

[40] The phrase *lōʾ-ābû šĕmôaʿ tôrat yhwh* (v. 9) is sometimes translated "who refuse / to obey the law of the Lord," as in the *NAB*, but the broader context of Isaiah and the immediate context in this passage indicate it is a case of instruction rather than of law. See above, Chapter Seven n. 21 on the use of *tôrâ* in the generalized sense of "law." As legal terminology *tôrâ* in the singular, in this earlier period, would only refer to an individual provision of law (e.g., the *tôrâ* of the guilt offering). In the current passage the reference to children who will not listen to/hear instruction brings us clearly into the sphere of wisdom instruction.

[41] The historical background of the piece is the determination of Judah's leaders to defy Assyria, trusting in help from Egypt, in the revolt of 705–701. The *tôrâ* in v. 9 is Yhwh's "instruction," delivered through the prophet, dealing with how Judah should conduct itself in this crisis. For details see Jensen, *The Use of tôrâ by Isaiah,* 112–20.

[42] The verbal root is *yrh,* from which *tôrâ* is derived.

experienced in his own time, it is because he expects that God will do something to make the human heart more receptive, much as Hosea, Jeremiah, and Ezekiel did.

Of the passages that deal with the ideal king of the future, it is worth noting the importance of the theme of peace in 8:23–9:6 (*NRSV* 9:1-7). The wonderful new king is called "prince of peace" (v. 5) and it is said that "his dominion will be vast and forever peaceful" (v. 6). Another of his titles (along with "prince of peace") is "wonder-counselor" (v. 5), which suggests that he would not be dependent on the sort of royal advisers who had been the downfall of the kings Isaiah knew. The same point emerges in 11:1-9, where the king has all the charismatic gifts necessary to enable him to formulate his own counsel and more (v. 2). The positive qualities of right judgment are emphasized (in the familiar terminology of *šāpaṭ, ṣedeq,* and *ʾĕmûnâ*). Again we note the great attention given to peace, described in paradisiac terms, and finally attributed to "knowledge . . . of the LORD" (v. 2). Here it may also be mentioned that the Immanuel whom Isaiah speaks of in 7:14-16 will acquire the knowledge to reject evil and choose good;[43] in this he will be the antithesis of what Isaiah had said of Israel in 1:2-3, that it did not know, did not understand.

APPLICATION

Much of what Isaiah has to say needs no "translation" to make it applicable to our own situation, especially with reference to social justice. But what about what he says about "policy"? Many would call (and have called) it impracticable, utopian. These include those many politicians and statespeople and even clergy who, while giving high-profile lip service to the Bible, think security is to be placed in missiles, bombers, missile shields, etc., and thus implicitly reject the very core of what Isaiah would teach us. Is what he had to say impracticable and utopian? The three "messianic" passages discussed above each emphasizes peace, and it is of interest to note that in his historical circumstances Isaiah's advice would have withheld Judah from a violent course. We can discern something very positive for ourselves and not at all impractical by thinking deeply on what Isaiah had to say about YHWH's "policy" (*ʿēṣâ*). Given the expanded view we now have through the completion of scriptural revelation, we need to expand the concept of YHWH's *ʿēṣâ* accordingly. The divine plan, ultimately, is the establishment of God's kingdom. Since

---

[43] For the arguments for this interpretation of the text see Joseph Jensen, "The Age of Immanuel," *CBQ* 41 (1979) 220–39.

it is to be a kingdom of justice, everything we can do now to help establish justice on earth (in the full biblical sense of *ṣĕdāqâ*)[44] promotes God's kingdom. It is to be a kingdom that embraces in unity all of humankind in love and in peace. From that point of view the escalation of the arms race can never be part of YHWH's *ʿēṣâ*. YHWH is not a nationalistic God but Lord of all the earth and of all peoples. To abandon the arms race involves a willingness to trust others, and that may involve some risk. Undoubtedly Ahaz thought that what Isaiah demanded of him involved risk, but by refusing to accept a risk he established the conditions for later destruction. The willingness to take that risk some might call idealism, but I think it is what Isaiah would have called faith, and it is the sort of thing expected and even demanded of those committed to the "good news" of the Bible.

---

[44] This sense of "justice" would, for example, call upon the affluent nations to do all they can to eliminate world famine and help the third-world nations to become more productive.

Chapter Nine

MICAH

This prophet, though assuredly an important one, will be dealt with relatively briefly since his principal concern, social justice, has already been treated in some detail in the preceding chapters.

Micah is, again, an eighth-century prophet, close in time to the three we have been looking at; he is more closely associated with Isaiah than with Amos or Hosea, frequently being designated as Isaiah's "younger contemporary," though his message is more often compared with that of Amos. Like Amos he was from a small town of Judah (Moresheth) and had harsh words for the life of the big cities. His ministry seems to have fallen within that of Isaiah. He must have been called to the prophetic ministry before 721, since Samaria is referred to as still standing (1:5), and he must have continued at least until 701, since 1:8-16 seems to have an invasion of Sennacherib as background and 4:14 [*NRSV* 5:1] is apparently an allusion to Sennacherib's siege of Jerusalem.[1]

Micah does not seem to have had the broad interests in "policy" we find in Isaiah. He was single-mindedly interested in social justice, as Amos was. But he does attend to what is going on in the capital cities, which appear to him to be hotbeds of corruption, and he foretells the destruction of both Samaria and Jerusalem (1:5-6; 3:12). Wolff argues that he was an elder of Moresheth and that, as such, he represented his town to the Jerusalem authorities; he was an official spokesman for his people,

---

[1] This, at least, is the more usual dating. Hans Walter Wolff, *Micah the Prophet* (Philadelphia: Fortress, 1981) 3, apparently basing his position on the inscription of the book (1:1, which lists Jotham, Ahaz, and Hezekiah as the kings in whose days he prophesied) says that Micah appeared on the scene at the very latest in 734 and was active at least until 728. But he also identifies Sennacherib's siege as the occasion for 4:14 (5:1), which would therefore have to be dated to 701.

so to speak. This hypothesis would help to explain his very bold address to the leaders of Jerusalem and also his frequent references to "my people." The claim is that Micah's words, while addressed in the main to the ruling classes of Jerusalem, often relate to oppressive measures taken against the populace of his own town. Wolff would also explain from his position as elder the instances of "clan wisdom" he detects in Micah's words.[2] I would agree that there are wisdom overtones, but it may be that Micah is throwing in the faces of the Jerusalem officials their rejection (in practice) of the right teaching they received (and theoretically approve) in the Jerusalem school that court officials attended.

A very simple division of the materials in the book would go something like this:

I. Punishment of Israel's Sins:
    Judgment to come: chapter 1
    Social evils: chapter 2
    Present leaders: chapter 3
II. The New Israel:
    The people: chapter 4
    The future king: 4:14–5:14 (*NRSV* ch. 5)
III. Admonitions and Threats: 6:1–7:7
IV. Future Mercy: 7:8-20

It seems evident that there is a deliberate attempt to alternate good news and bad news. This is the work of those who edited the book. There is considerable dispute over the authenticity of much of the material in Micah, especially that which offers hope for the future. We will be dealing mainly with his denunciations and so the material covered will be little affected by questions of authenticity.

The book opens (after the inscription) with a judgment theophany of YHWH (1:2-4) followed by an explanation that this judgment is provoked by sin (vv. 5-7). The capital cities of Samaria and Jerusalem are said to be the focus of evil and the overthrow of Samaria is foretold. The only crime that is explicitly referred to here is idolatry. The force of what Micah is saying is perhaps lost on us because of our callousness and because of the poetic diction in which it is couched, but the lament to which the prophet gives expression (vv. 8-9) is intended to make us feel some of

---

[2] Wolff draws this conclusion from the "disputation style that occurs in 2:6ff." and "the antithetical explication of injustice in 3:2a ('hate what is good and love what is evil'), which reminds us of the antithetical explication of injustice in Amos 5:14f." (p. 24).

the impact. After further descriptions of calamity, which now appears in the form of an enemy invasion (vv. 10-15), the listeners are invited to join in the expressions of grief (v. 16). This evil "has come down from the LORD" (v. 12b) and is because of "the crimes of Israel" (v. 13c).

The detailing of crimes becomes much more explicit in chapter 2, and here we see Micah's great concern for social justice and the manner in which he identifies with the suffering of his people. The leaders are the ones who are blamed. They are sarcastically described as not able to plan enough evil during the daylight hours, so that they lie awake at night plotting more. Amos had, in similar fashion, depicted the merchants as anxious for the Sabbath to be over so they could resume their cheating (Amos 8:4-6). Micah adds "in the morning light they accomplish it" (v. 1). As in Amos (and Isaiah) a major crime is the taking over of the property of others, no doubt that of the poorer people. The verb "covet" in 2:2 is the same as that used in the Decalogue *(ḥāmad),* and again Micah explicitly notes that the desire is put into action. The verb used here for "seize" *(gāzal)* suggests something more violent than simply acquiring by legal means. The reference to inheritance *(naḥălâ)* reminds us of the Naboth story (1 Kgs 21:3). But there is perhaps a stronger allusion to Joshua 13, where *naḥălâ* applies to the portion assigned to each tribe by lot; this suggestion is reinforced in vv. 4-5, where it is a matter of punishment being administered through the stripping away of ill-gotten lands by an enemy.[3]

Verses 6-11 again contain a strenuous indictment. It begins with a quotation from Micah's critics, who want him to stop preaching; evidently his reprimands aroused opposition rather than repentance and amendment. Micah sarcastically concludes that the only preacher acceptable to them would be one who spoke of wine and strong drink. Apparently they wanted to hear reassuring words that they are God's people and are safe in God's protection, words such as those Micah quotes them as saying at 3:11: "Is not the LORD in the midst of us? No evil can come upon us!" Micah responds that the good have nothing to fear, but what one sees is the despoiling of the poor, expulsion of the helpless from their homes, and the exacting of crippling pledges for loans. Those who do such things can expect to hear about them. Religion does not consist in hearing reassuring words nor does the prophetic vocation consist in pronouncing them. In our own day we have heard priests told to "stick to the gospel" when they preach against segregation and discrimination

---

[3] Cf. Isa 34:17, where, with similar imagery, it is the Lord who redistributes Edom's territory.

and bishops criticized as leaving their proper sphere when they write pastorals on the economy and nuclear arms.

It is specifically to the rulers that the prophet addresses himself in 3:1-4, a passage notable for the manner in which it depicts violence against the poor as a kind of cannibalism, even to the point of describing the preparation of their flesh for the stew pot. Micah's criticism of the leading elements extends to the prophets; he speaks sarcastically of those who give oracles in return for gifts and adjust their message to the offering they receive (3:5). The Old Testament does not use the term "false prophets," but there could hardly be any stronger contrast between those he criticizes / and what he says of himself: / he is filled with "the spirit of the LORD, / with authority and with might; To declare to Jacob his crimes / and to Israel his sins" (3:8). In such words we have a characterization of his mission as he conceived it.

The following verses (vv. 9-12) continue much the same theme, only more systematically; the rulers (literally "heads"), priests, and prophets are all accused of venality and perverting the exercise of their office for the sake of money. The fact that all three groups could be "bought" would again give the rich terrible leverage over the poor. Here also Micah startles us with the violence of his imagery, as he speaks of them as people "who build up Zion with bloodshed" (v. 10).[4] The passage concludes with the famous prophecy of the destruction of Jerusalem (v. 12). Many years later it would be cited in defense of Jeremiah (Jer 26:18), who also threatened the Holy City. Like Jeremiah on that occasion (Jer 7:4), Micah rejects the idea that YHWH's presence would protect them from the punishment their crimes deserve (Mic 3:11).[5]

The best known and perhaps most important passage in Micah is 6:1-8, containing, as it does, one of the few "essential definitions" of religion that we find in Scripture. We will here treat these verses together, though many authors point to the likelihood that vv. 6-8 originally formed a unity distinct from vv. 1-5.

Verses 1-5 are in the *rîb*-form in the sense that they use courtroom imagery: YHWH is to bring an accusation against Israel; the mountains and the foundations of the earth are called in as witnesses. Yet in fact no

---

[4] Wolff sees here a reference to blood drawn by the lash of the overseer of forced labor; that may well be correct, though the parallel expression ("and Jerusalem with wickedness") does not favor this. More probably the reference is to oppression in a general sense, though oppression so severe that it can be compared to the violent shedding of blood.

[5] It is a point worth noting, and here clearly illustrated, that Micah seems almost always to use Jacob/Israel terminology (cf. v. 11) even when he is clearly referring to Judah.

accusation is leveled. Instead, several incidents from Israel's salvation history are detailed, and are then characterized as "the just deeds of the LORD" (*ṣidqôt yhwh*—again a reminder of the overtones of *ṣĕdāqâ*). (On my rejection of the "covenant lawsuit" sometimes proposed for this text, see above, Chapter Two, n. 15, and Chapter Seven, n. 16.) In view of the other accusations in the book it is not hard to understand why a specific listing of crimes can be dispensed with here. And saving history is brought in, no doubt, for much the same reason it was in Amos, namely, to demonstrate what they owe YHWH and how they are to behave toward others—something given special point by the reference to the *ṣidqôt yhwh*. In vv. 6-8 we are presented with an Israel well disposed and wanting to respond to YHWH, acknowledging sin and asking how to atone for it. The reply to this question accords very well with other prophetic passages up to a point in that it presents moral dispositions, rather than sacrifices, as what God requires:

> You have been told, O man, what is good,
>   and what the LORD requires of you:
> Only to do right and love goodness,
>   and to walk humbly with your God (v. 8).

The "right" and "goodness" are *mišpāṭ* and *ḥesed,* and so we can find this a very good parallel, in a general sense, to Hos 6:6 ("For it is love that I desire, not sacrifice"). Yet most of the other prophetic passages that favor moral dispositions over sacrifice are strongly polemical and often harsh in their wording;[6] this one is more calm and pacific: the questioner sincerely wants to know and deserves a good answer. Since the demand for *mišpāṭ* and *ḥesed* have been there from the beginning, the "you have been told" is appropriate. But the Micah passage goes beyond those other passages that ask for moral dispositions rather than sacrifice on the point of "walk[ing] humbly with your God." Unfortunately the word we translate "humbly" (*haṣnēaʿ*) occurs nowhere else in the Masoretic text,[7] so the exact meaning is obscure and there are no parallels to help us out. However, the call to "walk with your God" is itself a very significant expression. To Abraham, God's special friend, it was said "Walk in my presence and be blameless" (Gen 17:1). To "walk with God" suggests familiar friendship and fellowship. It also implies

---

[6] Cf. especially Amos 5:21-24; Isa 1:10-17.

[7] It does occur twice in the fragments of the Hebrew text of Sirach that have been recovered (16:25; 35:3) but with a meaning that would not fit here.

walking in the way God walks, being with him, being like God, imitating him. Hardly anything more challenging or more consoling has come from any prophet.

Chapter Ten

JEREMIAH

Since Jeremiah's call came in 627, the thirteenth year of Josiah (Jer 1:2), he is the better part of a century later than the cluster of prophets we have been looking at. The inscription of the book (1:1-3) tells us that he was of a priestly family from the town of Anathoth in Benjamin. This puts his roots in northern territory and northern traditions. Anathoth was the home of Abiathar, who, before he became David's priest, had ministered at the shrine of Shiloh and therefore appears to have belonged to the priesthood of Israel's old Tribal League. Jeremiah may well have been of the same priestly family. Thus, though like Isaiah he preached in Jerusalem, the native soil that nourished him was far different. The kings under whom Jeremiah prophesied, according to the inscription, were Josiah (640–609), Jehoiakim (609–598), and Zedekiah (597–587); there were, in fact, two other kings during this period: Jehoahaz, who reigned briefly after Josiah, and Jehoiachin, who reigned equally briefly after Jehoiakim.

The period of Jeremiah's ministry was a troubled time. It saw the fall of the Assyrian empire to a coalition of Medes and Babylonians (Nineveh, the Assyrian capital, fell in 612, and Haran, the last stronghold, in 609), the annihilation of Egyptian power in the area by the Babylonians (at the battle of Carchemish in 605), the passage of Judah to Babylonian vassalage (precise date unknown), the revolt of Jehoiakim against the Babylonians (598) and the first deportation to Babylon that it entailed (597), and the revolt of Zedekiah, which occasioned the destruction of Jerusalem and the second deportation to Babylon (587). The later chapters of the book tell of Jeremiah's unwelcome ministry among the remnant of Judah that fled to Egypt, dragging Jeremiah with them, after the assassination of Gedaliah, the governor set over Judah by the Babylonians (chs. 39–44). According to Jewish tradition it was there that he died at the hands of his own people.

MATERIALS IN THE JEREMIAH COLLECTION

The book of Jeremiah is a long one but it is not, like the book of Isaiah, to be split up into collections coming, often enough, from later hands; aside from chapters 46–51 ("oracles against the nations") most of the remaining chapters relate directly to Jeremiah.

Bernhard Duhm, early in the twentieth century, had distinguished Jeremiah's poetic oracles, material supplied by Baruch, and later expansions (comprising almost two-thirds of the book). Sigmund Mowinckel found three types of material, which he designated as A, B, and C. A represented poetic oracles of Jeremiah, B the work of an author (not Baruch) who told related experiences of the prophet, and C was made up of long speeches with a deuteronomic flavor from a much later time than Jeremiah. When John Bright wrote his commentary he considered it traditional to distinguish three types of materials: (1) poetic oracles, generally attributed to Jeremiah, in which the prophet speaks in the first person; (2) biographical prose, usually attributed to Baruch, Jeremiah's secretary and disciple; and (3) prose discourses, sermons based on the words of Jeremiah but as remembered and passed on by the circle of friends and followers—passages that often overlap, as to content, with the poetic oracles.[1] Although Bright describes the view of three types of material "as universally agreed" (p. lx), some years later Ernest Nicholson argued[2] that the prose materials, including what others have labeled biographical prose and prose discourses (for which distinction he finds no basis), are composed by the deuteronomists. He argued that the function of such narratives corresponds closely in thrust to those found in deuteronomic history, that they betray the same interest in the function of God's word through the prophet, its fulfillment, human reaction to it, etc. Basically he argues that the words of Jeremiah have been used as a basis for deuteronomic sermons to the exiles of the Babylonian captivity, sermons that set forth fundamental deuteronomic themes of obedience to the Law, results of disobedience, etc. Nicholson does not doubt that such sermons were based on genuine words of Jeremiah or that the events depicted rest on real happenings; he further holds that both the words of Jeremiah and the accounts of his life have been medi-

---

[1] John Bright, *Jeremiah.* AB 21 (Garden City, NY: Doubleday, 1965) lx–lxxiii.

[2] Ernest W. Nicholson, *Preaching to the Exiles: A Study of the Prose Tradition in the Book of Jeremiah* (Oxford: Blackwell, 1970).

ated through Baruch.[3] More recent commentators have proposed far more refined explanations of the origin of the book and attribute the great bulk of it to the time of Jeremiah; see especially the commentaries of William Holladay[4] and Jack R. Lundbom.[5]

We should remember that Jeremiah's own background (in the north, in priestly circles going back, very possibly, to the old tribal league) relates him to northern traditions of covenant, Sinai, Exodus, and law. Along with this is the fact that during his ministry Deuteronomy came to light (in 622, the eighteenth year of Josiah), and this could well have reinforced his native traditions. What is clear is that we find different preoccupations in Jeremiah's thought than in Isaiah's; he is not concerned with the Davidic kingship, the election of Zion, or other traditions at home in Jerusalem, as Isaiah was.

TEACHINGS

The early years of Jeremiah's ministry seem to have been in part concerned with the pagan encroachments under Manasseh and Amon and apparently continuing under Josiah. Here we find use of the bridal imagery introduced by Hosea, with some evident dependence on Hosea; this is not surprising, since they were both northern prophets. Many of his words at this time were directed against Baal worship and other pagan practices. In the early chapters we also find reference to *the foe from the north.* These may have been from his early period, though the dating of these oracles is disputed, some authors holding that they reflect the new situation after Babylon had crushed Egypt in the battle of Carchemish in 605. Presumably Josiah's reform did much to eradicate pagan practices. It is generally assumed that Jeremiah was sympathetic to the deuteronomic reform of Josiah, though he may have become disenchanted with it (cf.

---

[3] It should be noted that Nicholson follows Martin Noth in seeing deuteronomic history composed during the exile rather than, as is probably more commonly held, passing through two editions, one completed during the lifetime of Josiah and then a later one during the exile. One could accept much of Nicholson's argument regarding deuteronomic influence but see it already operative during Jeremiah's ministry and in the earliest formulation of the Jeremianic materials.

[4] William L. Holladay, *Jeremiah 1: A Commentary on the Book of Jeremiah, Chapters 1–25.* Hermeneia (Philadelphia: Fortress, 1986), and *Jeremiah 2: A Commentary on the Book of Jeremiah, Chapters 26–52.* Hermeneia (Minneapolis: Fortress, 1989), especially pp. 15–24 of the later volume.

[5] Jack R. Lundbom, *Jeremiah 1–20.* AB 21A (New York and London: Doubleday, 1999), especially pp. 92–101.

8:8), possibly because it could affect only externals, tearing down altars and other cult paraphernalia, but could not change the heart, where Jeremiah saw the problem to lie (see below). Not many of his oracles can be attributed to the time of Josiah with any security.

Jehoiakim is judged as wicked by the deuteronomic historians, and apparently Jeremiah concurred. The "woe" pronounced upon him in 22:13-19 is an important passage for a number of reasons: it demonstrates something of Jeremiah's heroic courage in speaking such strong words against a tyrannical king who was willing to use his power unscrupulously (cf. his treatment of the prophet Uriah in 22:20-24), it demonstrates the kind of social abuses that were found in Judah at this time, and it provides a kind of "essential definition" of true religion (cf. Mic 6:8). It also illustrates that the *content* of a prophetic word is more important than whether certain externals that are predicted find fulfillment. The oracle blames Jehoiakim for oppressing his subjects through forced labor in order to build a magnificent palace for himself, an action that leads Jeremiah to suggest sarcastically that he thought thereby to demonstrate what a great ruler he was. The Hebrew term for the "neighbor" *(rēaᶜ)* who is forced to work without pay often refers to the person who stands next to one in a crowd rather than one who lives next door; it might be better translated "his fellow man." Obviously those compelled to do forced labor were the lower classes, but Jeremiah, with this term, puts them on a level with the king (or vice versa) and in so doing harks back to the egalitarian ideal of early Israel. The prophet contrasts the selfish and oppressive behavior of Jehoiakim with that of his father, Josiah. The "he did what was right and just" of v. 15 is explained in v. 16 as "he dispensed justice to the weak and the poor," and Jeremiah asks rhetorically, "Is this not true knowledge of me?" As we have already seen, "to know the LORD" is the equivalent of practicing true religion (cf. Hos 2:21-22 [*NRSV* 2:19-20]; 6:6). The oracle ends with a promise that Jehoiakim will be unlamented and unburied at his death. Whether or not that prediction was literally fulfilled,[6] the truth and value of what Jeremiah has to say here relates to the judgment he makes on vice and virtue and to the punishment or reward they deserve.

Other oracles from the time of Jehoiakim suggest that the populace in general could be accused of social crimes and of paganism. His famous "Temple sermon" (7:1-15), dated to the accession year of Jehoia-

---

[6] 2 Kings 24:5 mentions Jehoiakim's death ("he rested with his ancestors") but not the burial that is regularly reported of other kings of Judah.

kim (26:10), i.e., to 609, excoriates the people of Judah for oppressive social behavior and for pagan practices, warns against naïve trust in the Temple and YHWH's presence there, and threatens destruction for the Temple and city.[7] Elsewhere Jeremiah pronounces the most pessimistic judgment imaginable upon the people in general: the presence of only one just person in Jerusalem would cause the Lord to spare it, but such cannot be found (5:1); the corruption is found in both the high and low of society (5:4-5) and in all members of the family: father, mother, and children (7:18). And Jeremiah, in spite of his constant calls for repentance, expects improvement no more than he expects the Ethiopian to change his skin or the leopard his spots (13:23).

An example of Jeremiah's call for conversion is seen in 4:3-4:

> Till your untilled ground,
>   sow not among thorns.
> For the sake of the LORD, be circumcised,
>   remove the foreskins of your hearts.

This call for "circumcision" of the heart points to the interior aspect of Jeremiah's teaching. The heart is something he keeps coming back to. The call in this text to circumcise the heart corresponds to the accusation that Israel (along with other peoples) is "uncircumcised in heart" (9:25; *NRSV* 9:25-26). He speaks also of the heart of the people that is "stubborn and rebellious" and keeps them from having the reverence and fear of the Lord they ought to have (5:22-24). But it is perhaps especially in 17:9-10 that the mystery involved is commented on:

> More tortuous than all else is the human heart,
>   beyond remedy; who can understand it?
> I, the LORD, alone probe the mind
>   and test the heart,
> To reward everyone according to his ways,
>   according to the merit of his deeds.

All of this would leave us to think that there is no remedy, that the situation is hopeless. But Jeremiah, like Isaiah, knows a God whose power has no limits, and in the end he has some important things to say about God making things right, even in the human heart, the only place things can be made right. These texts (24:7; 31:33; 32:39) will be treated below.

---

[7] Jeremiah's defense of his message in the parallel account of 26:1-19 emphasizes that the threat is conditional, that destruction can be averted through repentance and conversion.

This interior aspect of Jeremiah's teaching is drawn, no doubt, from his own experience, an experience that was forced upon him by the circumstances of his vocation. We learn of the difficulties he experienced through passages such as 16:1-9, in which we are told that Jeremiah was isolated from normal human companionship (marriage, raising children, joining with those who mourn or celebrate) so that his life could be a sign, and 36:5, in which we learn, quite incidentally, that Jeremiah was forbidden to go to the Temple. And we may think of the many passages that detail the imprisonings and beatings he underwent (20; 32:2; 37:11-21; 38:1-13, 28). But most especially we have the so-called "confessions"[8] of Jeremiah: 11:18–12:6; 15:10-21; 17:14-18; 18:18-23; 20:7-13, 14-18. Such passages indicate that Jeremiah was excluded from much normal human companionship, even from certain aspects of Judah's religious life, and that he thus turned to the Lord in intimate communion. From such passages we also learn of the fidelity with which Jeremiah carried out his vocation, even though it came unasked and undesired and brought many trials upon him. These passionate appeals to the Lord for vindication brought him little consolation; indeed, at one point the Lord indicates that Jeremiah has further need of conversion before he will be fully a prophet (15:19). Von Rad is correct in saying that in Jeremiah prophecy reached a new development in that the prophet's message was contained not simply in his words but in his life itself.[9] We could perhaps more accurately say that Jeremiah is unique in this regard, for there is hardly another Old Testament prophet whose life we know in sufficient detail for this to be the case.

Another important area for our study of ethics can be seen in what Jeremiah has to say about Judah and the Babylonians, which corresponds fairly well to what was said of "policy" in Isaiah, though the *ʿēṣâ* terminology is found sparingly in Jeremiah. At the beginning of his ministry Assyria was still in charge, but by 612 Nineveh had fallen, by 609 the remnant of

---

[8] The term is applied by analogy with St. Augustine's *Confessions*. The term does not suggest confession of sins but comes from the Latin *confessio*, which indicates a giving of glory to God for the action of God that Augustine perceived in his own life.

[9] Gerhard von Rad, *Old Testament Theology* (Edinburgh and London: Oliver and Boyd, 1965) 2:36: "Jeremiah the man and his *via dolorosa* are now really described for their own sake. This . . . is closely connected with the fact that with Jeremiah prophecy entered upon a critical phase of its existence, and that a new concept of prophet was beginning to appear. . . . There was more to being a prophet than mere speaking. . . . [The account of the prophet's life] is given because in his case his life had been absorbed into his vocation as a prophet, and made an integral part of the vocation itself."

the Assyrian troops had been wiped out at Haran, and in 605 the Egyptians had been administered a staggering blow at Carchemish. Shortly after this (the sources do not give explicit information) Judah became a vassal of the Babylonians. We have already spoken of the "foe from the north" in the early chapters of the book, which may or may not refer to the Babylonians. But in 605 (see 36:1-7) Jeremiah dictated anew to Baruch all the oracles he had been speaking in the twenty-two years since his call in 627 and had him proclaim them in the Temple. Jeremiah charges Baruch with this task because he himself was not allowed to enter the Temple (36:6). No further explanation is given, but presumably the prohibition stems from official displeasure over the sort of things Jeremiah had been proclaiming. The obvious explanation for this new action is that the emergence of Babylon as a clear threat, thanks to their victory at Carchemish, would give special point to all he had been saying. Jehoiakim burned the scroll, which was brought to him after Jeremiah and Baruch had been warned to go into hiding; it seems to have had no effect on him, for he revolted against the Babylonians in 598. But from the time the Babylonians stormed down and obtained the city's surrender and took away Jehoiachin and thousands of others, Jeremiah did not cease to insist that the only course for Judah was submission to the Babylonians. He even went about wearing a wooden ox-yoke to illustrate the point and declared that YHWH had delivered all into the hands of the Babylonians (chs. 27–28).

Obviously this was not a popular message with the political and military leaders. Jeremiah was looked upon as a traitor.[10] No doubt he was considered a coward and worse. To encourage resistance is always considered much more acceptable and courageous, a course that leads to being esteemed as brave and patriotic. To do it in the name of religion, because "God is on our side," is even better. In fact, however, it often requires far greater bravery to risk being called a coward and a traitor, and sometimes it is the more religious thing to do. Other prophets contradicted Jeremiah,[11] displaying the sort of nationalism that goes all the way back to the very origins of Israelite prophecy. The nationalistic spirit lies very close to the surface, and people who esteem religion are often too prone to equate the national cause with God's cause, to identify the national enemy as God's

---

[10] Again we can think of Isaiah, who apparently was accused of conspiracy because of his opposition to official policy (Isa 8:12-13).

[11] The clearest example is seen in the encounter between Jeremiah and Hananiah in ch. 28, but in all probability the same sort of conflict lies behind the accusations Jeremiah levels against prophets who promise peace, who have not stood in the circle of YHWH's intimates *(sôd)*, in 23:16-18.

enemy. Popular voices such as those of Jerry Falwell and Hal Lindsey, influential in some circles, easily come to mind. Jeremiah's call was simply to carry the message the Lord gave him in these circumstances; the message was one of submission, and that encouragement to trust in God above all no doubt took greater courage than to urge resistance. Prophecy had come a long way since Samuel sent Saul to utterly wipe out the Amalekites. If *we* are to carry on the prophetic tradition, we need to be aware of the dangers of a nationalistic fervor that equates our nation's interest (often conceived very narrowly or shortsightedly) with the good; the "good" is always going to be that which promotes *global* peace and *global* justice.

THE NEW COVENANT: 31:31-34

Earlier we spoke of the emphasis Jeremiah places on the human heart as both the cause of the trouble and the place where correction must take place. Thus when Jeremiah speaks of restoration, the heart is where some of the important action occurs. This is seen in 24:7, where Jeremiah calls the exiles of 597 "good figs" (contrasted with the "bad figs," the people who remained in Judah) and says that YHWH "will give them a heart with which to understand that I am the LORD. They shall be my people and I shall be their God, for they shall return to me with all their heart" (v. 7). In 32:39 YHWH promises that "one heart and one way I will give them, that they may fear me always, to their own good and that of their children after them." But the most important oracle in this line is undoubtedly that of the "new covenant" in 31:31-34.[12] The passage speaks in a very positive

---

[12] Many question the Jeremian authorship of this piece. For Nicholson (*Preaching to the Exiles*, 82–84) this oracle is the work of the deuteronomists, and he points to passages in Deuteronomy that speak of the Law being in the heart (6:6 and 30:14) and of passages in the deuteronomic history that speak of covenant renewal. Against this it must be asserted that there is no deuteronomic parallel for the covenant coming to an end; covenant renewal is not the same as a new covenant—in fact, they are mutually exclusive ideas. The Jeremiah passage emphasizes the fact that the old covenant has come to an end and the new covenant is not like the old one. Many have seen the single reference to "the house of Judah" as a later addition to an oracle originally directed to the northern kingdom, and this too would militate against Nicholson's position. An article by H. D. Potter ("The New Covenant in Jeremiah XXXI 31–34," *VT* 33 [1983] 347–57) sees this oracle explicitly directed *against* the deuteronomic position. See also Moshe Weinfeld ("Jeremiah and the Spiritual Metamorphosis of Israel," *ZAW* 88 [1976] 17–56), who argues that the new covenant passage is distinctly different from Deuteronomy and reflects a certain disappointment with the literary-religious activity that failed to improve the spiritual attitude of the people; covenant would no longer be enforced from without through learning and indoctrination but would be implanted in the heart, whence it would not depart. This arose,

sense of what Yʜᴡʜ is to do in the future, making his *tôrâ* immediately present to each one, interiorly, not on tablets or any document, not even having to be communicated from someone else. The central provision of the covenant ("I will be their God, and they shall be my people," 31:33), which can hardly be improved upon, remains the same. But the result of Yʜᴡʜ's *tôrâ* [13] being immediately present is that they shall *know* him, and we have already commented on the significance of knowing the Lord.[14] And along with knowledge of God, which is virtually synonomous with true religion, goes forgiveness of sins.

The stark contrast between what Jeremiah experienced in his own ministry, in terms of the human reality, and what he expects for the future is as great as it was in the case of Isaiah. All that Jeremiah has to say about the universal sinfulness of the people he preached to, the perversity of the human heart, the pointlessness of expecting any change, suggests a despair of anything better for the future. The fact that Jeremiah does indeed paint a picture of far better things to come is a testimony to his faith in the power and goodness of God. What is of particular interest for our study is that most of the improvement Jeremiah looks to for the future relates to moral conversion. He has only a word or two about an ideal king to come, nothing about extraordinary fertility, no return to paradise, no reign of universal peace. But he does look forward to a time when the nations "will walk no longer in their hardhearted wickedness" (3:17), when the people of the northern tribes will again go on pilgrimage to Jerusalem (31:6), when Ephraim will return in repentance (31:18-19), when Judah's exiles will return to the Lord with all their heart (24:7; 29:13-14), and when the Lord will give them a heart to fear him (32:39).

he says, as a reaction to the failure of Josiah's reform and was inspired by the teaching of Hosea (cf. Hos 2:21-22; *NRSV* 2:19-20). Holladay holds that "the likeness to Deuteronomic diction, notably in the first half, is deliberate, since the setting proposed is the recitation of the Deuteronomic law during the feast of booths (tabernacles) in the autumn of 587, after the destruction of Jerusalem," *Jeremiah* 2:197.

[13] Most discussions seem to take as unquestioned that *tôrâ* here means "Law," but that is by no means clear. With the advent of Deuteronomy *tôrâ* can be used as a single term to sum up the whole complex of laws, but it could equally well have the more generalized meaning of "instruction," as it does, e.g., in Isa 2:3.

[14] See above, p. 138, on 22:15-16, with reference to Josiah.

Chapter Eleven

EXILIC PROPHECY:
EZEKIEL AND DEUTERO-ISAIAH

Some scholars have suggested that the phenomenon we call classical prophecy was restricted to the period of the monarchy. Bruce Vawter, although he ends his own presentation with Jeremiah, more correctly asserts that prophetism "did not perish with the exile. Ezekiel is the bridge from the prophetism of Israel to the prophetism of Judaism; there is true continuity, even as the postexilic religion was a legitimate offspring of preexilic Israel. With changed conditions there was a change in prophetic emphasis, but the tradition went on." Of the parts of the Isaianic collection we call Deutero-Isaiah and Trito-Isaiah he says that they "are in many respects among the most important of the Old Testament, fully worthy to stand with the great Isaiah as those who continued his work . . . and who perfected it."[1] Although in terms of outstanding personalities, originality of themes, and extent of material it would be hard to match the period of the monarchy with any later time, the period of the Babylonian exile provides us with two outstanding prophets, each of whom made his own inestimable contribution to the prophetic heritage. In addition, during the exile much work was done on earlier prophetic books, collecting, editing, arranging, and supplementing the materials that came to make up the books as we have them, much of it done by personalities themselves embued with prophetic charisms.

EZEKIEL

Ezekiel was one of those led into Babylon in the first deportation (597); it was there, in the fifth year, i.e., 593, that he received his call to

---

[1] Bruce Vawter, *The Conscience of Israel: Pre-exilic Prophets and Prophecy* (New York: Sheed & Ward, 1961) 182.

prophecy (Ezek 1:2). A very simple division of his book would distinguish three major sections:

(1) Chapters 1–24: oracles against Judah and Jerusalem
(2) Chapters 25–32: oracles against the nations
(3) Chapters 33–48: promises of restoration, namely:
    Chapters 33–37: restoration oracles of a general nature
    Chapters 38–39: Gog oracles
    Chapters 40–48: the new theocracy

On the basis of the content of the book and its organization one can distinguish two phases of Ezekiel's ministry: first a period in which he must warn the exiles that Jerusalem will surely fall; then, after the fall of the city, the time to encourage the exiles with promises of something better for the future. The second section (oracles against the nations) probably does not represent a particular phase of his ministry, but in the organization of the book functions as a transition from the first part to the third: destruction will surely come upon Judah because of its past wickedness, but the nations are no less guilty and deserve punishment no less than Judah.[2] Thus, before speaking of the good things YHWH has in store for Judah in the future, account is given of how God will deal with the sins of the nations. We conclude to this transitional character of the oracles against the nations because of their location between threats to Judah and promises for its future, and this location is owing to the organization imposed on the book by its editors. No doubt these oracles (those that are authentic) were uttered at various times during Ezekiel's ministry.

Ezekiel was a bizarre prophet in some ways. At times he seems almost to glory in describing the punishment to come, as in the "Song

---

[2] We see counterparts of this section in the collections of "Oracles against the Nations" in Isaiah (Isaiah 13–23) and Jeremiah (Jeremiah 46–51) and in some other books, especially Nahum, which, sometime before the destruction of Nineveh in 612, exults over the coming downfall of the mighty Assyrian empire, wicked destroyer of nations. In a sense such oracles give an answer to the poignant question Habakkuk directs to the Lord: "Why, then, do you gaze on the faithless in silence / while the wicked man devours / one more just than himself?" (Hab 1:13). In a long response (2:2-19) the prophet describes in detail the punishment to come upon the wicked nation. There is irony here, however. The very terms used to describe the tyrant's behavior seem to echo condemnations of Israel's rulers (cf. Hab 2:12: "Woe to him who builds a city by bloodshed, / and establishes a town by wickedness!" with Mic 3:10: "Who build up Zion with bloodshed, / and Jerusalem with wickedness!"). Thus on one hand and the other—punishment on Israel, punishment on the nations—the Lord is seen to be the vindicator of the weak against those who exploit them through the unjust use of power.

of the Sword" (21:13-22). At the death of his wife he manifests none of the customary signs of mourning (24:15-18); this is, however, one of his prophetic acts, intended to signify the Lord's indifference over the fall of Jerusalem (vv. 19-23). In addition to the more conventional type of oracle he used a range of prophetic acts, allegories, and visions, many of them strange and unusual, in which to couch his message. Some of his visions betray features later to become standard in apocalyptic.

Although Jeremiah was of a priestly family (Jer 1:1), little of this came through in his oracles. Ezekiel's priestly background (Ezek 1:3), however, is very prominent in his teachings. With him there is much emphasis on ritual cleanness, on certain kinds of ritual defilement, on keeping the Sabbath, emphases we have not found before.

With reference to the first part of the book, "Jerusalem must fall," Paul Joyce says:

> The first twenty-four chapters of the book of Ezekiel contain one of the most sustained and vehement declarations of judgment to be found anywhere in the prophetic literature of the Old Testament. These chapters assert in an unqualified way the responsibility of Israel for the fate which has befallen her. In so doing they offer a rationale for exile which is also a theodicy: Yahweh is indeed still both powerful and just and he is punishing his own people for their outrageous sins.[3]

In this, of course, Ezekiel was very much in the line of Jeremiah, though he expresses himself far more violently, without any hint of the grief that characterized to such an extent Jeremiah's oracles of doom. Joyce speaks of the violence of Ezekiel's depiction of disaster, then explains: "However, it must be read in the perspective of the catastrophic events which had already come upon Israel, events which demanded theological interpretation. Ezekiel offers a key to understanding the disaster which had engulfed the nations: this is not, he asserts, meaningless chaos; it is the just punishment of a sinful people by their powerful God."[4]

Ezekiel is pitiless and unrelenting, in this first part of the book, in his denunciation of the sins that are to bring about Israel's downfall. At times he can be specific, but more frequently his accusations are couched in general terms. He repeatedly complains about idol worship, all but a handful of the references being in the first twenty-four chapters. Somewhat surprisingly, he does not use the more common terms for idol, but rather *gillûl*,

---

[3] Paul Joyce, *Divine Initiative and Human Response in Ezekiel.* JSOTSup 51 (Sheffield: Sheffield Academic Press, 1989) 34.

[4] Ibid.

a term otherwise relatively rare. Jeremiah, his near contemporary, whose ministry overlapped his and who foretold the downfall of the kingdom in part for the same sort of sins, speaks much less frequently of idols, and in rather different terminology.[5] Again, usually in a fairly general way, Ezekiel speaks frequently (about forty times) of the "abominable things" (e.g., 8:17) Israel has done *(tôʿēbôt)*. This word, which, in the singular, can be used to designate a specific thing as taboo or forbidden (Lev 18:22; cf. Gen 43:32; 46:34), Ezekiel uses almost always in the plural in a more general sense.[6] Again, Jeremiah's usage is very different; the word is found only four times in his collection,[7] probably not all attributable to Jeremiah. To ground the reference to "abominable things" Ezekiel will often refer generally to "not living by my statutes nor fulfilling my ordinances" (5:7), though sometimes reference is made specifically to idolatry (8:6, 13, 15; 14:6), to infant sacrifice (16:36; 23:39), to adultery and/or incest (22:11; 33:26), to admitting foreigners into the sanctuary (44:7). Many of these generalized references to idolatry and abominable behavior occur in the three chapters in which Ezekiel reviews, from his own unique point of view, Israel's history, two of the chapters utilizing the "Israel as Yhwh's bride" theme (chs. 16; 23),[8] the other (ch. 20)[9] in more prosaic terms. This is all part of the prophet's

---

[5] Jeremiah's idol terminology may be said to be functional rather than technical. While *pesel* and *pāsîl* are found in his collection occasionally (8:19; 10:14; 50:37; 51:17, 47, 52—including passages not usually attributed to Jeremiah), more frequently they are referred to as emptiness or vanity *(hebel:* 2:5; 10:8; 14:22; 16:19), deception *(tarmît:* 8:5; *šeqer:* 13:25), detestable thing *(šiqqûṣ:* 7:30; 16:18; 32:34). Only once do we find *gillûl,* in 50:2, among the "oracles against the nations."

[6] The exceptions, accepting the masoretic pointing, would be 16:50; 18:12; 22:11; and 33:26. This accords with the generalized usage found in Lev 18:26, 29, 30, and differs from the singular to specify a particular act as forbidden ("You shall not lie with a male as with a woman; such a thing is *tôʿēbâ"*—Lev 18:22). See earlier discussion on *tôʿēbâ* in Chapter Eight, pp. 118–119.

[7] 6:15 ǁ 8:12; 44:4, 22.

[8] The first of these speaks of one woman espoused to Yhwh, as in both Hosea and Jeremiah; the other speaks of two sisters, representing the northern and southern kingdoms, as in Jer 3:6-10. Hosea and Jeremiah utilized the theme to underline both the personal character of Israel's rejection of its loving God and God's continued love and longing for Israel. In Ezekiel's treatment, however, the emphasis is almost exclusively on Israel's infidelity, which the prophet describes in crude detail, and the punishment it deserves.

[9] In addition to the accusation of idolatry, formulated in various ways, Ezekiel also makes reference in this chapter to violation of the Sabbath (vv. 13, 16, 20-21, 24) and to infant sacrifice (v. 31)—which, illogically, is also attributed to Yhwh's giving them "statutes that were not good, and ordinances through which they could not live" (vv. 25-26). This is a *crux* into which we need not enter.

strategy to point to the inevitable punishment of destruction to come upon the people.

Chapter 22 is somewhat reminiscent of chapter 20 in its blanket condemnation of Jerusalem for idolatry, but here the crimes are given in far richer detail. There are the multiple references to idolatry, but only one reference to "abominable deeds" (v. 2). Beyond that, we find reference to bloodshed (vv. 3, 4, 6, 9, 12, 13, 27), despising of parents (v. 7), extortion from resident aliens and oppression of widow, orphan, and the poor and needy (vv. 7, 29), violation of the Sabbath (vv. 8, 26; cf. also 23:38), sexual abuses (vv. 9-11), acceptance of bribes (v. 12), exaction of usury (v. 12), and failure to distinguish between the sacred and profane, between the clean and unclean (v. 26). In all this Ezekiel manifests his priestly concerns, but also his concerns for what we call social justice, much in line with the earlier classical prophets.

Ezekiel also goes into greater detail of what he considers wrongdoing in those passages in which he speaks of individual responsibility and the need for and possibility of conversion. This matter is dealt with in depth in chapter 18, where the starting point is a proverb then making the rounds, "Fathers have eaten green grapes, / thus their children's teeth are set on edge" (v. 2; cf. also Jer 31:29-30). The proverb tended to absolve the exiles of guilt and to complain that they were suffering for the sins of previous generations. Ezekiel's reply is that punishment does not pass from generation to generation. An individual is rewarded or punished in accord with his own deeds. The virtuous man, in Ezekiel's description, is (negatively) not guilty of idolatry, adultery, oppression, or robbery, and (positively) returns the pledge and judges honestly—all things relating to Israel's legislation (cf. "if he lives by my statutes and is careful to observe my ordinances," v. 9). But the virtuous man also manifests the sort of concern for the lowly that can hardly be legislated: "if he gives food to the hungry and clothes the naked" (v. 7). Therefore we again have a mix of concerns that can be characterized as both priestly and related to social justice. To illustrate the point that each one bears the responsibility for his/her own sins and receives the reward of his/her own merit, Ezekiel then runs through the case of a wicked son of such a virtuous man, a son who commits all those crimes the father avoided; Ezekiel asserts "he shall surely die; his death shall be his own fault" (v. 13). A third case is the son of a wicked father, who, although having the example of his father, pursues a virtuous life: "this one shall not die for the sins of his father, but shall surely live" (v. 17).

Now the question arises of whether or not the point Ezekiel is here insisting on relates to individual retribution. Joyce does not think so, but asserts that it is by no means clear that Ezekiel 18 asserts "individual responsibility" in the sense he defines it ("the moral independence of contemporary individuals; in other words, that particular men and women are judged in isolation from their contemporaries"). He believes that the chapter is intended "to demonstrate the collective responsibility of the contemporary house of Israel for the national disaster which she is suffering." He goes on to assert that "it is the cause of the nation's predicament that is being explored; the proverb blames the sins of previous generations for the sufferings of the present, and accordingly the individuals of the test-cases each represent a generation."[10] Specifically of what happens to the righteous son of a wicked father, he says: "we see that he is asserting that if the present generation were righteous they would not be suffering; since they are suffering, this must be because of their own sins. Thus Ezekiel's hearers cannot be the righteous sons of wicked men as they suppose themselves to be."[11]

The position taken by Joyce is certainly defensible, but there are points at which it can be questioned. The teaching in chapter 18 echoes that of 33:10-20. "Echoes" is used designedly, for Blenkinsopp has argued that 33:10-20 is the source from which chapter 18 is taken. For him the location of that pericope, "the postcatastrophic situation . . . serves as a point of transition between judgment (chs. 1–24) and restoration (chs. 34–48)." He says that "the despairing cry of the community shows that the disaster at last brought home to them the consciousness of sin. . . . It seems, then, that Ezekiel's preaching has at last begun to take effect and that they are disposed to listen."[12] And the emphasis in this pericope is to give answer to their question: "How can we survive?" (33:10)—an answer given in the Lord's statement, "I take no pleasure in the death of the wicked man, but rather . . . that he may live. Turn, turn from your evil ways! Why should you die, O house of Israel?" (33:11).[13] Joyce may be correct in asserting that individual responsibility is something presupposed in Ezekiel (p. 72), but while Ezekiel may have presupposed it, the proverb about green grapes suggests his contemporaries did not. Yet Joyce's reconstruction supposes they did, since it is taken as the major

---

[10] Joyce, *Divine Initiative*, 36.

[11] Ibid. 46.

[12] Joseph Blenkinsopp, *Ezekiel. Interpretations: A Bible Commentary for Teaching and Preaching* (Louisville: John Knox, 1990) 147–49.

[13] Joyce asserts that "the final section of [chapter 18] explores the theme of repentance" (p. 34) but that "the purpose of the chapter is to demonstrate the collective responsibility" (*Divine Initiative*, 36).

premise in his syllogistic argument: each one is punished for his or her own sins, but the exilic generation is being punished; ergo, they must have sinned.

Two other passages incline toward the same conclusion. The vision of the avenging angels in chapter 9 puts a clear emphasis on the distinction between the innocent and the guilty and on the deliverance of the former from the punishment that is to fall upon Jerusalem. The supposition underlying the scene is that the great mass of people are guilty of the crimes of idolatry that have been shown to Ezekiel in vision (8:3-18); therefore it is only the others, those who "moan and groan over all the abominations that are practiced within [Jerusalem]," whose foreheads are marked with the tau by the scribe-angel (9:4) who will be spared. Clearly this is a one-to-one sort of retribution, with no reference to different generations or any debate about one generation suffering for the sins of another. Individual retribution again comes to the fore in 14:12-20. Ezekiel is not speaking of successive generations, but uses legendary figures, people famous for their virtue—somewhat surprisingly, all non-Israelites. The figure of Noah is particularly apposite in this context because although the biblical text, while speaking of universal corruption, says that "Noah found favor with the LORD" (Gen 6:8) and the Lord says "you alone in this age have I found to be truly just" (7:1); Noah's wife, sons, and daughters-in-law are preserved along with him. In the new situation Ezekiel describes, however, "these three men . . . [could] save only themselves by their virtue. . . . They could save neither sons nor daughters" (Ezek 14:14, 20, 16). Joyce maintains also in this passage that individual responsibility "is taken for granted," but concedes that "it is certainly the case that the passage asserts that this principle is to be operated with unprecedented rigour."[14] Blenkinsopp, more accurately in my opinion, says: "His solution to the problem, which is basically a problem of theodicy, is consistent with his teaching on personal accountability which will be set out schematically in chapter 18. . . . The situation addressed by Ezekiel called for emphasis on personal accountability and the acceptance of responsibility, and this is the main point of the case history presented here."[15] Note that this is a far cry from the assertion of Jeremiah that the Lord would spare Jerusalem if only one just person could be found in it (Jer 5:1). Although this passage might be a shaky foundation on which to erect a theological argument, given the colorful

---

[14] Joyce, *Divine Initiative*, 72.

[15] Blenkinsopp, *Ezekiel*, 73–74.

rhetoric of the piece, it certainly does not rest on a presupposition such as Joyce sees in Ezekiel. To justify the destruction of all, Jeremiah argues for the wickedness of all (Jer 5:1-5; 7:16-18).

Ezekiel's restoration material, while continuing to echo the more external, often priestly, concerns such as idolatry, ritual cleanliness, and Sabbath observance, also contains elevated and interior elements. Yhwh excoriates the unworthy "shepherds" (i.e., leaders and rulers) for having exploited those under their charge rather than nurturing them (34:1-10). Although generally Ezekiel is intent on emphasizing the transcendence of Yhwh,[16] condescension and immanence are in evidence as Yhwh himself comes into the midst of his sheep and himself acts as shepherd, gathering the scattered sheep, tending and pasturing them, binding up their wounds (34:11-16).

Jeremiah had recognized that the problem of sin and evil was rooted in the human heart and had spoken of God's stratagem for healing the evil at its source (see Chapter Ten). Ezekiel, too, sees the need for a change of heart and uses the bold image of "taking from your bodies your stony hearts and giving you natural hearts" (36:26)—part of an all-encompassing program that involves cleansing from all impurity with clean water and giving not only this new heart, but also a new spirit (v. 26),[17] which is specified as "my spirit" and appears to be the force that will enable them to walk in God's statutes, to observe and do God's decrees (v. 27). Such gifts will enable them to be truly a covenant people, and Ezekiel repeats the covenant formula, "you shall be my people, and I will be your God" (v. 28). What Israel had been exhorted to do in 18:31 ("Cast away from you all the crimes you have committed, and make for yourselves a new heart and a new spirit"), but could in no way do by its own power, is here granted by the grace of God.

---

[16] As seen, e.g., in the constant address to the prophet as "son of man" (= "mortal," as opposed to the divinity who addresses him), in the frequent explanation, even in oracles of restoration, that Yhwh acts "for the sake of my holy name," etc.

[17] It would be difficult to do justice to the important and multifaceted role of the spirit in Ezekiel. It is the spirit that provides the motive force for the cherubim of the chariot that provides the Lord's transportation (1:12, 20), that transports Ezekiel himself (8:3; 11:1, 24; 37:1; 43:5), that enables him to prophesy (11:5), and that gives life to the dry bones that represent Israel (37:5, 6, 9-10). This last scene, in which new life is given to Israel, is a sort of reprise in symbolic terms of the more prosaic promise in 36:25-28, as can be seen in 37:14: "I will put my spirit in you that you may live" (cf. also 39:29).

Ezekiel recognizes the evil that lay behind the division of Israel into two nations, which, one can conclude from the biblical accounts, was occasioned by Solomon's oppression through taxation and forced labor and perpetuated by Jeroboam's desire for power. Presumably the thought that any true restoration would include a righting of that primeval wrong is what led Ezekiel to postulate a reunion of Judah and "Joseph" (= Israel) in 37:15-28. While the restoration of Judah to its own land could be conceived (and in fact took place), it required a healthy imagination (which Ezekiel certainly had) to conceive of a restoration and reunion with Judah of a nation that had ceased to exist well over a century before. Jeremiah, too, had spoken of the restoration of the northern kingdom (much of the material in Jeremiah 31), or at least, more credibly, of the return of a remnant (Jer 3:14). The division and its continuation was wrong and unnatural, the result of sin and rivalry, and both of these prophets believed in a God who could right all wrongs.

Ezekiel's description, in chapters 40–48, of what may be termed the new and ideal theocracy again betrays his priestly concerns, but at the basis of it lies the conviction of God's holiness and the need for Israel to live in a way consonant with being in the presence of the holy God. This concern can be seen especially in chapter 44, but in one way or another it pervades this whole section. It is interesting to note that while some earlier passages looked for an idealized Davidic ruler ("I, the Lord, will be their God, and my servant David shall be prince among them," 34:24; cf. 37:22, 24-25), the utopian vision of chapters 40–48 is somewhat more realistic. It provides detailed instructions for the role of the "prince" (never "king") in the cult, but also lays down prohibitions against the use of his power to exploit the people or deprive them of their property (cf. 45:8, 9; 46:18).

DEUTERO-ISAIAH

By Deutero-Isaiah (or Second Isaiah) is meant, of course, the extraordinary prophet responsible for chapters 40–55 of the book of Isaiah, whose ministry dates to the years of the exile. The general consensus of scholars is that his ministry was exercised in Babylon, during the closing years of the exile. Presumably the meteoric rise of Cyrus of Anshan in Persia, vassal king within the empire of the Medes, and the success of his revolt against the Medes, was seen by this prophet as the beginning of the fulfillment of Yhwh's promises of liberation and restoration. Probably Cyrus' capture of Ecbatana, capital of the Medes, was the signal to Deutero-Isaiah that his vocation to console and strengthen the exiles could begin.

This background helps explain why the work of Deutero-Isaiah was so different in so many ways from the prophets who preceded him. They, for the most part, excoriated Israel for its sins and threatened punishment to come. But now the blow had fallen, so the time to threaten was past; the time to strengthen the weak knees and faint heart had come, lest remorse be replaced by despair. Thus the tirades present in all the prophets we have studied from Amos through Ezekiel are largely absent from Deutero-Isaiah.

Instead, the Lord is presented as the deliverer of the weak and oppressed, much like the God who delivered Israel from slavery in Egypt. Indeed, the theme of the Exodus is evoked more than once. The deliverance of the weak and enslaved was clearly an important theme in the traditions that form the accounts of Israel's oppression in Egypt and the Exodus narrative (cf. Exod 3:7-10), but was not very much in evidence as Israel dispossessed the native Canaanites to take over the land of promise or in the days when David was subjecting neighboring peoples to Israel's rule. And though Israel soon became the vassal of larger and more powerful nations, the emphasis, at least in the prophetic books, was usually on the sins of God's people that deprived them of God's help, rather than upon Israel as an oppressed people. Ezekiel even accuses Judah of treachery for rebelling against Babylonia and transferring loyalty to Egypt (17:1-21). But in Deutero-Isaiah Judah in exile is again the object of Yhwh's compassion and saving deeds. Isaiah of Jerusalem saw the nations as Yhwh's instruments to punish a guilty Judah (5:26-29; 7:18-19, 20; 10:5-15), but now Cyrus the Persian is his instrument for overthrowing Babylon, to the end that Judah should be released (41:1-5, 25; 44:24–45:8).

Because Judah is held captive by the power of a mighty nation, its deliverance can be thought of as a new Exodus. The poet dramatically depicts the return across the Syro-Arabian desert, the people led and indeed carried by Yhwh (Isa 40:3-5, 10-11; 41:17-20), much like Israel being led across the desert of Sinai. But, perhaps because of greater sophistication, it is now not a matter of Yhwh effecting the release by means of plagues directed against the captor nation but rather by means of another nation, Persia, utilized as Yhwh's instrument. Thus although we see Yhwh here as deliverer of the captive Israel, it is not exactly the same sort of recital of saving history as what we saw in Amos, which showed Israel how it was to behave through "imitation of God" (cf. Amos 2:9-10 and pp. 13, 81, 90 above).[18] In the Exodus event, although God's election of Israel and love

---

[18] Relevant here is Thomas Leclerc's observation highlighting the difference between *mišpāṭ* in Isaiah and in Deutero-Isaiah with three observations: the hendiadys *mišpāṭ*

toward the people provide motivation, the oppression and cruelty of the Egyptians and the desire to free Israel from slavery form a much more prominent motive. In Deutero-Isaiah, on the other hand, since Israel is in captivity because Yhwh is punishing it for sin, much less attention is paid to the concept of deliverance from slavery and oppression,[19] much more to God's tender and totally unmerited love for Israel.

If this prophet gives less in the way of material for the "imitation of God" theme, he perhaps compensates with a clearer indication of what, for lack of a better term, may be called "grace." The references to God's saving acts in the past are invoked more as a paradigm of what God is about to do, rather than as a paradigm of how Israel ought to behave, based on the example of divine behavior. While Israel's sinfulness, past and present, is bluntly acknowledged,[20] the tender mercies of the Lord in loving, redeeming, and restoring Israel are everywhere insisted upon.[21] It is precisely where the recipients are incapable of helping themselves that grace is most clearly manifested, so that, paradoxically enough, words such as "worm" and "maggot" function as terms of endearment by stressing simultaneously Israel's helplessness and Yhwh's redeeming help (41:14). In some cases these "grace" passages are in fact continuations of passages that speak of Israel's sinfulness, so that Yhwh's gracious response to Israel's need is quite explicit. Although occasionally we find God's blessings presented as contingent on Israel's obedience (48:18-19), normally the good things of the future appear as absolute promises. This sort of love and grace is calculated to evoke a response of love, commitment, and loyalty far freer, deeper, and longer lasting than that evoked by simple gratitude for deliverance from slavery.

However, if we shift our perspective from a national or communal level to the individual level, we can say that Deutero-Isaiah's utilization of the theme of Israel as Yhwh's bride can be very instructive. Hosea and Jeremiah used the theme in what might be called a bipolar fashion, to emphasize both the heinous nature of Israel's apostasy and the constancy of Yhwh's love and tenderness; Ezekiel, on the other hand, used it quite

ûṣĕdāqâ does not occur in Deutero-Isaiah, but rather ṣĕdāqâ is often paired with yešûʿâ; the social aspect recedes into the background, and the idiom of the courtroom moves to center stage (*Yahweh is Exalted in Justice: Solidarity and Conflict in Isaiah* [Minneapolis: Fortress, 2001] 92).

[19] This is not wholly lacking, however; cf., e.g., 51:21-23.

[20] E.g., 40:2; 42:18-25; 43:22-28; 44:22; 48:1-11; 50:1; 51:17-20 (though not explicitly stated, the Lord's wrath referred to in this last text was undoubtedly occasioned by Israel's sins).

[21] E.g., 41:8-12; 42:16; 43:1-8; 44:1-5; 46:3-4, 12-13; 49:8-18; 51:14-16, 21-23; 54:4-17.

single-mindedly to drive home the lesson of Israel's infidelity.[22] But Deutero-Isaiah uses it only to point up Yʜᴡʜ's love and forgiveness (54:4-8). There is here no reference to Israel's sins or to anything that would have provoked or justified the "divorce"; Israel is "a wife forsaken and grieved in spirit" (v. 6), from whom Yʜᴡʜ hid his face "in an outburst of wrath" (v. 8)—almost arbitrarily, one might conclude. But if we are to forgive, that is the way forgiveness should be, not laced with grievances over past wrongs, not recalling past injuries; it should simply be total and unconditional. In this way Yʜᴡʜ's reconciliation with his bride is a paradigm to be imitated for all human reconciliation, including, but not restricted to, the case of estranged spouses.[23] And this accords with the merciful nature of Yʜᴡʜ as everywhere attested in the Old Testament, beginning with the self-revelation to Moses on Mount Sinai (Exod 34:5-7) and echoed elsewhere, especially in the Psalter.

Earlier prophets had inveighed against idolatry, especially Ezekiel,[24] but Deutero-Isaiah's explicit monotheism gives a particular edge to his words.[25] In addition to the religious infidelity involved in idol worship, it is now claimed to involve the foolishness of worshiping a non-entity or, more accurately, it is now said that it is only the material idol, the product of a worker's hands, that is worshiped, since there is no other reality behind it. So Deutero-Isaiah does not so much inveigh against Israel for worshiping idols as satirize both the process of manufacturing them and of putting trust in them.

---

[22] See Ezekiel 16 and 23. Ezekiel also departs from Hosea and Jeremiah in not seeing the Exodus period as a honeymoon of faithful response (Hos 2:17b [*NRSV* 2:15b]; Jer 2:2); for Ezekiel, Israel's infidelities began before the departure from Egypt (cf. Ezek 23:3; cf. 20:6-9).

[23] Too often human "forgiveness" is tempered with the reservation, whether expressed or not, "I'll forgive but I won't forget." Forgiveness without forgetting is no forgiveness at all.

[24] The term "idolatry" as the object of prophetic condemnation is often used in a very broad sense to cover almost any kind of religious infidelity. What Hosea polemicizes against, to avoid this broad usage, is "pagan worship," with no emphasis on idols themselves (which may not have been present at all, since many authors think Israel's crime was syncretistic worship of Yʜᴡʜ rather than outright Baalism). Ezekiel and Deutero-Isaiah, on the other hand, make frequent reference to the idols themselves.

[25] It is incomprehensible, at least to me, that some will not admit explicit monotheism in the teaching of Deutero-Isaiah, in spite of passages such as 43:10b; 45:5, 21-22; 46:9. If this is only "incipient monotheism," as some have termed it, it may be asked what would be required for full-blown monotheism.

The evil involved in idol worship is heightened by the contrast with the matchless majesty of YHWH that Deutero-Isaiah so eloquently depicts, as in 40:12-26, a passage that describes the making of an idol, a creature of wood and metal, produced by human hands (vv. 19-20),[26] to underline the difference from YHWH, and that twice hurls the challenge "To whom can you liken God/me?" (vv. 18, 25). While the pagan gods' inability to do *anything* shows that they are nothings (41:21-24), YHWH presents himself as Lord of history, bringing about those things he has been able to foretell precisely because he is the power that brings them to pass.

Although, as previously noted, Deutero-Isaiah's mission is not primarily to reproach his hearers for their sins, some elements of his ethical teaching do emerge from the culpable behavior he refers to. Generally speaking, however, the allusions are too vague to allow us to speak of specific vices. The people see without taking note (42:18-20, 25),[27] refuse to walk in the Lord's ways (42:24), fail to call upon him and offer him fitting worship (43:22-24),[28] invoke God without sincerity *(lō᾿ be᾿ĕmet)* or justice *(wĕlō᾿ biṣĕdāqâ)* (48:1), are stubborn and treacherous and a rebel from birth (48:4, 8), might attribute YHWH's acts to its idols had he not foretold them (48:5), do not heed his Servant and therefore walk in darkness (50:10-11).

The virtues most esteemed by Deutero-Isaiah are manifest in what he says of the Servant of the Lord,[29] namely, that he establishes the Lord's

---

[26] The *NAB* joins to these verses, as part of the same anti-idol polemic, 41:6-7.

[27] In this we are reminded of Isaiah's strictures on the people of Judah, especially the leaders, for failing to see, to hear, to understand, to be aware of what the Lord was bringing to pass (1:3; 5:12-13, 19; 6:9-10).

[28] This detailed listing of acts of worship reminds us of Isaiah, but by way of contrast: Isaiah similarly listed various acts of sacrifice, prayer, and worship, not by way of blaming Judah for not offering them, but only to say that they were unacceptable to the Lord because right dispositions, especially those relating to social justice, were absent (1:10-17).

[29] That is, the figure depicted in 42:1-4; 49:1-6; 50:4-9; 52:13–53:12. Modern attempts to lay the Servant to a final resting place have been no more successful than those of the fourth song who assigned him "a burial place with evildoers." In spite of Tryggve Mettinger's confident dismissal (*Farewell to the Servant Songs: A Critical Examination of the Exegetical Maxim* [Lund: Gleerup, 1983]), authors continue to debate the figure and its significance. There is no need for the present work to enter into the thorny question of the identity of the Servant, e.g., whether a personification of a collective Israel, an individual, a "corporate personality," etc., since we are only looking at the traits manifested in the descriptions of the Servant. On the other hand, the position taken here is that these ideal portraits stand in contrast to the characterization of Israel found elsewhere in Deutero-Isaiah; further, it is held that these passages do come from the author of Isaiah 40–55 and are not interpolated from some other context or by some other hand.

judgment *(mišpāṭ)* and instruction *(tôrâ)* throughout the earth (42:4), toils and spends his strength and undergoes sufferings in the mission entrusted to him (49:4; 50:6), has an "open ear" for hearing (= obeying) and (unlike Israel) does not rebel or turn back (50:5), submits meekly to harsh treatment (53:7); sinless himself, he patiently gives his life for the sins of others (53:4-5, 10-12). However we interpret this mysterious figure, it is clear that he demonstrates the ideal of what the prophet believes Israel should be. Whereas Israel is basically a passive recipient of the grace, forgiveness, and deliverance of the Lord (aside from the call to bear witness, as in 43:12; 44:8), the Servant actively pursues a mission of establishing the Lord's rule. Moreover, in the Servant we learn that, however generous the Lord is in granting grace and forgiveness, sin is not lightly disposed of; somehow, mysteriously, the Lord requires that the Servant be his instrument for atoning for sin through innocent suffering.

Chapter Twelve

POSTEXILIC PROPHECY

The great themes of Israel's prophetic heritage belong mainly to the period of the monarchy and, to a lesser extent, to the exile. Postexilic prophecy continues to present many problems and puzzles that intrigue scholars, but it clearly does not gain attention comparable to that enjoyed by the earlier periods.[1] Whether we know the names of the figures that stand behind some of the prophetic collections of this period is questioned. The name Malachi means "my messenger" and could be simply a creation to go with the collection rather than a historical recollection of its originator.[2] The same could be said of Obadiah, a name that means "Servant of YHWH." In the Book of Zechariah it is usual to distinguish two collections, chapters 1–8 and chapters 9–14, the latter designated as Deutero-Zechariah and often further subdivided into smaller compositions from various periods.[3] In the realm of ethical thought we shall not find here a great deal to add to what has been covered in the preceding chapters. The great themes of social justice, submission to the Lord's

---

[1] Joseph Blenkinsopp, *A History of Prophecy in Israel* (rev. and enlarged ed. Louisville: John Knox, 1996), is quite correct in taking issue with "the once commonly accepted assumption that for all practical purposes prophecy came to an end with the Babylonian exile" (p. 195). His own book devotes 146 pages (48–193) to the period from the beginning through Deutero-Isaiah, plus a generous fifty-two pages to cover the later period (194–245). Bruce Vawter speaks of "the vigor of postexilic prophecy" but says that it "did not long survive the postexilic restoration" (*The Conscience of Israel* [New York: Sheed & Ward, 1961] 283).

[2] Indeed, David L. Petersen, *Zechariah 9–14 and Malachi: A Commentary.* OTL (Louisville: Westminster John Knox, 1995) treats the last part of Zechariah and the book of Malachi as a single composition.

[3] For some of the debate on whether Zechariah 9–14 should be considered prophetic literature see Petersen, *Zechariah . . . Malachi,* 23–24. His own conclusion is that "Zechariah 9–14 possesses the essential hallmarks of prophetic literature."

plan, and action in history reappear to an extent, but much less that is new will be gleaned for our study of prophetic ethics. Since the present work is designed to emphasize what is unique in the contribution of each prophet, without going over the same sort of material in different prophets, we will here glean only a few points that have not already been elaborated.

HAGGAI AND ZECHARIAH 1–8

These two prophets are very close in time chronologically and in some of the themes they treat. The first group to return to Judea from Babylon came in 538, their repatriation allowed by the decree of Cyrus published that year. The altar of burnt offerings seems to have been re-built almost at once, the cult resumed, and a beginning made on building a new Temple. However, opposition from the Samaritans (the Israelite remnant in the northern territories) and surrounding peoples, and dis-couragement stemming from multiple causes, brought the work to an end. Haggai and Zechariah appear on the scene almost simultaneously, around the autumn of 520, and both exhort the people to resume work on the Temple. Haggai attributed the drought and other trials the returnees were experiencing to indifference to the project; he promised speedy relief if they would hasten its completion (Hag 1:2–2:4). Zechariah's exhortations were less direct, largely implied in promises of restoration and future glory for the land, but with some explicit references to the rebuilding, usually under the hand of Zerubbabel, governor and Davidic heir (Zech 1:16; 4:9; 6:12-13, 15; 8:9).

In these postexilic prophets we see a new emphasis. Whereas the prophets of the monarchy, and here we may mention Amos, Hosea, Isaiah, Micah, and Jeremiah in particular, were at pains to warn Israel against naïve trust in the cult and in the Temple—even in terms that seemed almost to condemn the cult itself—these two make the rebuild-ing of the Temple an important goal. This new emphasis illustrates the fact that the mission of the prophet is dependent on the conditions of time and place. Those who had returned from exile needed a focus and an identity, and in urging the rebuilding of the Temple, Haggai and Zechariah were helping to make sure that focus would be religious and in the line of the traditional faith. Other considerations were also pres-ent. There was a serious temptation to despair, which their promises of a glorious future would help to counter. And the promises of a glorious future spoken earlier by Ezekiel and Deutero-Isaiah were tied up with a restored Zion and could hardly be a source of hope as long as the Temple lay in ruins.

In 520 there was also the hope that the Persian empire was collapsing, and such collapse could be thought to presage the establishment of the new order expected by the prophets and implied in the words of Ezekiel and Deutero-Isaiah. In 522 the Persian king Cambyses committed suicide on his way back from a campaign in Egypt,[4] and Darius, a general of royal blood, was proclaimed king by his fellow officers. With a usurper on the throne and a new claimant far afield the situation was ripe for uprisings throughout the vast Persian empire, which appeared to be shaken to its foundations.[5] The expectations of great things about to happen (Hag 2:20-22) were soon extinguished, as Darius showed himself capable of putting down the rebellions and restoring order (Zech 1:7-17). Nevertheless, the efforts of these two prophets indicate how important true worship is to the prophetic spirit. Each sees that "that day of small beginnings" was prelude to great things to come (Zech 4:10). And Zechariah, at least, exhorts the people by reminding them of the words of the former prophets concerning true judgment and compassion for the weak and lowly, tells them that punishment came because Israel had neglected those words (7:7-14), and instructs them how they are to behave in this new time of grace (8:14-17).

MALACHI

As suggested earlier, the *malʾākî* of the inscription of this book (1:1) probably is to be understood literally as "my [i.e., Yhwh's] messenger" rather than as a proper name. The period would seem to be after the rebuilding of the Temple and before the reforms of Ezra and Nehemiah, therefore during the first half of the fifth century. The harsh words about Edom in the opening oracle (1:2-5) reflect the hostility that had festered

---

[4] The reason for this would seem to be the report that a usurper was on the throne of Persia, a usurper who gave himself out to be the dead brother of Cambyses, whom Cambyses is thought to have murdered.

[5] It may have been these same circumstances that encouraged Haggai to think that the Davidic kingship would be restored in the person of Zerubbabel; cf. Hag 2:23 (see Jer 22:24-27 for the significance of the signet ring imagery). Assuming that v. 23 is a continuation of vv. 20-22, the reference to "the twenty-fourth day of the month" in v. 20 apparently links back to v. 18, which names the ninth month. However, this is generally taken as an error for "sixth month," i.e., August/September 520, at which time Darius was still quelling the rebellion. Zechariah seems to have entertained similar expectations for the restoration of the monarchy (Zech 6:9-15), though this oracle is not dated.

between Israel and Edom, supposedly related through their ancestors,[6] but also point up the gratuity of God's love for Israel, for which a love in return is to be expected.

In the case of Haggai and Zechariah we noted the shift in emphasis from the eighth- and seventh-century prophets: instead of warnings about the danger of putting trust in the Temple and the cult, their emphasis had been on the rebuilding of the Temple. In the collection that bears the name of Malachi we find some emphasis on propriety in the cult: Malachi, speaking in the name of the Lord, complains of the offering of defective animals as victims on the altar (1:6-9, 12-14), a practice forbidden in Lev 22:19-25. This does not reflect a merely ritualistic concern, but one that springs from a true religious spirit. To offer to God something less than perfect, something that would not even be acceptable to another human (cf. 1:8) is a departure from the reverence for the All Holy One. The defective gift reveals a defect in the intention of the giver. But Malachi's complaints have to do more with the priesthood than with the simple faithful (cf. 1:10-12). Criticism of the priests is implied also in the words concerning the messenger to come, part of whose task is to "purify the sons of Levi" (3:3).

In the teachings of the prophet Malachi we encounter an important point of social justice that we have not met before, relating to divorce. The subject is approached here not in terms of any Catholic-Protestant-Jewish controversy over divorce.[7] It is not a question here of the licitness or possibility of divorce, for Malachi speaks from an Old Testament perspective, and Mosaic legislation assumed that divorce could happen (Deut 24:1-4). Rather, it is a question of his recognizing that divorce can be a real injustice to one of the parties. The text, 2:13-16,[8] is corrupt and

---

[6] See also the short book of Obadiah, almost totally preoccupied with the same sort of hostility toward Edom and the anticipation of its destruction. The hostility between these two peoples, Israel and the Edomites, perdured throughout most of their existence and is retrojected back into the Genesis stories of the birth of their eponymous ancestors, Israel (Jacob) and Edom (Esau), as seen in Gen 25:19-26 (cf. 19:27-34; 27:1-45). Israel, under David, subjugated Edom, though later Edom won its independence. The venom against Edom in many exilic and postexilic passages would seem to be explained by the belief that Edom participated with the Babylonians in the destruction of Jerusalem in 587, but there seems no sure evidence that in fact Edom did so participate.

[7] For that matter there is no position on divorce, or at least on divorce with remarriage, universally accepted by all Protestants. Witness, e.g., the problems that have occasionally confronted the British royal families in matters of divorce among their members.

[8] Many translations and commentaries indicate the unit here to be 2:10-16, and indeed the reference to breaking faith (in *bgd* terminology) would seem to tie the verses together

questionable, and consequently the translation is uncertain in spots, though the general tenor would appear to be clear, even though it is often contested.[9] The *NAB* has it as follows:

> 13 This also you do:[10] the altar of the LORD you cover
>   with tears, weeping and groaning,
>   Because he no longer heeds your sacrifice
>   nor accepts it favorably from your hand;
> 14 And you say, "Why is it?"—
>   Because the LORD is witness
>   between you and the wife of your youth,
>   With whom you have broken faith
>   though she is your companion, your betrothed wife.
> 15 Did he not make one being, with flesh and spirit:
>   and what does that one require but godly offspring?
>   You must then safeguard life that is your own,
>   and not break faith with the wife of your youth.
> 16 For I hate divorce,[11]
>   says the LORD, the God of Israel,
>   And covering one's garment with injustice,

by a sort of *inclusio*. Thus we would have two examples of breaking faith, one by taking a pagan wife (vv. 10-12) and one by divorcing "the wife of your youth" (v. 14). Note, however, that doubts have been raised about the authenticity of the phrase in which *bgd* occurs in v. 16; see note in *BHS*.

[9] For a well-documented and detailed discussion of Mal 2:10-16 see Gordon P. Hugenberger, *Marriage as a Covenant: A Study of Biblical Law and Ethics Governing Marriage Developed from the Perspective of Malachi*. VTSup 52 (Leiden, New York, and Cologne: Brill, 1994).

[10] These introductory words are treated as a later addition by some commentators.

[11] A reading from Qumran 4QXII^a would give a significantly different sense: *ky ʾm śnth šlḥ* (MT: *ky śnʾ šlḥ*), which would be rendered, "But if you hate [your wife], divorce [her]." The editor of this ms, however, holds that the MT is closer to the original. See Russell Fuller, "Text-Critical Problems in Malachi 2:10-16," *JBL* 110 (1991) 47–57. Some other authors read the text as conditional ("if one divorce his wife because of hatred") while still seeing a rejection of divorce ("then violence covers his garments"). See David C. Jones, "Malachi on Divorce," *Presbyterion* 15 (1989) 16–22; and idem, "A Note on the LXX of Malachi 2:16," *JBL* 109 (1990) 683–85. Hugenberger translates: "If one hates and divorces, says Yahweh, God of Israel, he covers his garments with violence, says Yahweh of hosts . . ." (p. 69). He sees the advantage of this rendering: taking the divorcing party as the subject of *śānēʾ* has the support of the versions. See also the rendering of Richard Deutsch and his comment that "The reason for this new and much stricter approach in Mal 2:14-16 must be sought in the theological and moral developments which had taken place during the Exile in Babylon," in Graham S. Ogden and Richard R. Deutsch, *A Promise of Hope—A Call to Obedience: Joel and Malachi*. ITC (Grand Rapids: Eerdmans; Edinburgh: Handsel, 1987) 96.

> says the LORD of hosts;
> You must then safeguard life that is your own,
>   and not break faith.

The fact that their behavior occasions the Lord's rejection of their sacrifices puts us in mind of similar passages from Amos and Isaiah that condemn in strongest terms sacrifices and other rites offered by those guilty of oppression (cf. Amos 5:21-24; Isa 1:10-16). We can conclude that this puts the behavior here condemned in line with oppression of the widow and orphan, despoiling of the poor, etc., as a form of social injustice; the Lord takes the part of the weak against the strong. Although Israelite legislation covered some aspects of divorce, there was only limited protection against a man divorcing his wife.[12] Since the grounds for divorce in the primary text, Deut 24:1-4, were rather vague,[13] there was little to prevent a man from divorcing his wife on capricious or nonexistent grounds. This very text from Malachi may be taken as proof that this, indeed, did happen. It could come to pass that a man, after years of struggle to raise a family and attain economic prosperity, finds a younger, more attractive woman with whom he "falls in love," and is led to repudiate the "wife of his youth," though she had borne his children and shared his early trials. It happens in modern times and no doubt happened then. In cases such as these the divorced partner is truly the injured one and may suffer the pain of rejection, humiliation, social stigma, and financial insecurity to an excruciating degree. The prophet sees God as the guardian of the initial pact and presents violation of it ("covering one's garments with injustice [literally 'violence,' *ḥāmās*]") as making sacrifice as unacceptable as does any other kind of oppression of the weak. What *NAB* renders as "your betrothed wife" is more literally "the woman [wife] of your covenant."[14] Where covenant

---

[12] Some safeguards were that a man who falsely accused his wife of not having been a virgin at the time of marriage could be chastised and fined and could not later repudiate her (Deut 22:13-19); the man who rapes a young woman who is not betrothed must pay a fine to the father and cannot divorce the woman (Deut 22:28-29).

[13] *ʿerwat dābār*, usually translated "something indecent," at least in later times, was interpreted in widely divergent ways; cf. the famous disagreement between the schools of Hillel and Shammai on this point. It is likely that it was often interpreted rather broadly also in earlier times.

[14] The theme is discussed by S. L. McKenzie and H. N. Wallace, "Covenant Themes in Malachi," *CBQ* 45 (1983) 549–63. However, when the authors assert that "the covenant of marriage is contained within the section relating to the violation of the covenant of the fathers (2:10-16)" (whom they take to be Jacob and Levi, p. 552), and conclude therefore that

is involved, faithfulness and loyalty are obligations rather than counsels of perfection. This passage in Malachi concerning divorce is a rather isolated one in the Old Testament and, while steeped in Israel's history, has a strangely modern, poignant tone.

Verses 13-16, as already mentioned, may be related to vv. 10-12, in which it is said that Judah has broken faith by marrying an idolatrous woman (literally "the daughter of a foreign god"). The connection of vv. 10-12 with vv. 13-16, some claim, is that the dismissal of the "wife of your youth" is occasioned by marriage with a foreigner and therefore does not relate to the matter of divorce *per se*. This is neither obvious nor even likely.[15] The concern for the danger to racial and religious purity through marriage with foreigners, so eloquently attested for this period in the books of Ezra and Nehemiah, is sufficiently dealt with in the reproach of vv. 10-12;[16] and the threat directed in v. 12 against those

"it is thus an example of the greater issue, the profaning of the covenant of the fathers" (p. 558), the conclusion can be disputed. The expression "the woman [wife] of your covenant" does not in any way suggest subordination to or dependence upon any other covenant.

[15] This assertion is made, e.g., in the treatment of Beth Glazier-McDonald, "Intermarriage, Divorce, and the *BAT-ʾEL NEKAR*: Insights into Mal 2:10-16," *JBL* 106 (1987) 603–11. She frequently alleges that Malachi's reference to "the covenant of our fathers" (2:10) "expressly forbade intermarriage" (pp. 606, 607, 610), in each case citing Exodus 34 and Deuteronomy 7. However, those texts (presumably Exod 34:16; Deut 7:3-4 are intended) are simply deuteronomic exhortations about how pagans are to be treated and are no more part of a covenant text than the associated exhortations about destroying pagan cult objects. McKenzie and Wallace give a totally different interpretation of the "covenant of our fathers" reference in Mal 2:10; see above, n. 14. In her fuller presentation, *Malachi: The Divine Messenger*. SBLDS 98 (Atlanta: Scholars, 1987) 98, Glazier-McDonald states explicitly, "in the covenant concluded with the fathers (Mal 2:10, cf. Exod 34 and Deut 7) the Israelites agreed not to intermarry because foreign women go astray after their own gods . . . and cause Israelite men to do the same." She stresses that the subject of divorce begins not here [v. 13], but in v. 14 (p. 99; cf. pp. 115, 116). This is misleading in that Malachi's procedure (statement [here, v. 13] which provokes a question, which occasions an answer [here, both question and answer in v. 14]) already opens the topic in v. 13. In order to sustain her thesis that the covering of the altar with tears of v. 13 relates to weeping for the dead god in the fertility cult, she asserts of v. 14 that "although the question has already been answered . . . a second reason is tendered here . . ." (p. 100). Objection may also be raised to the close connection she draws between Malachi's words on divorce and the preceding on intermarriage, as well as to other points of her presentation.

[16] The samples referred to above by no means exhaust the range of opposing interpretations. Petersen, *Zechariah . . . Malachi*, 193–204, for example, argues that in vv. 13-15a Israel is being reproached for the worship of Asherah, a female fertility deity. But this conclusion is reached through a series of questionable, not to say unlikely, arguments. It involves, e.g., emending ʾăšer in v. 11 to ʾăšerâ, without any textual evidence, arguing

guilty in this matter seems to bring that passage to a satisfactory end. While Ezra and Nehemiah are adamant about the dismissal of foreign wives, there is no suggestion that marrying them was at the expense of repudiating Jewish wives.

Malachi concerns himself with other moral themes as well. The later part of the book condemns those who defraud the hired man of his wages, those who defraud widows and orphans, those who turn aside the stranger. Malachi characterizes those who do such things, and sorcerers, adulterers, and perjurers as well, as "those who do not fear me" (3:5).

JOEL

In spite of its location in the canon, between Hosea and Amos, the book of Joel would seem to belong to the postexilic period, though evidence for dating is indirect. The fact that there is reference to the Temple but none to the personnel of a royal court, even where it would be expected (Joel 1:13-14), suggests the period of the Second Temple. Since there are no references to the abuses corrected by Nehemiah's reform, a date after that reform is indicated; this, along with the fact that Tyre and Sidon are still standing,[17] suggests a date from the middle of the fifth to the middle of the fourth centuries.

The limited scope of the present work dispenses us from having to take a hard position on the thorny and still debated question of the composition of the book, the more so because it would add little to our study. The elements that are clearly present in chapters 1 and 2 are descriptive of the devastation from a locust plague, in places depicted as an enemy invasion, and from drought; these are at times identified as "the day of the LORD" (1:15; 2:1). People are urged to call upon the Lord (1:13-14; 2:12-17), and a favorable response is received (2:18-27). Chapters 3 and

---

that the tears on YHWH's altar (v. 13) are from the rite of lacrimation over the fertility deity (Tammuz/Dumuzi), that the "wife of your youth" (v. 14) is YHWH (with a reversal of gender language as Israel now becomes the male in the YHWH-Israel spousal relationship, YHWH the female)—which also involves the unlikely scenario of YHWH acting as witness between Israel and himself, if he is "the wife of your youth." Verses 15b-16, which again use phrases from the earlier verses, Petersen acknowledges to treat of "family integrity," but judges them a later addition of "some epigone." Not surprisingly, none of the modern, mainline translations *(NAB, NRSV, JPS, NIV, NBJ, REB)* reflect positions such as those of Glazier-McDonald or Petersen in their renderings.

[17] Destroyed in 332 and 343, respectively.

4 are mostly descriptive of events of the end time: the gift of the Lord's spirit (3:1-5),[18] judgment upon the nations and deliverance for Judah.

Although some passages of the book are used for lectionary readings for Lent and lend themselves to use in penance ceremonies, the ethical content is modest. The first call to prayer (1:13-14) seems wholly inspired by the loss of vegetation (1:5, 11, 16-18). A better note is struck in 2:12-14, where there is an implied suggestion that the trials are punishment for sin: the people are invited to "return to me with your whole heart, / with fasting, and weeping, and mourning" (v. 12); true repentance is called for in the words "rend your hearts, not your garments, / and return[19] to the LORD, your God" (v. 13); and a reminder is given of the merciful nature of the Lord.[20] It is also edifying that a primary concern of the prayer to spare the greenery has to do with being able to make "offerings and libations / for the LORD, your God" (2:14). The prayer is presented as having moved the Lord (2:18), and from this point on the book is wonderfully positive, with the Lord reversing the trials of locust and drought and visiting just judgments upon the sinful nations, blessings upon his people.

It is somewhat remarkable that, although much of the book reads like a lamentation about a terrible scourge that has come upon the people, very little is said of the nature of any sins of the people that might have provoked such a scourge. It is noteworthy that the attacking "army" is said to be led by the Lord himself and does his bidding (2:11).

The one specific moral note is the condemnation of slave trade, though this is against Tyre and Sidon for having sold the people of Judah as slaves (4:6). So also violence and the shedding of innocent blood is referred to, again as a crime against Judah done by Egypt and Edom (4:19).

---

[18] Chapter and verse citations are given according to the Hebrew, which is followed by the NAB and *JPS*. The *NRSV* and most other English translations follow the Vulgate arrangement, which has only three chapters instead of the four of the Hebrew: 3:1-5 of the Hebrew are added (in *NRSV*) to ch. 2 as 2:28-32, and 4:1-21 of the Hebrew becomes 3:1-21 in the *NRSV*.

[19] In each of the quotations "return" is the familiar *šûb*, encountered so often in Jeremiah and the other prophets.

[20] The phraseology used here (2:13), "For gracious and merciful is he, / slow to anger, rich in kindness, / and relenting in punishment," is, of course, intended to echo Exod 34:6-7. Much of the irony of the book of Jonah stems from the fact that the description of this merciful character of the Lord becomes, in the mouth of Jonah, an accusation by a prophet who does not wish to see such mercy manifested toward the pagan Ninevites. In Joel both the call to penance and the reminder of the Lord's mercy are in the mouth of the prophet (presumably, though cf. v. 17), whereas in Jonah it is the king of Nineveh who must give the call to repentance (Jonah 3:7-8).

TRITO-ISAIAH

The oracles that make up Isaiah 56–66, the collection usually referred to as Trito-Isaiah (or Third Isaiah), stem from a time after the Babylonian exiles have been allowed to return to the land of Judah, which remains under Persian domination—a rather benign domination, as attested in the books of Ezra and Nehemiah. These oracles proceed from a school of prophets rather than from an individual, prophets who appear to be consciously continuators of Isaiah and Deutero-Isaiah, probably disciples of the latter; thus the oracles easily bear the designation of Isaian. The oracles of this collection are rather mixed and do not have the clearer focus of Deutero-Isaiah; they seem to alternate between exhortation, promise, and threat. In so doing, however, they do give us some indications of the moral situation of those whom the prophets address, primarily the exiles returned from Babylon, but also the remnant that had remained in the land. We learn of the moral situation in part through what the prophetic group responsible for these passages saw fit to condemn, in part through the better things they hoped for in the future. Indeed, one can say they saw a close connection between the two:

> Observe what is right, do what is just;
> > for my salvation is about to come,
> > my justice, about to be revealed (56:1).[21]

Observance of the Sabbath, which had become one of the particular features of Judaism during the period of the exile, now calls for prophetic attention.[22] In two texts Sabbath observance is explicitly noted as

---

[21] Thomas L. Leclerc, with reference to this verse, compares the concept of justice in Isaiah and in Trito-Isaiah: "For first Isaiah, the doing of justice is the concretization of salvation; for Third Isaiah, the coming of God's salvation is the motive for enacting justice." *Yahweh Is Exalted in Justice: Solidarity and Conflict in Isaiah* (Minneapolis: Fortress, 2001) 137.

[22] We have already noted in the previous chapter Ezekiel's frequent reference to the Sabbath. This is not to suggest that the Sabbath was not observed from early times. But at the time of the Babylonian exile, when so few of Israel's religious practices could be observed, those practices that could be, such as circumcision and observance of the Sabbath, took on a special significance as being the mark of the Jew, as distinct from others around them who did not observe them. Of course, without the Temple the Sabbath could not be observed in terms of the customary sacrifices, but the prescription of not working could be kept, and no doubt communal prayer and study services, leading ultimately to the development of the synagogue as a regular feature of Jewish life, came into vogue at this time. Ezekiel, the prophet whose interest runs so much in the way of ritual, cultic, and priestly concerns, in addition to blaming the Israelites for lack of observance in their own

a characteristic of those singled out for praise (Isa 56:2, 4, 6; 58:13), and in 56:6 it will be one of the marks of the non-Israelite who converts to Judaism. Another universalistic passage specifies "from one sabbath to another" as the time when "all mankind shall come to worship / before me" (66:23). The eighth-century prophets had mentioned the Sabbath only as background for condemnations: Isaiah (1:13) lists it along with other observances that Yhwh cannot bear because of sinful behavior, and Amos (8:5) notes the grudging observance by the merchants who cannot wait for the Sabbath to be over so they can resume their cheating practices. In these passages (cf. also Hos 2:13) the prophets testify to the fact that the Sabbath was observed. But they do this not to manifest any prophetic enthusiasm for the institution or testify to any special virtue therein; like the offering of sacrifice, its value was dependent on the dispositions with which it was observed. With Trito-Isaiah, however, Sabbath observance has obviously taken on a new importance.

One is reminded of the parallel case of the Temple: whereas Nathan had said David was not to build it (2 Sam 7:5-7), Jeremiah had warned against naïve trust in it (Jer 7:4), and Micah and Jeremiah had foretold its destruction (Mic 3:12; Jer 7:12-14; 26:6), the exilic and postexilic prophets, as we have had occasion to note, saw it as the necessary condition for the fulfillment of the messianic promises. Thus for Deutero-Isaiah the mission of Cyrus was not only the deliverance of God's people from captivity, but also the rebuilding of the Temple (Isa 44:28); the enthronement of Yhwh in the restored Zion was the ultimate goal of the procession from Babylon to the Holy Land, itself the culmination of the delivery from Babylonian exile (52:7-8). So now for Trito-Isaiah this new Temple will be the locus of pure worship and the rallying point for all the peoples (56:6-7; 60:5-7, 14; 65:25; 66:20-21). Thus Trito-Isaiah continues and develops a theme prominent in Isaiah (cf. especially Isa 2:2-4) and Deutero-Isaiah, though not in other early prophets, and so suggests one line of continuity within the Isaian collection.

In spite of all the work of God on their behalf, Trito-Isaiah depicts the people as wanton, disobedient children, accusing them of indulging in the fertility cult and in child sacrifice (Isa 57:3-13). A similar, though more obscure passage makes reference to offering sacrifices in the groves and burning incense on the mountains (65:2-7). The paralleling of these

---

land, makes frequent reference to it in describing the ideal theocracy of the restoration (Ezek 44:24; 45:17; 46:1-7, 12). Jeremiah 17:21-22, 24, 27 is generally judged to come from a much later hand—perhaps as late as the time of Nehemiah (cf. Neh 13:15-22).

practices with "the crimes of your fathers" (v. 7) would seem to identify them as pagan worship. Thus also the reference to eating swine's flesh, joined as it is with "carrion broth in their dishes" and "living among the graves" (v. 4), would probably not relate simply to unclean food but to pagan worship. Although God is prepared to respond graciously to the people, these and other pagan practices like them, which are seen as a continuation of the crimes committed by their ancestors, provoke wrath and punishment instead (Isa 65:3-7, 11-12). Such practices appear to have been a revival of pagan practices regularly condemned by the earlier prophets and perhaps practiced more particularly by those who had remained in the land than by those who had returned from Babylon and the exile. The exile had, in fact, brought about a renewal of religious fidelity, with a greater devotion to the worship of YHWH alone, greater observance of the Law, greater awareness of Jewish identity. Thus, although the hostility toward the Samaritans was to some extent a continuation of the hostility between north and south, occasioned by the division into two kingdoms, there is also the fact that the religious observance of those exiles who had returned from Babylon had taken a new turn and had reached a higher level compared to that of those who had remained in the land, whether in the northern territories or in Judea.

As in the case of the earlier prophets, much of the blame is laid at the door of the leaders (56:9-12). As in earlier days, the matter of social justice arises. Thus Trito-Isaiah sees avarice as an occasion for YHWH's punishment (57:17); the victims of avarice are "the crushed and dejected in spirit" (v. 15), whose part YHWH takes. With great condescension YHWH becomes their consoler:

> On high I dwell, and in holiness,
> and with the crushed and dejected in spirit,
> To revive the spirits of the dejected,
> to revive the hearts of the crushed (57:15bc).

The prophet apparently identifies avarice as one of the "stumbling blocks" (v. 14) YHWH commands to be removed from the people's path (57:14-18). And he speaks out against mistreatment of workers and the violence of one Israelite against another (58:3-4), commending instead acts of "releasing those bound unjustly / . . . / setting free the oppressed / . . . / sharing your bread with the hungry, sheltering the oppressed and the homeless; / clothing the naked . . ." (58:6-7). In 59:3-15 still greater violence is described, with reference even to the shedding of blood. Again, such crimes are given as the reason that the good things of the hoped-for restoration elude them: "the hand of the LORD is not too short to save / . . . / rather it is your crimes / that separate you from God" (59:1-2), "that is why right is far from us / and justice does not reach us. / . . . / We look for right, but it is not there, / for salvation, and it is far from us" (vv. 9, 11).

In spite of such denunciations and the threats that went with them, Trito-Isaiah contains some of the most beautiful and uplifting promises to be found anywhere. The "salvation [which] is about to come" (56:1) is extended even to those often excluded from the people (foreigners, eunuchs), so that God's house shall be called "a house of prayer for all peoples" (56:7). If the people will only heed God's word in caring for the needy, all manner of blessings shall be bestowed upon them (58:8-14). Far more often than in the earlier prophets, Trito-Isaiah ties words of threat to specific wrongdoing, and far more often connects promises of good things with right behavior in a sort of "if . . . then" pattern: "If you hold back your foot on the sabbath / . . . / then / . . . / I will nourish you with the heritage of Jacob, your father" (58:13-14).

But the promises can also be unconditional, as in 60:1-22; 61:1-11; 65:17-25; 66:7-14. This is a reminder of the sovereign freedom of YHWH to bestow graces regardless of merit, to create the dispositions to allow the people to receive such blessings. The arrangement of passages that describe sinful conditions, on the one hand, and others that promise great things for the future is far from easy to understand, but it is probably not by accident that it is in the midst of such passages that we have the matchlessly beautiful and moving confession of sin in 63:7–64:11. The prophet begins by remembering the Lord's glorious deeds on behalf of Israel in the past and then turns to Israel's infidelities, followed by a plea for help. Poignantly the petitioner asks "Why do you let us wander, O LORD, from your ways, / and harden our hearts so that we fear you not? / . . . / Would that you might meet us doing right, / that we were mindful of your ways!" (63:17; 64:4). The plea for help erupts in phrases like "Oh, that you would rend the heavens and come down" (63:19), and finally, "Can you hold back, O LORD, after all this? / Can you remain silent, and afflict us so severely?" (64:11). While this prayer is identified as a communal lament, as many of the psalms are, it would be difficult to find an adequate parallel to it in the Psalter.

Like some of the other prophets we have looked at, Trito-Isaiah knew what we might call grace, even if there was no developed terminology for the concept. The passages of promise contain extravagant claims that still other exiles will return to the homeland, that other peoples and lands will venerate Israel and its God, and they will render services to Jerusalem, the Temple, and Israel. But these passages also speak of Israel's right dispositions: "Your people shall all be just" (60:21); "They will be called oaks of justice" (61:3); wrapped "in a mantle of justice" (61:10); "They shall be called the holy people, / the redeemed of the LORD" (62:12). Like Jeremiah and Ezekiel, Trito-Isaiah promises a "lasting covenant" (61:8), which supposes a relationship of fidelity. The crowning testimony of YHWH's forgiveness and redeeming love is seen in his use of the YHWH-Israel bridal imagery: as in Deutero-Isaiah, it is utilized only to emphasize God's love for Israel (62:1-5). That YHWH receives Israel back with such tender love can only be because it returns in true repentance and fidelity.

Chapter Thirteen

RELEVANCE OF THE PROPHETS TO MODERN TIMES

What is the advantage to us, now in the twenty-first century, of study-ing the ethical teachings of prophets who lived almost three millennia ago and in a culture in many ways quite unlike our own? At least three lines of response are worth pursuing. First, from a purely historical point of view there is the strong influence that the Old Testament prophets have exercised upon the world and especially on the ethical praxis of western civilization; then, looking to the present, there is the concrete content of much of their teaching, which is applicable to us here and now, without need of "translation"; finally, looking to the future, principles derived from their manner of dealing with ethical concerns help us to discern the best ways, ethically speaking, of handling new problems that begin to emerge as our culture develops in ever new ways and directions.

Not too much need be said about the first of these, i.e., the prophets and their teaching taken in a purely historical perspective. We need al-ways to stay in contact with our roots if we would understand who we are, where we are, and how we got here. While there have been many influences on the ethical thought and praxis of the western world, few if any of them have equaled that of biblical religion. Although it could be claimed that this comes to many of us most directly from the Christian religion, that claim would have to be nuanced and carefully qualified, for New Testament ethical teaching leans very heavily on the Old Testa-ment. When Jesus is asked what one must do to possess everlasting life, his reply is, initially at least, in terms of provisions from the Decalogue (Mark 10:17-31; Matt 19:16-30, who adds love of neighbor from Lev 19:18; Luke 18:18-23). A different question on another occasion, about "which is the greatest commandment" (cf. Mark 12:28-34; Matt 22:34-40), obviously inquired about provisions found in the Old Testament, and so the reply necessarily came from there. Yet one does not have the impression that Jesus feels the Old Testament response, "Hear, O Israel! . . . you shall love the LORD, your God, with all your heart, and with all your soul, and with all your strength" (Deut 6:4-5), is wanting in any way. When he adds the commandment about loving one's neighbor as oneself (Lev 19:18), it is by way of complement rather than completion, and again the formulation comes from the Old Testament.[1]

Our investigation of Israel's prophets illustrates that ethical sensibilities developed and evolved in the course of history. We are disconcerted by the account of Micaiah ben Imlah and his explanation of the deceiving message given through the mouths of false prophets, that the Lord had sent a "lying spirit" (1 Kgs 22:22) into the mouths of the court prophets (1 Kgs 22:19-23). But another prophet a century later, Micah of Moresheth, explains false prophecy more acceptably by the accusation of venality (Mic 3:5, 11). And Jeremiah, a century later still, asserts that such prophets of deception speak "visions of their own fancy" (Jer 23:16), that the Lord had not sent them, that they had not stood in the Lord's council (Jer 23:16-18; cf. 28:15). Like Micah, he holds that the role of the prophet is to turn sinners back from evil ways, from their wicked deeds (Jer 23:22; cf. Mic 3:8). Sometimes the ethical judgment of the prophets stands high above that of their contemporaries or even of those who come later. The deuteronomistic author has nothing but praise for Jehu's bloody suppression of Ahab's line and his savage purge of Baal worshipers, and even reports without comment his pointless murder of Ahaziah, Judah's king. Hosea, on the other hand, in a word that no doubt refers to these incidents, condemns them in predicting punishment and destruction on the "house of Jehu" for the "bloodshed at Jezreel" (Hos 1:4).[2]

The same kind of advance can be seen in most of the prophetic references to an ideal king of the future.[3] Nathan's so-called dynastic oracle

---

[1] This provision from Lev 19:18 is often devalued on the claim that the "neighbor" one is to love as oneself is understood to be a fellow Israelite. Yet the same sort of admonition is found a little later in the same chapter: "You shall treat the alien who resides with you no differently than the natives born among you; have the same love for him as for yourself . . ." (v. 34). The same verb and form (*ʾāhabtā*) is found in both texts.

[2] If Jehu is carrying out a policy intended by Elijah and/or Elisha, as would seem to be the case (cf. 1 Kgs 19:5-18 and 2 Kgs 9:1-3), Hosea's condemnation of the policy would represent another example of ethical development within the prophetic line.

[3] The one who comes to be referred to as the Messiah. As is well known, the term "messiah" does not occur in the Old Testament in this technical sense of a future ideal

(2 Sam 7:8-17) was the seedbed for great expectations from the Davidic line and, ultimately, from one representative of that line. Those expectations, along with the exaggerated way of speaking of the king common in the ancient Near East ("court style"), led to the sort of diction found in the royal psalms. In those psalms the king's role as victorious warrior is frequently extolled, sometimes in bloody terms (Ps 2:8-9; 18:32-46; 45:4-6; 110:1-2, 5-7); in spite of this, the prophets often describe the future ideal king as a figure of peace (Isa 9:5-6; 11:6-9; Mic 4:19–5:4a [*NRSV* 5:2-4]; Zech 9:9-10). This last passage is especially interesting. It also presents the king as meek (or, more properly, poor —*ʿānî*—identified with the lowly of the land) as well as peaceful (banishing chariot, horse, and bow from the land and announcing peace to the Gentiles). The passage identifies the extent of his rule in the same terminology as that found in Ps 72:8 ("from sea to sea, / from the river to the ends of the earth"), a psalm in which, however, the king's enemies bow before him and lick the dust. Thus the Zechariah passage quotes the royal tradition of warlike domination while at the same time transforming the king into a bringer of peace.

On the second point, the application without "translation" of the content of much of the prophetic ethical teaching to our present situation, one undoubtedly thinks first of all of what the prophets have to say in the area of what we call "social justice." As in the days of eighth-century Israel/Judah, much of what we deplore relates not so much to the provisions of legal justice as to the crass indifference to the plight of the poor on the part of those well able to help them, not to mention those who grow rich by exploiting the poor. What choice words would Amos have had for those men who buy automobiles with a $50,000–$100,000 price tag and yachts costing many times that much, or to the women who buy gowns (or even swimming suits!) that cost in the thousands, while in the same city mothers work at two jobs in order to feed their children—these being the lucky ones, because others go hungry, without medical aid, without shelter, without hope. An apartment owner charges whatever rent he can get, whether his/her tenants can afford it or not. A factory owner closes down his business in order to relocate to a place where he can pay the workers less, without concern for the unemployed he leaves behind. Sometimes terrible disruption is visited upon the poor for the sake of hydroelectric developments, developments unfortunately

royal figure, though it is used in that sense in the intertestamental literature, in rabbinic writings, and in the New Testament.

sometimes supported financially by prestigious organizations such as the World Bank. An article by Colman McCarthy some years ago detailed the displacement of village or tribal populations, sometimes numbering in the hundreds of thousands, in Thailand, India, and Brazil, as the people were ejected from fertile river valleys where business interests wanted to build dams, people for whom no adequate resettlement had been arranged—despite the pledges of the power companies who profit most from such projects.[4]

All such practices relate directly to the prophetic condemnations of the rich who acquire still greater riches at the expense of the poor—no violation of law, perhaps, but surely a violation of ṣĕdāqâ. The prophets, as I have argued, rarely rest their case on legal prescriptions; they speak, rather, of how God has acted in Israel's history, and they take over the diction of the wisdom tradition, in which God is the vindicator of the poor and the judge of those who oppress them.

The third point referred to above has to do with deriving principles from the prophets' manner of dealing with ethical concerns that can help us discern the way of dealing with new problems that emerge in our developing culture; this does require some "translation." First, since this book deals with the Old Testament prophets we should take to heart Brevard Childs' caution cited earlier[5] about using the term "prophetic" too loosely, e.g., by applying it to any progressive modern moral ministry. We are looking to the words of people who were called and empowered to say "thus says the LORD" in ways that we are not.

Speaking, then, of the ancient prophets, we might consider especially matters relating to peace and war. None of the prophets has left us an abstract declaration about the morality of war, and one might come to the conclusion that war was simply accepted as a fact of life, perhaps was even regarded as necessary or, at worst, as morally indifferent. Sometimes the early prophets themselves were the instigators of violence; we can think of Elisha's machinations to have Hazael crowned king of Aram, in the knowledge that he would wage war on Israel. Ahijah's instigation of Jeroboam's revolt did not lead directly to war, but it did provoke a schism that often enough occasioned war between the sister kingdoms.

---

[4] Colman McCarthy, "Peasants Swept From Progress's Path," *The Washington Post*, March 10, 1992. No doubt large numbers may benefit from such power projects, but they should not be advanced without adequate plans to avoid misery, despair, and starvation for displaced populations. Even the lowly snail darter was given more consideration than these!

[5] See Chapter Five, n. 8.

And certainly even the classical prophets presented the Lord as waging war against Israel's or the Lord's enemies, or even against Israel, in actions often described in very violent and bloody terms. There is ample material on the Lord waging war against the nations in the collections of "oracles against the nations" (especially, though not exclusively, Isaiah 13–23, Jeremiah 46–51, Ezekiel 25–32, and Amos 1:3–2:3). In general the collections of the "oracles against the nations" speak of judgment, often in military terms, sometimes by the hand of earthly enemies, sometimes by the hand of the Lord.[6] Not infrequently these oracles issue from an Israelite prophet crying for the downfall of an aggressor nation attacking or lording it over Israel. Thus there is a negative aspect in that these passages sometimes stem from a nationalistic zeal and tend to equate Israel's enemies with the Lord's enemies.

Even here positive aspects can be discerned: such oracles include the condemnation of aggression and campaigns of conquest by rich and powerful nations; the punishment of the mighty is seen as punishment for sinfulness and pride.[7] Where this is not expressed, it may often be inferred. Not infrequently the harsh punishment is mitigated, usually by an addition by a later hand.[8]

Often enough, however, God's action is directed against Israel itself, the nations functioning as the Lord's instrument to punish. Isaiah, emphasizing the disciplinary aspect, calls Assyria the Lord's "rod in anger" and "staff in wrath" (Isa 10:5-15; and cf. 5:26-29; 7:18-19, 20). Jeremiah, too, considers the punishment to come upon Judah by the "enemy from the north" as sent by the Lord in retribution for Judah's conduct (Jer 4:13-18; and cf. all he has to say about Nebuchadnezzar's dominion being the Lord's doing, chs. 27–28 and elsewhere). Ezekiel, acting in the person of the Lord, goes through the motions of laying siege to Jerusalem to indicate symbolically that the Babylonian attack on the city is the Lord's

---

[6] The fact that much of the material in these sections cannot be attributed to the prophets in whose books they are found is beside the point. Some of these materials do find reasonably close parallels in the authentic words of the classical prophets. More importantly, these words are part of the canon of Scripture, among the prophetic books, and by and large need to be treated with what Israel took to be prophetic teaching.

[7] E.g., Isa 13:9, 11; 14:5-6; 23:8-9; Jer 48:29-30; 49:4, 16; 51:5b, 24, 34-37, 49; Ezek 25:3-17; 28:2-10, 15-19; 29:6-9; 31:10-11; 32:32.

[8] E.g., Isa 16:3-5; 17:7-8; 18:7; 19:18-25; 23:17-18; Jer 46:26b; 48:47; 49:6, 39; Ezek 29:13-14. This last passage is intended to mitigate the harsh judgment proclaimed in 29:1-12. But it would seem a still later author added the final words of v. 14, plus vv. 15-16 to give the knife another twist, so to speak.

own attack and that its fall will be the Lord's own doing (Ezek 4:1-3). Ezekiel's "song of the sword," directed against Judah, has something almost sadistic about it (Ezek 21:13-22). Such oracles directed against Israel/Judah indicate that the Lord's militaristic action is intended for punishing evil and rectifying wrongs rather than simply establishing the claims of a chosen people, while at the same time demonstrating that YHWH is the Lord with power over history.

The same conclusion, though arrived at from a very different direction, is seen in Deutero-Isaiah. He sees the military victories of Cyrus, granted by the Lord, specifically as the means of delivering Judah from exile in Babylon; the Lord can use pagan nations as instruments to effect the divine plan, whether it be to chastise a people or to deliver them.

Two points in particular are worth noting: on the practical level the effect of the message of the prophets on many occasions would have been to turn Israel/Judah away from armed conflict, and on an ideal level the pictures they painted of the future often had universal peace as a prominent feature. Isaiah could be considered inconsistent in that he opposed Judah's submission to Assyria in the days of Ahaz, but on later occasions, in the days of Hezekiah, he opposed revolt against Assyria (Isaiah 20; 30:1-17; 31:1-3). Isaiah was, in fact, being consistent in following the same single principle in each of these judgments, namely, that YHWH is the Lord of history who guides events in wisdom and power and that any actions that do not take into account what the Lord has planned are bound to end in disaster; there is further consistency in that his advice in each case would have spared Judah involvement in disastrous hostilities—hostilities that did come when the message had been rejected. In a similar fashion Jeremiah preached the message of submission to the Babylonians as the will of God. This was a most unpopular message and exposed the prophet to hostility and ridicule, but, as in the case of Isaiah, it would have spared Judah and Jerusalem disastrous military operations. Again, rejection of this message led to the siege and surrender of Jerusalem in 597, along with the first deportation, and to the destruction of Jerusalem and the nation and the second deportation in 587. These prophetic messages were based on the conviction that the Lord was at work in human history, that the great world powers were instruments of the divine plan, and that wisdom lay in recognizing these facts.

The inspiration for the statue in front of the United Nations building in New York, that of a man beating a sword into a plowshare, is from a prophetic oracle (Isa 2:2-4; Mic 4:1-3), a powerful symbol of the longing for universal peace. "Longing" is, in fact, too weak a word; the word of the Lord is promise, and the fact that universal peace is the will of the Lord and something divinely promised is what sustains us in hope amid the failures that would tempt us to despair. Perfect peace comes only with the eschaton, of course, but the blueprint of the kingdom we have been given lays upon us the obligation of seeing it realized to the extent possible now.

In this same vein, the three most explicitly messianic texts in Isaiah all give a prominent place to peace. We have briefly mentioned Isa 2:2-4, the vision of all nations beating their swords into plowshares, no longer raising their weapons against each other, and no longer training for war, a beautiful ideal[9] the United Nations would like to see realized in practice. The U.N. is a human institution and therefore imperfect. However, it is the one institution that has as its goal establishing peace and coopera-tion among nations; no doubt it can go a long way toward reaching that goal, but only if all its member nations, especially the most powerful, cooperate. The starting point for the Isaiah oracle, and that which makes the whole scenario possible, is the willingness of all nations to turn to the Lord for instruction. Not only do the nations accept the Lord's authority to judge between them and to impose terms of peace; they even take the initiative in streaming to Jerusalem in order to obtain instruction in walk-ing in God's ways. So also, as previously mentioned, Isaiah's description in 8:23–9:6[10] and 11:1-9 of the ideal king to come places a strong emphasis on peace. In the first of these passages Judah is delivered from Assyrian oppression, possibly by a violent defeat of the Assyrians, since there is reference to the smashing of the yoke of servitude and the rod of domi-nation, along with a holy war allusion ("day of Midian"), i.e., probably to Gideon's victory over the Midianites in Judges 7; but this is through YHWH's act, as is regularly the case in the holy war tradition, rather than through human warfare. The burning of the military boots and bloody

---

[9] Some authors, though not the majority, are unwilling to attribute this ideal to Isaiah for various reasons, often having to do with doubts that this sort of messianic expectation arose before the exile. This is not the place to review all the arguments in favor of and against authenticity, but it can be said that there is no vocabulary in it that would be out of place in an eighth-century oracle and no theme in it that is foreign to Isaiah's thought. On the contrary, the concern for the Zion tradition, YHWH as source of wisdom and ruler of the nations, and concern for peace all fit well into the teachings of Isaiah in his eighth-century ministry.

[10] According to Hebrew and *NAB* numbering; 9:1-7 in *NRSV* and most Protestant versions.

garments (9:4) bespeaks a distaste for the trappings of war, and "peace" is explicitly referred to twice in the two verses that follow: in the final element of the king's name ("prince of peace," 9:5) and in the description of his kingdom as enjoying peace without end. All this is attributable to the Lord rather than to the king ("The zeal of the LORD of hosts will do this," 9:6), who seems to accompany the action rather than bring it about. In 11:1-9 the king is much more to the fore and plays a more active role. Rather than being given names that characterize him, he is given charismatic gifts that equip him for the rule that is characterized by judgment, justice, and concern for the afflicted, and that is accompanied by paradisiac peace. This wonderful peace is attributed to knowledge of God filling the earth and corresponds well with the king's charismatic gifts. Although it is not explicitly worked out in the text, there is no doubt a connection between the peace that prevails in the days of this ideal king and the fact that he shall judge with justice (11:4) and be characterized by justice and faithfulness, and we are reminded of the motto, "If you want peace, work for justice."

Perhaps the most striking prophetic passage of all in regard to world peace is Isa 19:18-25.[11] Here we read of the Lord being worshiped in Egypt and sending Egypt a savior, revealing himself to Egypt, and Egypt "knowing" the Lord, and of a highway that unites Assyria with Egypt and leads to easy commerce. Especially precious are the final verses, in which Israel, Egypt, and Assyria make up, as it were, three-thirds of God's people, each designated by terms that, until now, had been reserved for Israel alone: Israel is "my inheritance," but Egypt is "my people" and Assyria "the work of my hands." It matters little whether, as some commentators hold, Egypt and Assyria stand for political entities that came into existence at a much later period (i.e., the Seleucids and the Ptolemies); what is clear is that the author has taken for his imagery nations that throughout much of Israel's history were inveterate enemies of each other and of Israel and has placed them on friendly terms and under the Lord's special protection. What the prophet can conceive of as God's will is something we can work for as a goal. While the U.N. exists in order to bring about peace among nations, its success depends upon the will of the nations to live in peace; the desire of an individual nation to live at peace with the others will often depend on the will of its citizens to live at peace with one another. The beating of swords into plowshares,

---

[11] These verses may be put together from as many as four smaller oracles (v. 18, vv. 19-22, v. 23, vv. 24-25). This is a late passage, certainly not from Isaiah himself.

we might say, begins in our own back yard. "If you want peace, work for justice" has implications on the international, national, and individual level. It is pointless to wish for or to expect peace on any of these levels as long as oppression and exploitation are allowed to flourish. The concern for the poor and downtrodden that so characterized Amos and other prophets, if it became the moving force of individuals and states, could ultimately eliminate the conditions that promote violence and would therefore make the longed-for peace possible.

BIBLIOGRAPHY

Achtemeier, Paul J., and James L. Mays, eds. *Interpreting the Prophets*. Philadelphia: Fortress, 1987.

Albright, William F. *From the Stone Age to Christianity*. Garden City, NY: Doubleday, 1957 (©1942).

Alfaro, Juan I. *Justice and Loyalty: A Commentary on the Book of Micah*. Grand Rapids: Eerdmans, 1989.

Allen, L. C. "Micah's Social Concern." *Vox Evangelica* 8 (1973) 22–32.

Alt, Albrecht. "The Origins of Israelite Law." In idem, *Essays in Old Testament History and Religion*. Trans. R. A. Wilson. Oxford: Blackwell, 1966, 79–132.

Andersen, Francis I. "The Socio-Juridical Background of the Naboth Incident." *JBL* 85 (1966) 46–57.

Andersen, Francis I., and David Noel Freedman. *Amos: A New Translation with Introduction and Commentary*. AB 24A. New York: Doubleday, 1988.

_____. *Hosea*. AB 24. Garden City, NY: Doubleday, 1980.

Anderson, Bernhard W. "The Holy One of Israel." In Douglas A. Knight and Peter J. Paris, eds., *Justice and the Holy: Essays in Honor of Walter Harrelson*. Chico, CA: Scholars, 1989.

_____. *Understanding the Old Testament*. 4th ed. Englewood Cliffs, NJ: Prentice-Hall, 1986.

Barton, John. "Approaches to Ethics in the Old Testament." In John Rogerson, ed., *Beginning Old Testament Study*. Philadelphia: Westminster, 1983, 113–30.

_____. "Understanding Old Testament Ethics." *JSOT* 9 (1978) 44–64.

_____. "Ethics in Isaiah of Jerusalem." *JTS* 32 (1981) 1–18.

_____. *People of the Book? The Authority of the Bible in Christianity*. Louisville: John Knox, 1988.

_____. *Oracles of God: Perceptions of Ancient Prophecy in Israel after the Exile*. New York: Oxford, 1986.

Bergren, Richard V. *The Prophets and the Law*. HUCAMS 4. Cincinnati: Hebrew Union College, 1974.

Birch, Bruce C. *Let Justice Roll Down: The Old Testament, Ethics, and Christian Life*. Louisville: Westminster John Knox, 1991.

_____. *What Does the Lord Require? The Old Testament Call to Social Witness.* Philadelphia: Westminster, 1985.

Blenkinsopp, Joseph. *Wisdom and Law in the Old Testament: The Ordering of Life in Israel and Early Judaism.* Oxford: Oxford University Press, 1983.

_____. *Prophecy and Canon: A Contribution to the Study of Jewish Origins.* Notre Dame: University of Notre Dame Press, 1977.

_____. *A History of Prophecy in Israel.* Rev. and enlarged ed. Louisville: John Knox, 1996.

_____. *Ezekiel. Interpretations: A Bible Commentary for Teaching and Preaching.* Louisville: John Knox, 1990.

Boecker, Hans J. *Law and Administration of Justice in the Old Testament and Ancient Near East.* Minneapolis: Augsburg, 1980.

Bosman, H. L. "Taking Stock of Old Testament Ethics." *Old Testament Essays 1* (1983) 97–104.

Breasted, James H. *The Dawn of Conscience.* New York: Scribners, 1934 (©1933).

Bright, John. *Jeremiah.* AB 21. Garden City, NY: Doubleday, 1965.

Brueggemann, Walter. *Jeremiah 1–25: To Pluck Up, to Tear Down.* Grand Rapids: Eerdmans, 1988.

_____. *Jeremiah 26–52: To Build, To Plant.* Grand Rapids: Eerdmans, 1991.

Childs, Brevard S. *Biblical Theology in Crisis.* Philadelphia: Westminster, 1970.

Clements, Ronald E. *Prophecy and Covenant.* SBT 1/43. London: SCM, 1965.

_____. *Prophecy and Tradition.* Atlanta: John Knox, 1975.

Clifford, Richard J. "The Use of *HÔY* in the Prophets." *CBQ* 28 (1966) 458–64.

Collins, John J. "Natural Theology and Biblical Tradition: The Case of Hellenistic Judaism." *CBQ* 60 (1998) 1–15.

Collins, Raymond F. *Christian Morality: Biblical Foundations.* Notre Dame: University of Notre Dame Press, 1986.

Craigie, Peter C. *The Problem of War in the Old Testament.* Grand Rapids: Eerdmans, 1978.

Crenshaw, James L. "Prohibitions in Proverbs and Qoheleth." In Eugene Ulrich et al., eds., *Priests, Prophets and Scribes: Essays on the Formation and Heritage of Second Temple Judaism in Honor or Joseph Blenkinsopp.* JSOTSup 149. Sheffield: JSOT, 1992, 115–24.

_____. "Education in Ancient Israel." *JBL* 104 (1985) 601–15.

_____. "The Influence of the Wise upon Amos: The 'Doxologies of Amos?' and Job 5:9-16; 9:5-10." *ZAW* 79 (1967) 42–52.

_____. "Amos and the Theophanic Tradition." *ZAW* 80 (1968) 203–215.

Cross, Frank M. "Kinship and Covenant in Ancient Israel." In *From Epic to Canon; History and Literature in Ancient Israel.* Baltimore and London: Johns Hopkins University Press, 1998.

_____. *Canaanite Myth and Hebrew Epic.* Cambridge, MA: Harvard University Press, 1973.

Daly, Robert J., *et al.*, eds. *Christian Biblical Ethics: From Biblical Revelation to Contemporary Christian Praxis: Method and Content.* New York and Ramsey, NJ: Paulist, 1984.

Daniels, Dwight R. "Is There a 'Prophetic Lawsuit' Genre?" *ZAW* 99 (1987) 339–60.

Davies, Eryl W. *Prophecy and Ethics: Isaiah and the Ethical Tradition.* JSOTSup 16. Sheffield: JSOT Press, 1981.

Dever, William G. *What Did the Biblical Authors Know, and When Did They Know It? What Archaeology Can Tell Us about the Reality of Ancient Israel.* Grand Rapids: Eerdmans, 2001.

Driver, Samuel Rolles. *An Introduction to the Literature of the Old Testament.* 10th ed. revised and enlarged. New York: Scribner's, 1902.

Dupré, Louis. *Transcendent Selfhood.* New York: Seabury, 1976.

Eichrodt, Walther. "Covenant and Law." *Int* 20 (1966) 302–21.

_____. *Man in the Old Testament.* SBT 1/4. Chicago: Regnery, 1951.

_____. "Prophet and Covenant—Some Observations on the Exegesis of Isaiah." In John J. Durham and Joshua R. Porter, eds., *Proclamation and Presence. Old Testament Essays in Honour of Gwynne Henton Davies.* Richmond: John Knox; London: SCM, 1970.

_____. *Theology of the Old Testament.* Vol. 1. London: SCM, 1961.

Falk, Zeʾev. *Religious Law and Ethics: Studies in Biblical and Rabbinical Theonomy.* Jerusalem: Mesharim, 1991.

Fensham, F. Charles. "Widow, Orphan and the Poor in Ancient Near Eastern Legal and Wisdom Literature." *JNES* 21 (1962) 129–39.

Fey, Reinhard. *Amos und Jesaja.* WMANT 12. Neukirchen-Vluyn: Neukirchener Verlag, 1963.

Fichtner, Johannes. "Die 'Umkehrung' in der prophetischen Botschaft: Eine Studie zu dem Verhältnis von Schuld und Gericht in der Verkündigung Jesajas." In idem, *Gottes Weisheit: Gesammelte Studien zum Alten Testament,* ed. Klaus Dietrich Fricke. Stuttgart: Calwer Verlag, 1965, 44–51. Reprinted from *TLZ* 78 (1953) 459–66.

_____. "Jesaja unter der Weisen." *TLZ* 74 (1949) 75–80.

Fitzgerald, Aloysius. *The Lord of the East Wind.* CBQMS 34. Washington, DC: Catholic Biblical Association of America, 2002.

Föhrer, Georg. "Das sogenannte apodiktisch formulierte Recht und der Dekalog." *KD* 11 (1965) 49–74. Reprinted in idem, *Studien zur alttestamentlichen Theologie und Geschichte (1949–1966).* BZAW 115. Berlin: de Gruyter, 1969.

Fuller, Russell. "Text-Critical Problems in Malachi 2:10-16." *JBL* 110 (1991) 47–57.

Gammie, John G. *Holiness in Israel.* Overtures to Biblical Theology. Philadelphia: Fortress, 1989, esp. Ch. 3, "The Prophetic Understanding of Holiness."

Gamwell, Franklin I. *The Divine Good: Modern Moral Theory and the Necessity of God.* With a foreword by David Tracy. San Francisco: HarperSanFrancisco, 1990.

Gemser, Berend. "The Importance of the Motive Clause in Old Testament Law." International Organization for the Study of the Old Testament, *Congress Volume.* VTSup 1 (1953) 50–66.

Gerstenberger, Erhard. "Covenant and Commandment." *JBL* 84 (1965) 38–51.

———. *Wesen und Herkunft des "apodiktischen Rechts."* WMANT 20. Neukirchen-Vluyn: Neukirchener Verlag, 1965.

———. "The Woe-Oracles of the Prophets." *JBL* 81 (1962) 249–63.

Glazier-McDonald, Beth. "Intermarriage, Divorce, and the *BAT-ʾEL NEKAR:* Insights into Mal 2:10-16." *JBL* 106 (1987) 603–11.

———. *Malachi: The Divine Messenger.* SBLDS 98. Atlanta: Scholars, 1987.

Glueck, Nelson. *Ḥesed in the Bible.* Cincinnati: Hebrew Union College Press, 1967; originally written in Hebrew in 1927.

Greene, William. B. "The Ethics of the Old Testament." *PTR* 27 (1929) 153–93, 313–66.

Gustafson, James M. "The Place of Scripture in Christian Ethics: A Methodological Study." *Int* 24 (1970) 430–55.

Hackett, Jo Ann. "There Was No King in Israel." *The Oxford History of the Biblical World,* ed. M. D. Coogan. Oxford and New York: Oxford University Press, 1998.

Häring, Bernard. *The Law of Christ: Moral Theology for Priests and Laity.* Trans. Edwin G. Kaiser. Westminster, MD: Newman, 1961–1967.

Harvey, Julien. *Le plaidoyer prophétique contra Israël après la rupture de'alliance.* Montreal: Les éditions Bellarmin, 1967.

———. "Le 'Rib-Pattern', requisitoire prophétique sur la rupture de l'alliance." *Bib* 43 (1962) 172–96.

Hayes, John H., and Stuart A. Irvine. *Isaiah, the Eighth-Century Prophet.* Nashville: Abingdon, 1987.

Heschel, Abraham Joshua. *The Prophets.* New York: Harper & Row, 1962.

Hillers, Delbert R. *Treaty-Curses & the Old Testament Prophets.* BibOr 16. Rome: Biblical Institute, 1964.

———. *Covenant: the History of a Biblical Idea.* Baltimore: Johns Hopkins University Press, 1969.

Hobbs, T. Raymond. *A Time for War: A Study of Warfare in the Old Testament.* Wilmington: Michael Glazier, 1989.

Holladay, William L. *Jeremiah 1: A Commentary on the Book of Jeremiah, Chapters 1–25.* Hermeneia. Philadelphia: Fortress, 1986.

———. *Jeremiah 2: A Commentary on the Book of Jeremiah, Chapters 26–52.* Hermeneia. Philadelphia: Fortress, 1989.

———. *Jeremiah: A Fresh Reading.* New York: Pilgrim, 1990.

Hoppe, Leslie J. *There Shall Be No Poor Among You: Poverty in the Bible.* Nashville: Abingdon, 2004.

Huffmon, H. B. "The Covenant Lawsuit in the Prophets." *JBL* 78 (1959) 285–95.

_____. "The Treaty Background of Hebrew *Yādaʿ.*" *BASOR* 181 (Feb. 1966) 31–37.

_____, and S. B. Parker. "A Further Note on the Treaty Background of Hebrew *Yādaʿ.*" *BASOR* 184 (Dec. 1966) 36–38.

Hugenberger, Gordon P. *Marriage as a Covenant: A Study of Biblical Law and Ethics Governing Marriage Developed from the Perspective of Malachi.* VTSup 52. Leiden, New York, and Cologne: Brill, 1994. [In paperback: Biblical Studies Library. Grand Rapids: Baker Books, 1994.]

Janzen, Waldemar. *Old Testament Ethics: A Paradigmatic Approach.* Louisville: Westminster John Knox, 1994.

_____. *Mourning Cry and Woe Oracle.* BZAW 125. Berlin: de Gruyter, 1972.

Jensen, Joseph. *The Use of tôrâ by Isaiah: His Debate with the Wisdom Tradition.* CBQMS 3. Washington, DC: Catholic Biblical Association of America, 1973.

_____. "The Age of Immanuel." *CBQ* 41 (1979) 220–39.

_____. "The Eighth Century Prophets and Apodictic Law." In Maurya P. Horgan and Paul J. Kobelski, eds., *To Touch the Text: Biblical and Related Studies in Honor of Joseph A. Fitzmyer, s.j.* New York: Crossroad, 1989.

_____. "Yahweh's Plan in Isaiah and in the Rest of the Old Testament." *CBQ* 48 (1986) 443–55.

_____. "Weal and Woe In Isaiah: Consistency and Continuity." *CBQ* 43 (1981) 167–87.

Johnston, Leonard. "Old Testament Morality." *CBQ* 20 (1958) 19–25.

Jones, David C. "Malachi on Divorce." *Presbyterion* 15 (1989) 16–22.

_____. "A Note on the LXX of Malachi 2:16." *JBL* 109 (1990) 683–85.

Joyce, Paul. *Divine Initiative and Human Response in Ezekiel.* JSOTSup 51. Sheffield: Sheffield Academic Press, 1989.

Kaiser, Walter C. *Toward Old Testament Ethics.* Grand Rapids: Zondervan, 1983.

Kapelrud, Arvid S. "New Ideas in Amos." VTSup 15 (1966) 193–206.

_____. "The Covenant as Agreement." *JSOT* 1 (1988) 30–38.

King, Philip J. *Amos, Hosea, Micah—An Archaeological Commentary.* Philadelphia: Westminster, 1988.

Klein, Ralph W. *Ezekiel: The Prophet and His Message.* Columbia, SC: University of South Carolina Press, 1988.

Koch, Klaus. "*ṣedeq.*" Ernst Jenni, ed., *Theologisches Handwörterbuch zum Alten Testament.* Vol. 2. Munich: Kaiser, 1976, cols. 507–530.

Kornfeld, Walter. "Old Testament Ethics." *Sacramentum Mundi.* Vol. 4. New York: Herder, 1980–82, 280–82.

Kraus, H. J. "Die prophetische Botschaft gegen das soziale Unrecht Israels." *EvT* (1955) 295–307.

_____. "Die prophetische Verkündigung des Rechts in Israel." *ThSt* 51; Zollikon: Evangelisher Verlag, 1957.

Leclerc, Thomas L. *Yahweh Is Exalted in Justice: Solidarity and Conflict in Isaiah.* Minneapolis: Fortress, 2001.

Lindars, Barnabas. "Torah in Deuteronomy." In Peter R. Ackroyd and Barnabas Lindars, eds., *Words and Meaning. Essays Presented to D. Winton Thomas.* Cambridge: Cambridge University Press, 1968, 117–36.

Lindblom, Johannes. *Prophecy in Ancient Israel.* Philadelphia: Fortress, 1965.

_____. "Wisdom in the Old Testament Prophets." In Martin Noth and D. Winton Thomas, eds., *Wisdom in Israel and in the Ancient Near East. Presented to Harold Henry Rowley.* Leiden: Brill, 1969, 192–204.

Lohfink, Norbert. *Option for the Poor.* Trans. Linda M. Maloney. Berkeley: BIBAL, 1987.

_____. "Der 'heilige Krieg' und der 'Bann' im der Bibel." *IKZ* 18 (1989) 104–12.

Long, E. L. "The Use of the Bible in Christian Ethics." *Int* 19 (1965) 149–62.

Lundbom, Jack R. *Jeremiah 1–20.* AB 21. New York and London: Doubleday, 1999.

Mason, R. A. "Some Echoes of the Preaching in the Second Temple? Tradition Elements in Zechariah 1–8." *ZAW* 96 (1984) 137–54.

Mays, James L. *Amos: A Commentary.* OTL. London: SCM, 1969.

_____. *Hosea.* London: SCM, 1969.

McCarthy, Dennis. *Old Testament Covenant: A Survey of Current Opinion.* Richmond: John Knox, 1972.

_____. *Treaty and Covenant.* 2d ed. Rome: Pontifical Biblical Institute, 1978.

McKane, William. *Prophets and Wise Men.* SBT 1/44. London: SCM, 1965.

McKeating, Henry. "Sanctions against Adultery in Ancient Israelite Society, with some reflections on Methodology in the Study of Old Testament Ethics." *JSOT* 11 (March 1979) 57–72.

McKenzie, John L. "The Four Samuels." *Biblical Research* 7 (1962) 3–18.

_____. "The Dynastic Oracle: II Samuel 7." *TS* 8 (1947) 187–218.

McKenzie, S. L., and H. N. Wallace. "Covenant Themes in Malachi." *CBQ* 45 (1983) 549–63.

Mendenhall, George E. "The Relation of Individual to Political Society in Ancient Israel." In J. M. Myers, *et al.*, eds., *Biblical Studies in Memory of H. C. Alleman.* New York: Augustin, 1960.

_____. "Ancient Oriental Law and Biblical Law." *BA* 17 (1954). Reprinted in E. F. Campbell and David Noel Freedman, eds., *The Biblical Archaeologist Reader,* Vol. III. Garden City, NY: Doubleday, 1970, 3–24.

_____. "Covenant Forms in Israelite Tradition." *BA* 17 (1954). Reprinted in E. F. Campbell and David Noel Freedman, eds., *The Biblical Archaeologist Reader,* Vol. III. Garden City, NY: Doubleday, 1970, 25–33.

Mettinger, Tryggve N. D. *Solomonic State Officials: A Study of the Civil Government Officials of the Israelite Monarchy.* Coniectanea Biblica, OT Series 5. Lund: Gleerup, 1971.

_____. *Farewell to the Servant Songs: A Critical Examination of the Exegetical Maxim.* Lund: Gleerup, 1983.

Miller, Patrick D. *Sin and Judgment in the Prophets: A Stylistic and Theological Analysis.* SBLMS 27. Chico: Scholars, 1982.

Nicholson, Ernest W. *God and His People: Covenant and Theology in the Old Testament.* Oxford and New York: Clarendon Press, 1986.

_____. *Preaching to the Exiles: A Study of the Prose Tradition in the Book of Jeremiah.* Oxford: Blackwell, 1970.

Ogden, Graham S. , and Richard R. Deutsch. *A Promise of Hope—Call to Obedience: Joel and Malachi.* ITC. Grand Rapids: Eerdmans; Edinburgh: Handsel, 1987.

Olivier, J.P.J. "Schools and Wisdom Literature." *JNWSL* 4 (1975) 49–60.

Patrick, Dale. *Old Testament Law.* Atlanta: John Knox, 1985.

Pedersen, Johannes. *Israel, Its Life and Culture.* 2 vols. London: Oxford University Press, 1926.

Petersen, David L. *Zechariah 9–14 and Malachi: A Commentary.* OTL. Louisville: Westminster John Knox, 1995.

Phillips, Anthony. *Ancient Israel's Criminal Law: A New Approach to the Decalogue.* New York: Schocken, 1970.

_____. "Another Look at Adultery." *JSOT* 20 (1981) 3–25.

Porteous, Norman W. "The Basis of the Ethical Teaching of the Prophets." In idem, *Living the Mystery: Collected Essays.* Oxford: Blackwell, 1967, 47–60.

_____. "The Care of the Poor in the Old Testament." Ibid. 143–55.

_____. "Ritual and Righteousness: The Relation of Ethics to Religion in the Prophetic Literature." Ibid. 61–75.

_____. "Actualization and the Prophetic Criticism of the Cult." Ibid. 127–41.

Potter, H. D. "The New Covenant in Jeremiah xxxi 31–34." *VT* 33 (1983) 347–57.

Rad, Gerhard von. *Old Testament Theology.* Vol. I. New York: Harper & Row, 1962.

_____. *Old Testament Theology.* Vol. II. New York: Harper & Row. 1965, 135–38, 149–55, 212–17.

_____. *Holy War in Ancient Israel*. Trans. and ed. Marva J. Dawn and John Howard Yoder. Grand Rapids: Eerdmans, 1990.

Richter, Wolfgang. *Recht und Ethos. Versuch einer Ortung des weisheitlichen Mahnspruches*. STANT 15. Munich: Kösel, 1966.

Roche, Michael de. "Yahweh's *rîb* Against Israel: A Reassessment of the So-Called 'Prophetic Lawsuit' in the Preexilic Prophets." *JBL* 102 (1983) 563–74.

Rogerson, John. *Theory and Practice in Old Testament Ethics*. JSOTSup 405. Ed. M. Daniel Carroll R. London and New York: T & T Clark, 2004.

Rowley, Harold H. *From Joseph to Joshua*. London: Oxford University Press, 1950.

Sakenfeld, Katherine Doob. *The Meaning of ḥesed in the Hebrew Bible: A New Inquiry*. HMS 17. Missoula: Scholars, 1978.

_____. *Faithfulness in Action: Loyalty in Biblical Perspective*. Philadelphia: Fortress, 1985.

Sauer, Georg. "Die Umkehrforderung in der Verkündigung Jesajas." In Hans Joachim Stoebe, ed., with Johann Jakob Stamm and Ernst Jenni, *Wort, Gebot, Glaube. Beiträge zur Theologie des Alten Testaments. Walter Eichrodt zum 80. Geburtstag*. ATANT 59. Zürich: Zwingli, 1970, 277–95.

Schüngel-Straumann, Helen. *Der Dekalog—Gottes Gebote?* SBS 67. Stuttgart: Katholisches Bibelwerk, 1973.

Seebass, Horst. "Der Fall Naboth in 1 Reg. XXI." *VT* 24 (1974) 474-88.

Seilhamer, Frank H. "The Role of Covenant in the Mission and Message of Amos." In Howard N. Bream, *et al.*, eds., *A Light unto My Path: Old Testament Studies in Honor of Jacob M. Myers*. Gettysburg Theological Studies IV. Philadelphia: Temple University Press, 1974, 435–51.

Smith, Terence. "Iran: Five Years of Fanaticism." *New York Times Magazine*, February 12, 1984.

Soggin, J. Albert. *Introduction to the Old Testament: From Its Origin to the Closing of the Alexandrian Canon*. Trans. John Bowden. 3d ed. Louisville: Westminster John Knox, 1989.

Sonsino, Rifat. *Motive Clauses in Hebrew Law: Biblical Forms and Near Eastern Parallels*. Chico: Scholars, 1980.

Spohn, William C. *What Are They Saying about Scripture and Ethics?* Fully rev. and expanded ed. Mahwah, NJ: Paulist, 1995.

Steiner, Richard C. *Stockmen from Tekoa, Sycamores from Sheba: A Study of Amos' Occupations*. CBQMS 36. Washington, DC: Catholic Biblical Association of America, 2003.

Stinespring, William F. "A Problem of Theological Ethics in Hosea." In James L. Crenshaw and John T. Willis, eds., *Essays in Old Testament Ethics*. New York: Ktav, 1974, 131–44.

Terrien, Samuel. "Amos and Wisdom." In Bernhard W. Anderson and Walter Harrelson, eds., *Israel's Prophetic Heritage; Essays in Honor of James Muilenburg.* New York: Harper, 1962, 108–15.

Tucker, Gene M. "Prophecy and Prophetic Literature." In Douglas A. Knight and Gene M. Tucker, eds., *The Hebrew Bible and Its Modern Interpreters.* Philadelphia: Fortress, 1985.

Vawter, Bruce. *The Conscience of Israel.* New York: Sheed & Ward, 1961.

Vawter, Bruce, and Leslie Hoppe. *A New Heart: A Commentary on the Book of Ezekiel.* Grand Rapids: Eerdmans, 1991.

Von Waldow, H. E. "Social Responsibility and Social Structure in Early Israel." *CBQ* 32 (1970) 182–204.

Walsh, James P. M. *The Mighty from Their Thrones: Power in the Biblical Tradition.* Philadelphia: Fortress, 1987.

Weinfeld, Moshe. "Ancient Near Eastern Patterns in Prophetic Literature." *VT* 27 (1977) 178–95.

_____. "Jeremiah and the Spiritual Metamorphosis of Israel." *ZAW* 88 (1976) 17–56.

Weiser, Artur. *The Old Testament: Its Formation and Development.* Trans. Dorothea M. Barton. New York: Association Press, 1961.

Westermann, Claus. *Basic Forms of Prophetic Speech.* Philadelphia: Westminster, 1967.

Whedbee, J. William. *Isaiah & Wisdom.* Nashville: Abingdon, 1971.

Whybray, Roger Norman. *The Intellectual Tradition in the Old Testament.* BZAW 135. New York: de Gruyter, 1974.

Wildberger, Hans. *Isaiah 1–12: A Commentary.* Trans. Thomas H. Trapp. Minneapolis: Fortress, 1991.

_____. *Isaiah 13–27: A Commentary.* Trans. Thomas H. Trapp. Minneapolis: Fortress, 1997.

_____. *Isaiah 28–39: A Commentary.* Trans. Thomas H. Trapp. Minneapolis: Fortress, 2002.

Wilson, Robert R. *Prophecy and Society in Ancient Israel.* Philadelphia: Fortress, 1980.

Wiseman, D. J. "Law and Order in Old Testament Times." *Vox Evangelica* 8 (1973) 5–21.

Wolff, Hans Walter. *Amos the Prophet. The Man and His Background.* Philadelphia: Fortress, 1973.

_____. *Joel and Amos.* Hermeneia. Philadelphia: Fortress, 1977.

_____. *Micah the Prophet.* Philadelphia: Fortress, 1981.

_____. "Die Begründungen der prophetischen Heils- und Unheilssprüche." *ZAW* 52 (1934) 1–22.

_____. "The Understanding of History in the Old Testament Prophets." In Claus Westermann, ed., *Essays on Old Testament Hermeneutics*. Richmond: John Knox, 1963, 336–55.

_____. "Das Thema 'Umkehr' in der alttestamentlichen Prophetie." *ZTK* 48 (1951) 129–48.

Würthwein, Ernst. "Der Ursprung der prophetischen Gerichtsrede." *ZTK* 49 (1952) 1–16.

Zimmerli, Walther. *The Law and the Prophets: A Study of the Meaning of the Old Testament*. Oxford: Blackwell. 1965.

AUTHOR INDEX

SCRIPTURE INDEX

TOPICS INDEX